Curio

or

Gloucestershire

THE COTSWOLDS

To Jack,
a constant source of inspiration and interference

First published in 1996 by S.B. Publications
c/o 19 Grove Road, Seaford, East Sussex BN25 1TP

ISBN 1 85770 100 3

Typeset, printed and bound by MFP Design and Print,
Longford Trading Estate, Thomas Street, Stretford, Manchester M32 0JT

Curiosities
of
Gloucestershire
THE COTSWOLDS

A County Guide
to the Unusual
by
Margaret Caine
and Alan Gorton

S.B. Publications

Cricket Pavilion, Stanway.

CONTENTS

Front Cover: The Giant at Warmley.
Back Cover: Montage of unusual signs.
Title Page: War Memorial, Stanway.

INTRODUCTION

This book is a collection of oddities and curiosities which can be seen by anyone visiting those parts of the Cotswolds which lie in Gloucestershire.

Though neither are native to the area, the authors have, for a total of over forty years lived in or near the region and been consumed by its cultural richness and its beauty.

> *How often have I poised on every charm,*
> *The sheltered cot, the cultivated farm,*
> *The never-failing brook, the busy mill,*
> *The decent church that top the neighbouring hill . . .*

Oliver Goldsmith's description of Cotswold villages still rings true two-hundred years after he penned these lines, but unlike a snapshot, the village picture is not static. As we muse over or smile about a building or an object, let us have more than a little thought for the men who made it so, and for the people to whom these clusters of cottages of golden local stone are home.

The area is rich in heritage and tradition, so the objects described represent only a small proportion of the fascinating hoard of folklore, legend, anecdote and local history awaiting the enquiring mind; as such a selection has been made to illustrate the type that can be found, whether it be a strangely shaped stone, a monument isolated in a wood, a building of no apparent purpose, or an item of street furniture now obsolete. Each has a history, perhaps amusing, perhaps tragic, certainly unusual, probably unique. Those depicted are so diverse as to defy any categorisation, and have been arranged according to locality.

In some cases, the curiosities are difficult to find: directions have been included. Distance between places has been an important consideration in organising this book, but not ease of access. The balance of chronological, thematic and topo–graphical interests should allow some planning ahead by the explorer. Ordinary touring maps will be of limited value. The best to use are the Ordnance Survey Landranger series; places quoted are given the grid reference to aid discovery.

This book will encourage you to explore the unexpected, the unexplained, the odd and bizarre; visit the little-known, the out-of-the-way, the secluded places; learn the astonishing local legends and folklore. Come on a voyage of discovery through the Gloucestershire Cotswolds, a land where genesis became geological fact, a region populated by eccentrics, demons and mysteries.

ACKNOWLEDGEMENTS

We owe grateful thanks to all those authors, known and unknown, of church guides which are such invaluable sources of information, and to church wardens and vergers who have let us into their churches when, regrettably, they have had to be made safe from predators. Our thanks are also due to those people we have met during our travels, whilst revitalising the inner man (and woman) in pubs and car parks where we ate our soggy tomato sandwiches, whose interest in our task has fortified us immensely — and whose guidance we have accepted almost invariably. To Ron Shipton of the Woodchester Mansion Trust, to Liz Foley of Stanway House, to the owners and gardener of Stancombe Park, to Prince and Princess Michael of Kent, and staff at Nether Lypiatt Manor, to Aylmer Blow of Hilles estate, and to Mark Griffiths of Stanley Mill, we owe especial thanks, not only for their interest in our book, but for giving their time so generously and for motivating us through their own enthusiasm and sense of devotion.

Hermit's cell, Badminton.

BROADWAY

THE HIGHEST FOLLY TOWER

> *Location:*   Off the A44, one mile south-east of Broadway.   Sheet 150 11263617

Because the Broadway Estate was held by Pershore Abbey prior to the dissolution of the monasteries by Henry VIII in 1539, the hill pastures surrounding the village remain in Worcestershire. The 'broad way' is the main street, wide to take huge flocks of sheep and droves of cattle which passed through on their way to the London markets.

It is though to the skyline in Gloucestershire that one's eye is drawn. Like a punctuation mark on Broadway Beacon, the north-westerly tip of the Cotswolds, stands a dark, Norman-style, battlemented tower.

It was built for George William, Sixth Earl of Coventry, whose family seat was at Croome Court, near Worcester. His second countess was a woman of great common sense who, when a shooting box in the form of a tower was suggested as a 'prospect', an improvement of the view from Croome, ordered a beacon to be lighted on the top of Broadway Hill, fifteen miles away, to make sure that a tower would indeed be visible — and when it was burning she travelled round to all the neighbours she wished to impress to ensure they could see it also.

In designing the Tower, James Wyatt followed the fashion set by Launcelot 'Capability' Brown for follies to be part of the estate landscaping, yet chose a darker limestone from further east than the native golden Guiting stone, in order to create an appearance of brooding maturity. Built from 1797, it is a castellated hexagon with three taller round towers at alternate angles. The design is rather ugly and stark, and the circular projections with battlemented turrets can be regarded as a figment of the imagination as the Tower stands alone in a field like a castle from some gigantic chess set.

At 1,024 feet (305 metres) above sea level, the second highest point on the Cotswolds, the 65-foot Tower commands a panoramic view; consistent with the aspirations of the Countess a rather excessive list of counties are visible from the top, thirteen instead of the usual modest seven or eight for most folly towers.

BROADWAY

DIRECTIONS FROM THE FISH

> *Location:*   On the A44, at the top of Broadway Hill.   Sheet 151 13223597

In these days of standardised tin-plate signs which dominate our roads, old sign-posts are a rare curiosity.

The sign-post at the top of Fish Hill, Broadway, is one of the oldest in the country. Dated 1669, and bearing the initials "N.I.", for Nicholas Izod, the local landowner who erected it, each of its arms terminate in a roughly shaped hand, pointing the way to Warwick, Oxford amd Gloucester.

The lovely spot on which the post stands had a less than happy history for it is the site of a former gallows. What frisson of fear and fascination must have rippled through the gathered crowd as the unfortunate Perry family, mother and two sons, were dragged from Gloucester gaol to be hanged here in 1660, still protesting their innocence of the murder near Chipping Campden of William Harrison — only to be proved correct two years later when Harrison walked back into his home, surrounded in the mystery of the 'Campden Wonder'. The site of the gallows was chosen specifically both to be near the scene of the murder and to be on a major route, 'pour encourager les autres'.

Why is it called Fish Hill? It is certainly a long way from the sea or nearest river. The quaintly styled pub at the top was an old charter house inn, one of the oldest in the country, and derived its name from the sign of the three fishes of Christianity of its former days as a priest house.

BUCKLAND

FOR LOVE AND FOR ART

> *Location:* St. Michael's church, Buckland, off B4632, one mile south-west of
> Broadway.   Sheet 150 08203600

For centuries it was the custom on the Cotswolds for young people who were
marrying to signify their mutual love by drinking, at some stage in the ceremony,
from a cup or a bowl. A great treasure in this church on the north wolds is just
such a vessel, the sixteenth-century Buckland Bowl, a bridal bowl of exceptional
charm which was used as a loving cup at village weddings. Made of maple and
with a silver rim, it has a disc in the centre showing a saint thrusting a staff into
a dragon's mouth. This is said to be St. Michael, but he looks decidedly feminine
in long flowing robes and it is easy to understand why some consider that it
represents the Virgin Mary or St. Margaret. One hardly associates the Virgin Mary
with slaying dragons, and after all the church's patron saint is St. Michael.

A treasure for which lovers of fine
art will seek out this church is its
rare east window, adjudged to be
the finest on the Cotswolds. Three
panels of stained glass by the
Malvern Priory School are part of
a window given originally by
William Graften, rector for forty-
four years from 1466 until 1510.
They represent three Sacraments
of the Catholic Church: Baptism
and Confirmation together, Holy
Matrimony, and Extreme Unction,
and in each case a bishop is
officiating. It is difficult to date
the glass precisely, but judging
from the bride's costume it would
be c.1475. The glass so
enraptured William Morris that he
had it restored at his own
expense in 1883.

The stone-built rectory is England's oldest and most complete medieval parsonage
used as such, until recently. A curious feature is the fifteenth-century stained glass
showing the courtship dance ('leck') of the blackcock, a display so complex that
these birds were suspected of being witches in disguise and so fiercely suppressed
that they disappeared from many regions. These particular blackcock though
dispel that suspicion by carrying in their beaks scrolls inscribed "In nomine Jesu".

3

STANWAY

AN ARCHITECTURAL GEM

Location: At Stanway, three miles north-west of Winchcombe.
Sheet 150 06103230

The view of Stanway from the B4077 nine miles west of Stow is one of the most enchanting in Britain. The village clusters close to its manor and both contain a number of impressive features.

Stanway House was built for the Tracy family in the sixteenth century on the site of the abbot of Tewkesbury's manor. Inside, a large landscape painting of 1748 by William Taylor of Worcester shows Stanway as it looked at that time. The Pyramid is a notable feature of the gardens on the east side, having been built by the inheriting twin Robert Tracy to commemorate his father, and a Cascade tumbles from it; this was later filled in but is in process of being reconstructed.

Amongst the two belts of trees stretching from the south lawn to the Pyramid is a tiny circular dog cemetary, surrounded by a tall yew hedge, and where has been raised a number of gravestones. One is to FAITHFUL STELLA, 1883–98, another to DARLING DANDY, 1930–44. The most elaborate is beautifully inscribed, now covered in algae. The epitaph, beneath a carved tin of dog food called PAD and crossed bones, supported on either side by hounds standing on their hind legs, reads:

Memoriae Fragranti Old Smelly
obit MCMLXXX aetatis XVI
canis sanguine quanuis ferocifacile redolentis
sauvitate tamensua quam stirpe redolentions
hoc qualecunque monumentum
JACOBUS NEIDPATH dominus
pronoptisque LITTLE SMELLY
sculptorque RORY YOUNG
pietas ergo erigendum curaverunti
anno salutis canum
MCMLXXXIV

Lady Hereford lived a long and melancholy widowhood at Stanway House, and she too adored her dogs, lamenting their deaths. When her favourite, Mignon, died, she ordered that he be buried in a place unknown to her so that she could not mourn over the grave, and wrote a poignant eulogy to be enclosed in the coffin:

> *He died the 27 September 1807 to her extream Agony.*
> *He was of exquisite and most uncommon beauty, with*
> *a peculiar elegance of motion, very small. I have*
> *suffered much in writing this paper.*

Lady Hereford beseeched whoever might come upon the coffin to replace her note, but this cannot have been done as the paper is now retained in the House.

The cricket ground is delightfully situated in a ridge and furrow field. The unique thatched wooden pavilion, set on staddle stones to keep it off the wet land, was given to the village by Sir James Barrie, celebrated author of *Peter Pan*, visitor to Stanway from 1921 onwards, and ardent cricket supporter.

Even the war memorial does not conform to the usual stone cross: Stanway's heroes are commemorated by an outstandingly splendid bronze sculpture by Alexander Fisher of St. George slaying the Dragon.

While the pet dogs at Stanway were treasured and remembered in different ways, such was not the case in the nearby village of Stanton: here the approach may have been more utilitarian but they were valued none the less.

The steady tread of centuries has worn the stone-flagged floor of St. Michael's church and beneath the oak gallery are medieval pews whose poppyhead benchends are deeply gouged by dogchains from the days when shepherds took their dogs everywhere. One wonders though whether those poor creatures had to suffer the doxologies lauded around them while their masters listened to the scriptures heaping contempt upon canines. Shepherds knew otherwise.

WINCHCOMBE

GARGOYLES AND TOBACCO

> *Location:* At Winchcombe, at the junction of the B4078 and B4632, seven miles north of Cheltenham.   Sheet 163 02402820

Sheltered under the bluff of the north-west hills, Winchcombe settled in its winding combe in Saxon times. The most important town in the Cotswolds for much of the period between Cirencester's desertion by the Romans and its wool-led revival in the early Middle Ages, Winchcombe was for centuries one of the main royal centres of the Hwicce, a sub-kingdom of Mercia, and controlled the northern approaches to the wolds. It was for a time capital of a separate shire, 'Wincelcumbe scire', but was amalgamated with Gloucestershire c.1017.

St. Peter's is one of the group of exceptional Perpendicular 'wool' churches found on the Cotswolds but displays a series of grotesque heads and carvings more curious than beautiful. The parapet alone bears forty of these bold sculptures. Why did the masons create them? One hypothesis is that they were intended to frighten away evil spirits, especially those who had followed the congregation and were lurking about to catch them after the service; a variation is that they were intended to remind parishioners of the monsters of the underworld, a place to be avoided; a further one, is that they represented the facial and postural distortions of people affected by the plague, especially at the time of the Black Death in 1349. Winchcombe has a different story still: the masons working on the church were so annoyed by a monk from the nearby abbey criticising their work that they caricatured him in a grotesque gargoyle. Approximately half of these grotesques represent demons and the remainder may well be caricatures of local dignitaries from the town and the abbey in the fifteenth century. The helmeted head on the south aisle is traditionally supposed to represent Ralph Boteler, lord of the manor, and the hideous figure above the east window the devil. One of these grotesques takes the unusual form of an anthropophagus, a cannibalistic monster eating a human being: one wonders what moral aspect that was meant to impart?

In a different medium, the curious carvings are continued inside. The medieval oak screen is very fine and bordered by beautifully carved representations of lizards, vines, grapes and roses. In one, the carver has cleverly placed a face, which has become known as the Winchcombe Imp. He really is a cheery chap.

The church has a number of striking monuments but one is quaintly amusing, even if unwittingly so. In Stuart fashion, Sir Thomas Williams is shown kneeling before an open Bible opposite the space which his widow's effigy should have come to occupy. But she remarried and is buried elsewhere. Sir Thomas' round-eyed stare suggests that he is waiting still.

Winchcombe's prosperity in wool and as a centre of pilgrimage suffered with the destruction of the abbey in 1539. The town looked to the land again, and developed an unusual trade. Tobacco was grown extensively as a crop in the neighbourhood, though successive governments tried to stamp it out in order to protect nepotism and the growth of plantations in the struggling colonies of Virginia and the Bermudas.

The first proclamation against the cultivation was signed by Queen Elizabeth, and in 1619 James I levied a tax on it of 3d in the pound, which gradually rose to 6s/10d. Despite this the venture in Winchcombe really became commercialised by John Stratford, who leased land in the town and at Hailes, successfully raised his first crop in 1622, and within a few years had made a fortune of £20,000. Though regarded as rather poor quality, the tobacco was cheaper than Virginian, selling at 3s per pound in 1636.

The uncertainties of profits drove Stratford into bankruptcy, but others persisted, despite the industry being prohibited yet again by Parliament in 1653 as a threat to English interests in the West Indies. The government repeatedly threatened to destroy the crop but had little support from local magistrates, though Samuel Pepys did write about the troops being sent to "Spoil the crop." Dragoons were deployed again in 1667 but the people of Winchcombe did not take lightly this interference with their livelihood. When a troop of Life Guards arrived in the district.

> . . . *the country did rise on them, above five or six hundred threatening to kill them, man and horse, so that they were constrained to depart.*

On this occasion unnecessary bloodshed was avoided but in the 1690s the cultivation of tobacco was finally stamped out. It is now recalled only in a few strange-sounding names for the Cotswolds, like Tobacco Field on the western outskirts of Winchcombe, and Tobacco Close nearby.

CHIPPING CAMPDEN

ARROGANCE, IMPATIENCE, HONESTY AND SADNESS

Location: St. James' church, Chipping Campden.   Sheet 151 15503960

On Campden wold the skylark sings,
In Campden town the traveller finds
The inward peace that beauty brings
To bless and heal tormented minds.

John Masefield certainly captured the essence of Chipping Campden, the most beautiful of all the market towns, for it wears its age with serenity. The church of St. James, at the westerly edge of the town, with its impressive pinnacled tower, is one of the finest of the Cotswold 'wool' churches and a veritable treasure-house of the town's past.

Curiously, several former inhabitants took opportunity on their monuments to blow their own trumpets about their achievements and to exort gratitude from the townsfolk for their gifts. Their motivation in doing so really must be questioned. One was William Grevel, a wool merchant, whose beautifully incised brass in the floor of the chancel is the largest in Gloucestershire and describes him as:

The flower of the wool merchants of all England

This tradition is continued in the Gainsborough mortuary chapel, which contains the exquisitely carved grey and white stone monument of Sir Baptist Hicks, later Viscount Campden, and his wife Lady Elizabeth, in their state robes. The remains of their house, destroyed during the Civil War, stands next to the church. Note the self-publicising epitaph to Lady Elizabeth, clearly written by herself before her death, and contrast this with the flinty look on her face: could she really be capable of such care and tenderness? Both the church and the town were indeed fortunate to have such benefactors but the eulogy, in Latin and translated below, is not exactly to modern taste, as she does not forget to include herself and attempts to pre-empt the Day of Judgment:

TO CAMPDEN
O FORTUNATE CAMPDEN, YOU POSSESS GREAT TREASURE
YOU WHO ENSHRINE THE BODY OF THE BEST OF YOUR PATRONS
O LORD RICH IN LANDS, WHO ALSO ADDED TO THOSE LANDS
NEW FLOWERS OF HONOURS. MAY YOU PROVIDE A BURIAL PLACE
FOR YOUR LORD. HE ADORNED YOUR LAND
WITH SPACIOUS BUILDINGS AND BEAUTIFUL GARDENS AND
DID NOT ALLOW THE HOUSE OF GOD TO BE NEGLECTED
BUT GAVE STRONG SUPPORT TO THE POOR. YOU WHO
WERE HIS DEVOUT PLEASURE IN LIFE BE A PLACE OF

REST TO HIM IN DEATH. HERE ALSO YOU HOLD THE
VIRTUOUS WIFE WHO WAS HIS PARTNER IN LIFE. CHERISH THIS TWIN
BODY WORTHY OF RESURRECTION
AND SHELTER THEM IN YOUR KINDLY BOSOM.

High upon a wall in the Chapel is the
bust of Penelope Noel, shown holding
her needlework equipment. Though
young, she was a keen and
accomplished needlewoman. She died in
1633 from blood poisoning, caused by
pricking her finger whilst embroidering
and being infected by the arsenical dye
used in those days.

Outside in the churchyard are some
interesting epitaphs, close to the
churchdoor. One is in memory of
Martha Hiron, who died aged forty-one
in 1708:

> *Here lieth a virgin pure and chaste*
> *Who did not want her time to waste*
> *She dearly longed to married be*
> *To Christ her Lord and none but he*
> *And now she has her soul at rest*
> *With glorious sounds for ever blest.*

But there are occasions when records
of the past leave so much untold.
One family lost four young children
in one year, 1759. A headstone
commemorates William, son of
Richard and Ann Keyte, who died in
June, aged eight; Jonathon, aged two,
died on the same day; Samuel, five
weeks old, had already died in May;
and Ann, aged five. Only details of
age and gender are given, but no
explanation of why they died within
a few days of each other, nor even a
few lines of doggerel to soften this
pathetic loss. Was no local poet
moved to praise the treasure of their
brief lives, nor versifier encouraged to
record the sadness and grief of their
parents? Was it not even talked about
at the time?

CHIPPING CAMPDEN

THE KIFTSGATE STONE

> *Location:* Three-quarters of a mile west of Chipping Campden, on the minor road to Saintbury. Sheet 151 13473900

On the Cotswolds, there are several stones of great historical significance, and this is one of them.

The Kiftsgate Stone, standing shyly in the undergrowth of the trees of Weston Park Wood, just inside a gap in the hedge on the side of the road to Saintbury, is a remarkable survival. It may not even be in situ, possibly having been removed from an original setting on Spelsbury ('speech hill'), adjacent to Kiftsgate Court above Mickleton. At this stone, on that hill, the Anglo-Saxon Hundred Court assembled to hold their routine inquisitions and make proclamations regarding important local and national issues: as such it is an ancient seat of British judgment. It is here that Saxon serfs came to pay homage and obtain counsel from the 'Witan', the forerunner of our Parliament. It has a hole in it where the chief of the Saxon Hundred stuck his sword when collecting dues from serfs and holding his court.

The 'gate' implies that it lay on a main thoroughfare serving the district comprising the Hundred, most likely in this case the White Way.

BLOCKLEY

MEMORIAL TO A FISH

Location:	Fish Cottage, Blockley, on the B4479, two-and-a-half miles south of Chipping Campden. Sheet 151 16483500

A former resident of Blockley, William Keyte, was devoted to an unusual pet — a trout. He trained it to take food out of a person's hand and though he never gave it a name — it was known simply as "The Old Fish" — such was his loving care that it lived for twenty years in a pond in the garden of Fish Cottage. When in 1865 it was found dead, believed killed by a stranger with a stick, it was buried with due ceremony, and William's son composed an epitaph which is carved on its headstone:

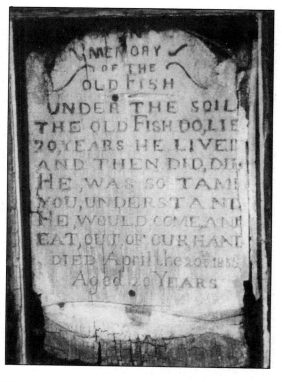

IN
MEMORY
of the
OLD FISH

UNDER THE SOIL
THE OLD FISH DO LIE
20 YEARS HE LIVED
AND THEN DID DIE
HE WAS SO TAME
YOU UNDERSTAND
HE WOULD COME AND
EAT, OUT OF OUR HAND.

DIED. April The 20th 1865
Aged 20 years.

Blockley was famous for another resident early last century. It was the home of Joanna Southcott, the prophetess who won national attention through her belief that she would bear Shiloh, the second Messiah. Her home, Rock Cottage, was the scene of many disturbing incidents unitl it was eventually destroyed by fire. Now rebuilt, it stands beyond gateposts marked with a commemorative plaque.

MORETON-IN-MARSH

THE MEETING POINT OF FOUR COUNTIES AND THE CURFEW TOWER

Location:	At Moreton-in-Marsh, at the junction of the A429 and A44.
	Sheet 151 23273220

One of the curiosities of this town is its name, often thought to be comical. Moreton derives from 'farmstead on the moor' but this 'marsh' has little to do with wet land, being a corruption of 'march', from 'mearc', meaning a boundary.

The town was indeed a very important junction of the boundaries of the four counties of Gloucestershire, Worcestershire, Warwickshire and Oxfordshire, recorded on the Four Shires Stone a mile eastwards on the A44. This is an eighteenth-century monument surmounted by a sundial and ball-finial with the names of the counties incised on appropriate faces. Though Worcestershire lost its right to be included with the tidying of county boundaries in 1931, it is a reminder that in the tenth century Edward the Elder determined to carve what is now the West Midlands into administrative divisions called shires, easily defended blocks based on the military centres of Gloucester, Worcester, Warwick and Oxford. For this purpose he disregarded the boundaries of ancient Kingdoms, but took note of existing estates. Boundaries may change but not stones.

Moreton-in-Marsh was founded in 1226 by the abbot of Westminster to exploit the junction of the Fosse Way (A429) with the major road between London and Worcester (A44). The oldest building in the town is the Curfew Tower. The 'curfew' dates to the Norman Conquest when a bell was rung to warn townspeople to 'cover-fire' for the night, but this Tower was built of stone in the sixteenth century, with a gabled turret and arched doorway. In the Tower is a bell dated 1633: it continued to be rung daily, at 5am and 8pm in summer and 6am and 8pm in winter, until 1860, as the result of a strange bequest. When Sir Robert Fry was returning to Moreton from London one foggy evening he became lost on the common but eventually found his bearing by hearing the curfew bell. In gratitude, he left an endowment of £1 for winding the clock, and 10s for ringing the bell.

On the wall on the High Street side is an interesting list of market tolls charged in the town, dated 5 August, 1905.

LOWER SWELL

AN ASPIRING SPA AND ENSURING FOOD

Location:	At Lower Swell on the B4068, half a mile west of Stow- on-the-Wold. Sheet 163 17912661

There are a number of curious houses on the Cotswolds. In some cases the reason for their oddity is clear, but in others too obscure to be recorded.

Lower Swell would have presented today a very different picture from the rural idyll had the chalybeate spring discovered last century been fully exploited. Certainly an attempt was made to do so, but too belatedly to compete with Cheltenham. The ornately-facaded Spa Cottage was built to attract the hard-

drinking squires of the area to take the fashionable spa waters. The Cottage looks very curious in the Cotswold countryside, and its oriental influence seems to have come straight from nearby Sezincote.

The twelfth-century church of St. Mary the Virgin has a Norman tympanum over the south door composed of ten stones, but wedged together so skilfully as to pass for one block. The unfinished carving is pagan in origin, showing a branching Tree of Life with a dove pecking at a side spray. Even more pagan in feeling are the twenty-six symbolic carvings round the former chancel arch: a continuous band is divided into boxes crudely carved with mannikins and what look like apples, interlinked rings, a fish, a hare, a salamander, and other devices. Carvings on the capitals are of people and serpents. This symbolism has never been explained satisfactorily: an uneasy Christian interpretation in the church's leaflet does not convince.

Dovecotes were a means of ensuring supplies of fresh meat and eggs. Many of them were very elaborate, designed as an integral part of the complex of buildings on an estate. In the nearby village, Lower Slaughter Manor (nothing to do with bloodshed but deriving from 'sloghtre', the sloe-trees which abound hereabouts) has a sixteenth-century dovecote which is the largest in Gloucestershire. It is built of stone, with twin columbaria in two equal gables with mullioned openings, and a small central Tudor entrance.

STOW-ON-THE-WOLD

THE OLDEST INN AND A SAVAGE BATTLE

> *Location:* Stow-on-the-Wold, at the junction of the Fosse Way (A429),
> A424 and A436.   Sheet 163 19102580

Various age-old jingles are well-earned by Stow:

Stow-on-the-Wold, where the wind blows cold

or the alternative:

At Stow-on-the-Wold the Devil caught cold.

At nearly 800 feet (246 metres) on the eastern plateau, it is the highest town on
the Cotswolds. Windswept throughout the centuries, its position exposes it to
chilling breezes, and in 1762 five soldiers died of exposure after being caught in
a blizzard near the town.

Founded by the abbot of Evesham to capitalise on the crossing of major routes
between Warwick, Gloucester, Worcester and Malmesbury, its exposed position
has no other advantage: "All roads lead to Stow" is another saying, and a total of
eight intersect here.

Originally 'Edwardsstowe' to recognise that it was founded specifically as a
market under King Edward and was already a holy place, it quickly became a
thriving market town and was given borough status and a market charter in 1107.
The market cross in the Square was renovated in 1878 to record the thanks of
the town to Joseph Chamberlayne whose gift of £1,000 provided regular supplies
of clean water for the first time; on one face of the gabled headstone is the
abbot of Evesham receiving the royal charter from Henry I.

Not surprisingly, a town of this nature and antiquity boasts a number of unique and
curious features. Even before the grant by Henry I, an inn had been established,
and still thrives. The Royalist was set up in 927AD and is the oldest in England.

At the other end of the green, the Crooked
House leans steeply because of subsidence;
now the Curiosity Shop, one wonders what it
was called before this happened to it?

The many inns and coaching houses that made
Stow a wealthy place in the past centre on the
green but on the front of the Talbot is a brass
box inscribed "For Corn Returns". This is a
reminder of the days when the building was

the Corn Exchange and farmers left sample packets of grain for the corn merchants to test and assess for quality. By the west wall of the Unicorn Hotel there remains an ancient mounting block for the use of horse riders.

While on the green, do not neglect the wooden stocks. They are remarkable for the unusually wide spacing of the two leg holes, and must have been most uncomfortable to sit in.

Near Stow on 21 March, 1646, 3,000 Royalists faced 3,500 Parliamentarians in what was to be the last important engagement of the first Civil War, as Prince Rupert attempted vainly to check the Parliamentary advance on Gloucester. The Royalists,

under the command of the aged Sir Jacob Astley, were defeated: the battle was bloody, the death total appalling, and Sir Jacob with 1,600 others were herded into St. Edward's church as prisoners. Those imprisoned were the fortunate ones as 200 of the wounded were put to the sword and others were dismissed to their homes that "they might perish." Many who were killed were buried where they died. Only one, Captain Keyt, has a tomb in Stow's church, a large slab engraved with a likeness of the young man in the dress of the period with, on each side, skulls and crossed bones, mailed gauntlets and a helmet. The inscription reads:

Sacred Memory
of the renowned leader Hastings Keyt
son of John Keyt of Ebrington in the
County of Gloucester
Knight, Commander of the Regiment . . .
on the King's side who fell in the
Battle of Stow on the 21st March 1645.

The troop of horse commanded by Hastings Keyt had been raised by his father — and it was his father who paid for his memorial.

On the outskirts of the town, on the A436, is Enoch's Tower, a castellated folly four storeys high and built in 1848, where a Mr. Enoch kept an unofficial museum.

BOURTON-ON-THE-HILL

STANDARD MEASURES

Location: St. Lawrence's church, Bourton-on-the-Hill, on the A44 two-and-a-half miles west of Moreton-in-Marsh.   Sheet 151 17503258

Medieval notions of measurement were sketchy and variable, there was no nationally accepted pattern and there were differences even from town to town. However, the system of weights and volumes developed at Winchester were of such practicability and consistency that they were taken to set the standard for the whole Kingdom — and became known as the Winchester Standard. These were enshrined in law when in 1587 Queen Elizabeth I granted a charter to that City and with it the Corporation received a set of Weights and Measures which, on account of their exactness, were fixed upon for the invariable rule throughout England and Wales. From then on they were used successively and enforced by Act of Parliament.

Subsequently, Stewards of Manors and Clerks to the Magistrates were directed by Statute to provide themselves with Standard Measures for use in dispute relating to corn rents and collection of tithes. In 1816 the Bench of Magistrates covering the Bourton-on-the-Hill area directed their Clerk (a solicitor from Shipton-on-Stour, Warwickshire) to procure a Standard, and these Bushel and Peck measures are retained in St. Lawrence's church. Made of bell-metal and inscribed:

Frederick Francis Findon, Clerk to the Bench
of Magistrates at Bourton-on-the-Hill, 1816

They were abandoned when the Imperial Bushel and Peck were introduced in 1826 in the reign of George IV.

At one time, the Winchester Standard measures must have been quite common but Victorian church 'restorers' too often disposed of such irreligious items. These, too, were lost for almost a century before being rediscovered and returned to their original place — a rare oddity indeed.

This church has another curiosity: an 1831 endowment of over £3,000 — a very substantial sum in those days — is painted on the wall. Rather than committed to the more usual legal deed and stored in some stuffy office, was this a case of good works not only being done, but being seen to be done?

SEZINCOTE

NORTH INDIA IN THE COTSWOLDS

Location:	Off the A44 Moreton-in-Marsh to Broadway road, three miles west of Moreton. Sheet 151 17383114

Sezincote is an experience, not a village. This latter was swept away by the early enclosures to make way for sheep, and its church was demolished in 1638. What we find in this quiet place, with its onion-shaped dome once burnished copper and now coated with verdigris, is a most eccentric Cotswold mansion, a touch of the exotic in the gentle countryside of the central wolds.

The Indian-inspired mansion, was remodelled in 1805 from an earlier country house and is the result, in combination, of the work of three people. Sir Charles Cockerell had made a fortune as an executive of the East India Company and wished both to enjoy his wealth and to demonstrate what it could do in the way of a country house, so the building was designed by his brother Samuel Pepys Cockerell, architect to the East India Company, and aided by the topographical artist Thomas Daniell, who was the most knowledgeable European of his day about Indian architecture and expert in oriental design.

Such was its impact, that Sezincote was visited by the Prince Regent in 1807 and gave him the inspiration for the Indianisation of the Brighton Pavilion.

Perhaps its design strength is that the house and its gardens appear to be a compromise between the Cockerell brothers' Indian interests and contemporary ideas of an English gentleman's residence, plus a few concessions to western European climate. Its large, round-headed windows are neo-classical in proportion but are embellished with decoration of Eastern origin; its onion-shaped dome rises between chimney-stacks that despite attempts to give them hints of the Orient persist in being chimney-stacks; its low-pitched roofs end not in traditional finials or classical figures but in diminutive minarets. Interestingly, the ornament is Mogul rather than Hindu style.

The illusion is carried to great lengths. To heighten the fantasy of the building and authenticate the colour of its material, the local stone was stained artificially to impart a more Indian orange tone. A formal garden with soaring Irish yews is overlooked by a grand sweeping conservatory with minarets, ending in an octagonal domed pavilion.

The drive to the house is over an Indian-style bridge by Thomas Daniell. The delightfully landscaped water-garden by Humphrey Repton has trees of enormous size. Sezincote means 'hillside of the oaks' and oaks are still plentiful in the acres of surrounding parkland; old woodland spreads all around studded with ornamental trees, which contrast wierdly with the exotic architecture.

These oriental garden features by Daniell still add charm. Beautiful gardens surround a stream which curves away from the house downhill to a pool, with many Indian details, such as the Indian Bridge with balustrade surmounted by cast-iron Brahmin bulls, and Temple Pool with the figure of Suraya, the Hindu sun god, in an Indian shrine, at the head of the little valley. Then behind the greenhouse is the Wellington Memorial, really the heating chimney for the greenhouse. Particularly clever is the choice of English plants arranged to give an oriental appearance, seen to best advantage in subdued light — few gardens can look so attractive in the rain!

Sezincote is thought to be the only Moghul building that has survived in western Europe: with its domed roof and Indian imagery it is certainly unique on the Cotswolds. Its oddity seems to express its originator's determination to show at all costs that he was no ordinary gentleman.

ODDINGTON

MEDIEVAL WALL PAINTINGS

Location:	Off the A436, two miles east of Stow-on-the-Wold. Sheet 163 23502568

St. Nicholas' church lies in an idyllic situation amongst trees, surrounded by fields, after being abandoned and isolated when the current village of Oddington moved to new ground in the early eighteenth century because of the Black Death, which played havoc with the people of Gloucestershire. The village was rebuilt on higher, drier ground and the old parish church left derelict. The roof and windows were broken and the outer walls matted with ivy. A vixen even raised her cubs in the richly carved Jacobean pulpit. But because it was left alone, it has remained rustic and unspoilt.

There are some very unusual features at this church. On the porch are three scratch dials, and the stone bench carries deeply incised lines where yeomen are said to have sharpened their arrows. Certainly the village was the scene of much fighting in the first Civil War and in 1643 the Royalists, under Prince Rupert, suffered a major defeat here.

Also incised on the porch bench are very puzzling outlines of the soles of two shoes, either both left feet or a very poorly crafted pair. Was this merely to wile away some time, or intended to signify a more lasting memorial before going into battle?

The principal interest in the church though is the wall painting. On the windowless north wall of the nave, a most unusual position for this subject, is a very large mid-fourteenth-century 'Doom', which had been whitewashed over in the seventeenth century, but was disclosed in 1913.

The execution of the painting is accomplished and the artist has allowed full play to his fancy and humour; in particular the torments of the damned are depicted with fearful realism.

Look for the wonderful images represented in this Last Judgment: Christ, attended by angels and Apostles, sits in judgment at the top; angels blow trumpets to summon the dead from their graves; the good are handed up into Paradise (castellated towers); the damned are herded by devils (two wearing smart stripes) into the mouth of Hell; a group of people are being boiled in a cauldron, with grotesque monsters in attendance, one of whom is blowing the flames with bellows while another carries lost souls in a wheelbarrow; repulsive monsters torture sinners, one being suspended from a gibbet with another unfortunate awaiting his turn while the hangman evidently enjoys immensely his gruesome task; the redeemed look on from the nearby heavenly city (which since it is of brick in a stone district suggests the artist was not a local man); a humorous detail is supplied by a figure clambering up the battlements, to whom an angel on the top extends a helping hand.

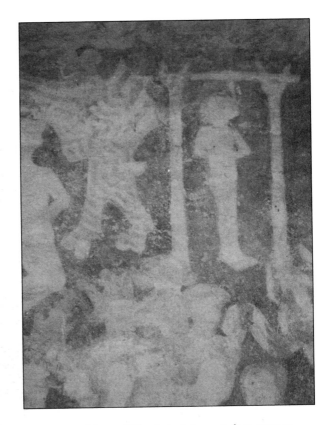

To the right of the Doom are various subjects difficult to interpret, but among them can be discerned a fox preaching, with a Franciscan in attendance: this is probably an attack on the Friars, of which a number of examples occur in English medieval art.

If the didactic moralising of the painting is not sufficient, there are yet other reminders of mortality in this church: an ancient wooden bier, inscribed "Death Shall Be Called", stands against the south wall, and on the north wall of the chancel a memorial plaque displays an eerie collection of leering skulls and broken skeletons.

WYCK RISSINGTON

A MAZE, A LIVING CROSS AND AN ECLIPSE OF THE SUN

> *Location:*   Two-and-a-quarter miles south of Stow-on-the-Wold, off the A429
> (Fosse Way).   Sheet 163 19102150

Wyck is one of the trio of Rissingtons, Little and Great being the others.

At the church of St. Lawrence the seventeen-year-old Gustav Holst had his first professional engagement in 1892–93 as organist and choirmaster; the organ he played is still in the church. During his time here, Holst was regarded by the squire as "a young man of great promise."

Canon Harry Cheales was rector here for thirty-three years. In 1947 he had a dream in which he received explicit instructions for the creation of an allegorical maze in the rectory grounds, representing man's journey through life and based on a series of lovely old carvings in the church.

It took over five years to construct the maze, with hedges seven-feet high and paths totalling 700 yards; along the way, various areas represented temptations and distractions, Death and Paradise. Treading the maze became traditional on the patronal saint's day, but over the years it became overgrown until the area was sold as a building site. Inside the church, though, is a mosaic copy which reproduces the exact course followed by the paths of the original.

The symbolism is continued in the churchyard with two unique trees. One of the first Wellington pines to be brought to this country, and now one of the largest with a circumference of thirty-three feet, has a life-expectancy of 4,000 years and is a fitting symbol of Eternal Life. The other is a yew, now nine-feet high, which has been shaped into a 'Living Cross'.

On the south wall of the chancel, a beautiful fourteenth-century stained-glass window depicts the Crucifixion, in which the cross is a rare green colour. The positioning of the sun, moon and two stars was influenced by a total eclipse of the sun in 1322, for here the moon is shown blood-red.

CLAPTON-ON-THE-HILL

LIBERAL INDULGENCES

Location: The church of St. James, Clapton-on-the-Hill, two miles south of Bourton-on-the-Water, off the A429. Sheet 163 16341811

It is difficult nowadays to imagine the terror with which the Penitential was regarded in medieval times. For then, if you had committed some wrong-doing, real or imaginary, and were desperate to save your immortal soul from torment in purgatory, repentance was not enough. God, as the injured party, must be recompensed. To this end, the Church had produced a neatly graded scale of penances, appropriate to every possible sin.

No believer was safe and the fearful possibility that the penitent might die before completing his allotted days of fast and abstinence led to alternatives — repetition of prayers by poorer folk, gifts of money or kind to the Church by richer ones, or even endowing a new abbey to safeguard oneself from Hell Fire.

St. James' church, Clapton-on-the-Hill, formerly known as Clapton super Montibus, was an early possession of Evesham Abbey. It is the smallest church on the Cotswolds: the chancel is fifteen feet by eleven, and the nave is thirty by thirteen and can seat forty-five people.

Carved in the stone chancel arch is a two-line inscription:

Qui ter devote P[ater] et Ave geneb[us] ip[se] dixerit,
en merces t[unc] ibi m[ille] dies

Whoever shall say three times devoutly a Pater and an Ave on his knees and in person — lo! There is a reward then and there of a thousand days.

It is known that when the new abbey church at Evesham was dedicated in 1239, the Bishop granted a series of indulgences. This carved inscription may well be the work of the local priest who took this means of publicising the Bishop's document. The terms do seem, though, somewhat liberal.

Because the village is so remote on its hillside, the carving escaped the ravages of the Reformation, and here still are the words which comforted many a contrite sinner almost 800 years ago.

COLD ASTON OR ASTON BLANK

THE VILLAGE WITH TWO NAMES

> *Location:* Two miles south-west of Bourton-on-the-Water, off the A429
> (Fosse Way).   Sheet 163 12871998

Cold Aston is often confused linguistically with Cold Ashton, but apart from their exposed upland positions (both stand at 700 feet above sea level) they have nothing in common. In fact, Cold Aston's nomenclature is even more confusing: it has laboured under two names for several hundred years — and still does, according to signposts, though even these are not sure which takes precedence!

Domesday is specific, using the name 'Eston', Aston. Episcopal records were the first to qualify it as 'frigida', in 1255, and that name remained, sometimes anglicised to 'cold', until in 1554 a Patent Roll announced the appointment of a vicar to 'Aston Blank'. The right of presentation had by then passed to the Crown but why that name was imposed on the village remains a mystery.

Aston Blank it became to all authorities, church, education, postal and Inland Revenue, but the inhabitants stuck stoically to Cold Aston, including those who embroidered the church banners, while the Ordnance Survey alternated the name on successive maps.

Even so, of paramount importance is that it is a complete village and on the tiny green stands a huge sycamore tree, one of the largest and oldest in England. The village's antiquity is also manifest in the mainly Norman church of St. Andrew, which has no east window: this is a rare unaltered feature of early Celtic origin found in only four other Cotswold churches: Baunton, Notgrove, Winstone and Brimpsfield.

The gravestone on the right of the porch is that of the last resident vicar — a man who not only loved his Lord and parishioners but also his cats — all twenty-seven of them!

COMPTON ABDALE

A CARVED STONE AND A VENGEFUL STONE

Location: Four miles west of Northleach, off the A40. Sheet 163 06311687

A spiritual association with springs and wells has a long history and it is not difficult to appreciate where a striking contrast with the bare, waterless Wolds all around emphasised their water as giver of life and bounty. Nor is it surprising that the imagination of the sculptor is manifest at these same springs, just as it was at the church he built.

Not for Compton Abdale the pumphouse on the green. Water enabled the settlement to exist, and where the road falls into the village the spring at the bottom must have refreshed many a dusty traveller long before the stone crocodile was born, and from whose mouth the water pours. No longer the amenity it was, the creature looks as though it has escaped from the company of the animals on the church buttress, but moss and fungi give it a strange prehistoric appearance.

Nearby, at the meeting point of the parishes of Yanworth, Stowell and Hampnett stands The Hangman's Stone, a monolith that tolerated no interference. A sheep stealer tied an animal's legs together so that he could carry it on his shoulders. Tired by its exertions, he rested against this stone, but was strangled by the thong as the animal continued to struggle. Justice was rough and swift in those days.

Preoccupation with judgment and death are visible in each of these parish churches. The consequences of Judgment features at St. Leonard's church, Stowell, where there is a twelfth-century 'Doom' wall painting depicting the sifting of souls, while angels and devils wait to collect their dues. A variation on this theme of visual symbolism of Death is continued at St. Michael's, Yanworth, where the tower arch has a sixteenth-century wall painting of a skeleton with scythe, shroud and sexton's shovel. However, not all local church paintings are old. In attempting to recreate the decoration that existed in all medieval churches, the Victorian rector had covered the whole of the chancel at Hampnett St. George's: whatever we may think of the result, the rector's courage and motives are worthy of admiration.

FARMINGTON

A DISTINCTIVE VILLAGE PUMP AND CHURCH GATE

> *Location:*　One mile north-east of Northleach, off the A40.　Sheet 163　15401360

Farmington is a delightful village with a distinctive pumphouse, an octagonal, many-gabled building erected as a shelter over the communal pump on the sloping green. It was built in memory of the squire, Edward Waller, who died here in March, 1828. Originally, it was roofed in thatch but when another Farmington, in the USA, was 300 years old in 1935 some of those citizens had the pumphouse re-roofed in Cotswold tiles and received, as a return gift, a bird bath of stone from the nearby quarry which now has pride of place in front of the library in Farmington, Connecticut.

When near the church of St. Peter, look closely at the gate: it is made from ninety old horse-shoes welded together, and is a work of true craftsmanship. Near to this gate is a headstone in memory of Henry Ruck, which reads:

> *A little while life's journey done*
> *We too shall reach the blissful shore*
> *And dwell while endless ages run*
> *With those not lost but gone before.*

The churchyard is though dominated by the enormous Waller tomb, which backs onto the tower and holds many of that family, their names carved on panels.

On the tower, two clocks have one hand only, a very rare and old feature. Other means of telling the time for Mass were the scratch dials which are still on the walls. Inside, the beautiful Norman chancel arch has orders of chevrons supported by pillars. Each pew is lighted individually by a candle held in a very old metal pole and standing at the bench end.

SHERBORNE

FUNEREAL ART

> *Location:*　Three miles east of Northleach, on the A40.　Sheet 163　16891478

The church of St. Mary's is joined by a corridor to Sherborne House so that the Dutton family, lords of the manor, could pass from one to the other without the inconvenience of having to step outside; they walked straight into a comfortable gallery which was solely for their own use. Sherborne is no longer their home, but the church is an awesome place still peopled by their ghosts and their monuments by the most famous sculptors of the day. For those visitors seeking social significance in funereal art and changes in symbolic presentation, there are few places better. The earliest monument, signed and dated 1661, is to Thomas Dutton:

> *. . . who was master of a large fortune and owner of a mind equal to it.*

In spite of his physical disability, 'Crump' Dutton was an active Colonel of Horse in the Royalist army yet friend of Oliver Cromwell to the extent that they proposed Dutton's son should marry Cromwell's eldest daughter — a match which never came to fruition. According to his contemporary Anthony a Wood, he was:

> *. . . a learned and prudent man, and as one of the richest, so one of the meekest in England.*

Rich he certainly was, for he could ride from Sherborne to Cheltenham, a distance of some sixteen miles, without leaving his land. Yet on one occasion he placed the whole estate on a single bet, and it was saved only by the swift action of his manservant.

When he died in 1657 he was buried in the church where his effigy portrays him standing in his shroud, following the fashion of Dr. John Donne in St. Paul's Cathedral, set in 1631.

Fashions change, and mortality is differently represented in the huge 1791 monument on the north wall of the Sanctuary. In this a buxom, life-sized marble angel, holding a medallion with profiles of the deceased James Lenox Dutton and his wife, tramples a prostrate figure of Death, but as she crushes the skinny skeleton with her foot, the skull only leers back at her.

James Bradley was arguably the greatest astronomer of the eighteenth century. Though buried at Minchinhampton, he was born at Sherborne in March, 1693, and in 1742 was appointed Astronomer Royal in succession to his mentor, Edmund Halley. Amongst his many discoveries were the abberation of light and the nutation of the Earth's axis; between 1750 and 1760 he also made a complete survey of the Northern sky. A plaque in St. Mary's commemorates his life and his achievements.

R. WESTMACOTT Fecit 1791.

To the Memory of
JAMES LENOX DUTTON Esq.

GREAT BARRINGTON

FIGHTING MEN AND FISHING MEN AND AGED MEN

| *Location:* | Three miles west of Burford, off the A40.   Sheet 163 20601350 |

The Barringtons, Great and Little, are synonymous with stone and the Strong family: both went from this quiet Cotswold corner to help Wren rebuild London after the Great Fire.

Until 1734 the Bray family owned Barrington Park. In the church of St. Mary, in a narrow space between the organ and the wall, is the life-sized recumbent effigy of Captain Edmund Bray, who died in 1620; here he is shown dressed in armour and with a ruff. Curiously, his sword is fastened on his right side so that he would have had to draw it with his left hand. Why is this so? In his youth, Bray killed a man in impetuous anger but was pardoned by Elizabeth I on condition that he always wore his sword on his right side to curb any repetition of thoughtless action. An alternative interpretation is that Bray vowed in gratitude for the pardon never to use his offending hand again. The reality may have been more prosaic: was he just left-handed?

Near the north door is a memorial exceptional for the superb marble sculpture of two Bray children.Here an angel is helping them, dressed as they are in their everyday clothes, to walk on the clouds and guides them heavenwards. The boy holds his sister by the hand, his eyes fixed on the guardian angel whose protecting wings overshadows them. The girl half-turns to look back as they walk among the clouds of heaven. These are two of a family of ten children who, the epitaph tells us, died of 'the Small Pox', Jane

> . . . *at her aunt Catchmay's in Gloucester*

in 1711 in her eighth year, and Edward at the Royal Academy at Angers in France in his fifteenth year on Christmas Day, 1720.

Charles Wingfield, squire and owner of most of the village, lived at Barrington Park, and rebuilt the house destroyed by fire in 1736. On the chancel wall is a tablet inscribed simply:

> *God Grant That I May Fish Until My Dying Day.*
> *And When It Comes To My Last Cast I Humbly Pray*
> *When In The Lord's Safe Landing Net I'm Peacefully Asleep*
> *That In His Mercy I Be Judged As Good Enough To Keep*
>
> Charles John Fitzroy Rhys Wingfield.

Pews in most parish churches are a relatively recent innovation. Previously the congregation stood throughout the service. Sometimes though a stone bench was specially provided, leaning against a wall, for the elderly and infirm to sit on. It is from this practice that the saying "the weak go to the wall" evolved. At this church is just such a bench, redundant for its original purpose, now standing outside against the churchyard wall. It is a long bench with elbow ends and was previously in the chancel.

Next to Great Barrington is its sister village, the Little one. The church has a superbly preserved twelfth-century doorway with deeply cut ornament, crisply carved foliage and a hideous head at the top. A beautiful Norman tympanum shows Christ in Majesty supported by two angels, each with a wing poised delicately behind Christ's haloed head to make a canopy.

This picturesque village has a unique claim to fame by having one of the oldest and smallest post-offices in Britain. There are other claimants to that title, but this one dates from 1643 and the public space is only a little over one yard square in extent.

WINDRUSH

EVIL-LOOKING BEASTS, PEACEFUL SHEEP AND A BRAVE MAN.

> *Location:* At the church of St. Peter, three-and-a-half miles east of Northleach, north of the A40. Sheet 163 19401310

Windrush is spread up the slope of the Windrush valley opposite Barrington Park. Here the stone is white and its name derives from the Celtic 'gwyn' coupled with 'riasc', morass. Its beautiful and well-preserved church has the most fascinating Norman south doorway, for it is completely surrounded by a double row of beakheads, less sophisticated and varied than Elkstone's and all the more alarming. These evil-looking carvings around the door are symbolic of demons waiting to snatch the souls of those attending in an irreverent or thoughtless spirit, but seem to have had little effect on the early incumbents.One vicar was made to carry a bundle of faggots three times round the cross at Burford as penance for keeping a concubine, and another was indicted by his servant for bemoaning the waste of his 18d on a pilgrimage to Hailes abbey and for declaring the sacred 'Blode of Criste' "a fabrication of men's hands."

Perhaps to make up for this, the church has had some outstanding curates. In 1817, Thomas Keble, brother of the famous John and later vicar of Bisley, was curate, and in 1829 Isaac Williams, another famous tractarian of the Oxford Movement, and who later attained very high office of the Church, served in that capacity.

This is of course wool country, and representations of sheep are to be seen everywhere. Inside the church are sheep's head terminals of c.1200. There are sheep carved on one of the splendid eighteenth-century tabletombs in the churchyard, alongside those with roll-tops and concave scalloped ends. Notice also the very early headstones which state simply K.F. 1694 and R.F. 1704.

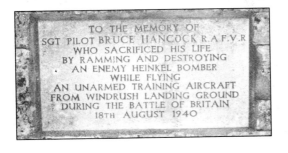

TO THE MEMORY OF
SGT PILOT BRUCE HANCOCK R.A.F.V.R
WHO SACRIFICED HIS LIFE
BY RAMMING AND DESTROYING
AN ENEMY HEINKEL BOMBER
WHILE FLYING
AN UNARMED TRAINING AIRCRAFT
FROM WINDRUSH LANDING GROUND
DURING THE BATTLE OF BRITAIN
18TH AUGUST 1940

Equally as simple, a more modern plaque is in remembrance of a very brave airman, Sgt. Pilot Bruce Hancock. On 18 August, 1940, he sacrificed his life by ramming and hence destroying a German Heinkel bomber while out flying his unarmed training aircraft.

ALDSWORTH

TWO LITTLE BOYS AND THEIR MOTHER

> *Location:*   Nine miles north-east of Cirencester, on the B4425.   Sheet 163 15481001

Sadness and grief are not confined to urban dwelling. In St. Batholomew's churchyard on the hillside outside this pretty village, two little brothers lie side by side. They were both born at Kilkenny, a small valley near where they rest, and lived their short lives in and around the farm in those mid-Victorian days when the substantial farmer lived a good life and was able to bring up his large family in well-fed comfort.

Following the fashion in the days of high infant mortality, they were both called Frederick Garne, for when the first son died in 1856 his name was given to the new-born baby brother. The first Frederick, sturdy, adventurous, climbing and exploring, was drowned at the age of eight when he fell headlong into one of the large vats of home-brewed beer made in those days on every farm of substance. The Garnes already had two girls but they were not expected to inherit the tenancy of the farm — a girl either married another farmer or stayed

to keep house for her ageing parents. Deeply distressed by this loss of their eldest son, the parents pinned all their hopes on the second Frederick who, like his brother, had the run of the farm and was full of the same spirit of adventure. At harvest time in 1863 he slid down from a rick where the labourers, having gone to dinner, left their pitchforks, prongs upwards, leaning against the stack, and was so badly injured that he died.

Now here they lie, two simple, indistinguishable grey stones marking their graves, both Frederick Garne, both eight years old, both dying in September, and next to them lies their mother, brought from South Cerney when she herself died some years later.

WINSON

THE SMALLEST POST OFFICE

Location:	Five miles north-east of Cirencester, off the A429 (Fosse Way). Sheet 163 09100869

Winson is a pretty little village upstream the Coln from Bibury, and achieved literary notice as the home of Robert Henriques, author of *Through the Valley*.

It has though other features worth a visit. Firstly, in a thatched cottage in a corner of the village is what is claimed to be one of the smallest post-offices in the West Country.

Then there are the marks on the shaft of the porch of St. Michael and All Angels. Nowadays one might call it vandalism, but the small, crudely scratched crosses are strangely moving in their simplicity. They are votive crosses, some initialled or with dates, thought to have been inscribed by parishioners about to embark on a journey or pilgrimage, as a pledge that they would make a gift to the church if they were spared to return.

Run your fingers along the line cut into the old grey stone and imagine yourself about to leave home, perhaps never to return — for those who set out from

medieval England on pilgrimage to the Holy Land took their lives in their hands facing robbery, hunger, sickness and perils of every kind as they made their painful way across Europe and maybe the small votive cross carved before leaving is the only memorial this pilgrim ever had.

What possessed them to go, to leave their own little village on the banks of the Coln, and journey off into the unknown? Was it simply a spirit of adventure, or for the expiation of some crime, or in the hope of glory to come in the Kingdom of Heaven?

While visiting the church, do not neglect the churchyard, for it contains some excellent tabletombs.

NORTH CERNEY

FEARSOME CREATURES

> *Location:*   Four miles north of Cirencester, on the A435.   Sheet 163 01890780

Here be fearsome creatures. Two carvings on the exterior of All Saints' church are thought to depict mythical creatures from the bestiaries. On the south-west buttress is the large incised drawing of an heraldic leopard passant guardant, its long tail between its legs, with small hoofs and a man's face. The other, on the south transept, is the grafitto of a Manticore, which was believed to have the head of a man, the body and legs of a lion, a scorpion's tail, three rows of teeth, a voice like the sound of flutes and trumpets, and a relish for human flesh!

The church was originally twelfth century, but the two drawings are post-Reformation, perhaps late sixteenth century, and must be masons' doodles.

Other faces peer down everywhere on this church, from gargoyles, roof-bosses and corbels, and four odd little human heads peer out from the lintel of the south doorway's Norman tympanum.

The magnificent carving is continued inside. The pulpit is of wine-glass shape, with a slim shaft spreading to form a base for the richly decorated bowl, carved from a single block of stone. Made c.1480, it is one of the finest on the Cotswolds.

When visiting North Cerney, a detour to Rendcomb will be repaid in your search for curiosities. Superbly situated in woodland in the steep Churn valley, the village is dominated by the vast and opulently Italianate mansion. Built in the 1860s for Sir Francis Goldsmidt, who twenty years earlier, had inherited a substantial fortune on condition that he spend a specified large sum on a country seat, the French-looking tower is said to have been a copy of that at Osborne House, by Victoria's Prince Consort on the Isle of Wight. Though designed for the impressions they would create, the towers on the house and stable block were judged necessary, for from their summits it can be seen that the copses of trees were planted not only to grace the park but in the shapes of Hebrew characters spelling out Sir Francis' name. Whatever is one to read into such a curious display?

33

BAGENDON

AN OPPORTUNITY TO BLOW HIS OWN TRUMPET?

Location:	Three miles north of Cirencester, off the A435. Sheet 163 01100660

There was a time when it was customary for people to prepare their own epitaphs before they died, and not surprisingly they took opportunity to emphasise those facets of themselves or their lives by which they wished to be remembered. Later, when this practice went out of fashion, others extolled the virtues of the deceased for them. In the tower of the little church of St. Mary is a memorial unique because it tells us little about Giles Parsloe, who died in 1728, but a great deal about his son who paid for the memorial and took opportunity to heap gratitude upon himself:

> *A dutiful son I have left behind.*
> *No man on earth could be more kind*
> *Than he was to me to my dying hour.*
> *He did for me that to his utmost power*
> *Nothing was me denyed that I would have*
> *In hopes to keep me longer from the grave.*
> *But God was pleased because he knows best*
> *To ease my pain and take my soul to rest.*

He who pays the piper calls the tune!

THAMESHEAD

THE SOURCE OF THE RIVER THAMES

> *Location:*   Three miles south-west of Cirencester, on the A433.
>   Sheet 163 98569916

With so many of the streams which feed the infant Thames springing up in Gloucestershire, it is not surprising that several remote localities claim to be the source of that river. The two strongest claimants, both with inscribed stone tablets to strengthen their arguments, are Thameshead, a short walk in fields behind the inn bearing that name, and Seven Springs, the unquestioned source of the river Churn, some eleven miles to the north, at the junction of the A436 and the A435 near Coberley.

Old Father Thames looks benignly from a sign at the Thames Head Inn, inviting the thirsty to stop and the curious and patriotic to find their way across the fields to where a statue of O Tamesine Pater used to recline stiffly in stone, a rather pompous patriarch to equate with the feeble embryo of the Thames, where only after heavy rainfall does one see even a puddle, as the water runs underground before asserting itself. But even if there is no gushing water, where is Old Father Thames now?

He is really a statue of Neptune, made c.1855 as decoration for the Crystal Palace. Rather larger than life, he reclines with his left hand on a bale, the other

behind him, and displays a shield bearing the arms of the City of London. The statue was set by the Conservators of the Thames at Thameshead in 1958 to mark the source of the river, but after being vandalised was moved to St. John's Lock at Lechlade: while not claiming to be at the source, at least he has a visible river to preside over.

Seven Springs (OS Sheet 163 96821723) is regarded by many as the true source of the Thames. Their argument claims that as the seven springs form the highest water rising of the Thames via the river Churn, its longest tributary, and the one furthest from the mouth, they must be the actual source. Thus on the wall of a tree-lined hollow, the spot is marked by a Latin inscription

HIC TUUS
O TAMESINE PATER
SEPTEMCEMINUS PONS

Here, thou, O Father Thames, has thy
sevenfold beginning.

Gurgling and bubbling, the infant Churn bounds away from the holes in the stone wall, through Coberley and then on to form the lakes at Cowley Manor. Even Lewis Carroll's Alice would have been amazed at Cowley's Wonderland of rare plants and birds had she known of it when she visited her uncle at the Rectory, where he was still the Revd Charles Lutwidge Dodgson.

While visiting either of these putative sources of the Thames, there are other curiosities to find.

At the crossroads near Seven Springs is a small round house, erected in 1840 by William Marshall, a wealthy industrialist and local squire. It was built so that people could leave parcels and messages which would be picked up by the passing carrier who called daily and charged 6d for the service. It is still used today, after restoration, though as a bus shelter.

There is another more than life-sized figure in Lechlade. A tall statue of a baker, rotund and smiling, stands in the road outside a shop in Burford Street, a reminder of the early days of advertising via street furniture.

SAPPERTON AND COATES

PORTALS TO A NEGLECTED CANAL TUNNEL

> *Location:*   Daneway is five miles west of Cirencester, north of the A419. Coates is
> three miles west of Cirencester, south of the A419.
> Sheets 163 94500349 and 96610068 respectively

Canal enthusiasts might well weep their way along the neglected route of the
Thames and Severn Canal from Lechlade westwards along the Thames watershed
and into the Golden Valley.

When construction started in 1783 the exciting ambition was to connect the
Severn via the Stroudwater Navigation to the Thames, and the spectacular
engineering was completed six years later, fulfilling the plan laid out by the poet
Alexander Pope and financed by the Lord Bathurst.

Never a financial success, the canal finally closed in 1933, but left many traces,
especially the Sapperton tunnel, regarded as a wonder of the age. Cutting
beneath the wooded Cotswolds south of Cirencester Park, the 3,817 yard (3,523
metre) tunnel is almost straight throughout. To consider that one canal is just like

any other is to neglect the
architectural and artistic designs
inherent in the structures. In the
case of this canal, the portals at
each end of the Sapperton tunnel
are unique.

The western entrance was of Gothic
Revival design, with battlements and
finials as decoration. Nearby stands
the Daneway Inn, built by the
Company for bargees to rest.
Unfortunately, this portal is still in a
state of sad neglect. The eastern
entrance, though, has been
renovated by volunteers and is most imposing. This one is in classical design,
with engaged Doric columns, niches, roundels, and a restricted archway with
keystone and voussoirs. Directly above it stands the Tunnel House inn.

Though beautifully designed, little thought was given to the bargees who had to
go through the tunnel. There is no towpath and the only way was for the men to
lie on their backs and propel the boat by walking, or 'legging', against the roof
or sides: it took five hours to 'leg' a laden eastbound boat against the stream, and
the prolonged activity caused a back complaint known inelegantly as
'Lighterman's bottom'.

Unique to the canal are the five classical, round lengthsman's houses which can be found at Chalford, Coates, Cerney Wick, Marston Meysey and Lechlade. They were built in 1790 to house watchmen whose duties included maintaining the towpaths in their section and ensuring the boatmen observed the Company's byelaws.

While in the area, a visit to St. Mathew's (note the spelling) church at Coates will reward the curiosity seeker. On the tower is a grotesque carving of an anthropophagus, a rare and frightening giant-like sculpture which holds in its teeth a naked form and is in process of swallowing it. This cannibal holds its victims by the legs and has engulfed him as far as his waist. What on earth, or not of this earth, possessed the mason to create such a monster? What message was he attempting to symbolise?

In the Baptistry of this church is an original stone seat. As there were no seats in the body of the church this would be used by the old and infirm; hence, in all probability, arose the saying, often wrongly used, "Let the weak go to the wall."

Look also in the Rectory garden, for you will see the most wonderful sculpture of a boar, larger than life, relaxing on the lawn and surveying his empire. Interestingly, an identical boar, of stone, sits on the island at Stanchcombe Park, and both are copies of that at the Uffizi theatre in Venice.

DRIFFIELD

WHERE IS 'BLUE' HANGER?

Location: Three miles south-east of Cirencester, east of the A419. Sheet 163 07459987

To Driffield, which time seems to have passed by, came 'Blue' Hanger to escape the plague rampaging in London. Later the 4th Lord Coleraine, he was nicknamed for his predilection to wear clothes of one colour only. In fact George Hanger would never accept the title when he inherited it, so that on his death it became extinct. His predecessors were notable for their unruly behaviour but George was the worst of the lot. He married a gypsy who eloped with a tinker, served in the Dragoons during the American War, and was a boon companion of the Prince Regent until notorious George's

. . . eccentric manners became too free and coarse even for the Prince Regent.

His extravagance was uncontrolled and he was committed to prison for debt; on his release he set up in business as a coal merchant. He died in 1824, but where was he buried? Prey to superstition, George, like other Regency rakes, had always maintained that if he was buried underground the devil would get him, so he requested to be buried above ground. There is a story that he was buried at Kempsford, his white marble coffin standing on a pedestal four feet high, but when the chapel was rebuilt in 1858 it was placed underneath the organ though with the top level with the floor. In his life he had many unsavoury distinctions, but in death did he become the only Irish peer to be buried beneath an organ in an English church? There is no notice of his burial, and his epitaph is in Driffield church, which must have the least distinguished tower on Cotswolds, and the porch is an example of early recycling. The epitaph reads, in apologia:

Near this place lieth the body of General George Hanger, Lord Coleraine. He lived and died a firm Believer in one God and in one God only. He was also a practical Christian as far as his frail nature did allow him to be so. He died 31 March, 1824 aged 73.

A predecessor had an equally enigmatic epitaph:

Here lieth in expectation of the last day Gabriel Hanger, Lord Coleraine, What manner of man he was That day will discover. He died 24 January 1773, aged 75.

CIRENCESTER

CAPITAL OF THE COTSWOLDS

Location: At the junction of the A429, A417 and A419.   Sheet 163 02500148

The claim of Cirencester to the 'capital of the Cotswolds' is not without foundation. As early as the fourth century, Corinium Dobunnorum was the capital

of the province of Britannia Prima and the second most important town of Roman Britain after London. During excavations prior to re-development in the town,a large mosaic pavement depicting a hare was discovered; the original is in the Corinium Museum but a reproduction was placed in the courtyard of the Old Brewery. It is the pivotal spot from which to follow the Roman roads and four meet here.

Cirencester is a place of superlatives. The Saxons built a church here which was in its day the longest in England; at the Dissolution, Robert Basinge bought the abbey and scrupulously obeyed instructions to leave not a single stone on top of another, so only the Norman gateway, incongruously called 'Saxon Arch', remains, though an enormous old mulberry tree thought to belong to the monks still stands, with much assistance from props under its branches. The cathedral-like parish church of St. John the Baptist is one of the largest in England; its magnificent three-storey south porch, erected as offices by the abbot and serving for centuries after the Dissolution

as the Town Hall, is the largest. The tower, at 162 feet, is the highest in Gloucestershire. It boasts the oldest peal of twelve bells in England, and observes some of the more ancient campanological customs, including the ringing of the 'Pancake Bell' on Shrove Tuesday, and the celebration of the Restoration on 29 May.

Fascinating features of this church continue. The open tracery of the fifteenth-century tulip-shaped painted stone pulpit is unique. The church holds the most interesting church plate in England, including the Boleyn Cup, with a hallmark of 1535, surmounted by the badge of Queen Anne's family, which was made for the Queen and given to Dr Richard Master in 1561. In the Lady Chapel is an ancient craftsman's joke, a carving of a cat chasing a mouse. On the exterior string-course are famous figures showing the Whitsun Ale procession, with many musical instruments. By the south door stands the painted eighteenth-century figure of a Bluecoat Boy which used to stand in the porch begging for the Powell's Schools.

In Cirencester Park, the town possesses one of the finest early landscape gardens in Britain, unspoiled by later changes in fashion. Allen Aspley, 1st Earl Bathurst, may have been his own architect for Cirencester House, the mansion in the Park, built between 1714-18, but his major achievement is the estate and gardens, laid out with the advice and collaboration of his literary friends, of whom the most intimate was the poet Alexander Pope. Pope wrote how he and his patron would

> . . . *draw plans for houses and gardens . . .*
> *all very fine and beautiful in our imagination.*

Letting their imagination have free rein,

> *Who then shall grace or who improve the soil*
> *Who plants like Bathurst or who builds like Boyle.*

The superlatives connected with Cirencester continue here also. An immensely tall semi-circular yew hedge separates the town from the Park and conceals its mansion. The hedge is one of the largest in the world, the gardeners needing a fireman's crane to clip the top. Laying out the Park was a massive operation. Ten rides segment it, radiating from the mid-point of Broad Avenue, which runs straight through the estate to Sapperton nearly five miles west (the Earl bought and demolished the Sapperton mansion to incorporate the grounds into his scheme) — the finest surviving example of formal geometric park planning.

The famous beech plantations attract foresters from all over the world, and we can marvel at the scale of Pope's recommendations:

> *Join Cotswold Hills to Sapperton's fair dale . . .*
> *Link towns to towns with avenue of oak,*
> *Enclose whole downs in walls, 'tis all a joke!*

As well as planting trees and laying out avenues, Bathurst littered his lands with romantic follies, the first to be seen in England and which, with the artificial lake and occasional serpentine walk, add a note of studied picturesqueness. There is little doubt that he designed these himself.

Alfred's Hall was begun in 1721 and is the ancestor of all the Gothic follies in Georgian parkscapes. It is a true sham. In an age of symmetry Bathurst abandoned all regularity and created "the real horrid feeling of conglomeration." Draped in ivy and enclosed in a grove of melancholy yews, its setting is still romantic.

The other follies are all very different. The Hexagon is a rusticated stone structure with six arched openings, built in 1736 to the north of Broad Avenue. 'Pope's Seat' is a small Doric temple facing south across Seven Rides down an avenue centred on Kemble church. The 'Horse Guards' are two ornamental arches, like a pair of gargantuan sentry boxes, at Ten

Rides. Still other buildings are part folly and part functional: the 'Round Tower', with narrow slits and castellations, is joined to a cottage; the 'Square House' is a cottage with a castellated parapet and a small tower just rising above the roof; 'Ivy Lodge' is a fantasy, half farmhouse and half farm buildings.

These are not the only unusual buildings in Cirencester. Just outside the Park, on a tree-clad slope at the edge of the Bullring is a tall eighteenth-century stone Obelisk. In Cecily Hill is an extra-ordinary embattled building of 1857 called the Barracks, though never used as such. Just outside the town, at Siddington, is another folly, a round tower.

AMPNEY CRUCIS

MEDIEVAL CROSS

> *Location:*   In the churchyard of Holy Rood, Ampney Crucis, three miles east of
> Cirencester, on the A417.   Sheet 163 08240155

In the churchyard recorded in Domesday as 'Omenie Holy Rood' can be found
the pride of Ampney Crucis (the 'p' is still not pronounced in any of the four
Ampneys). This is Saxon country but here is a medieval cross of c.1415, one of
the oldest and rarest in England, standing thirteen-feet tall above two steps. It is
covered with carved figures and has a gabled top holding a Crucifixion, St. John
and the Madonna.

It was not uncommon in Gloucestershire for parishioners to hide items from their
church which they valued and wished to protect from the iconoclasts. This cross
survived by being walled up inside the rood loft, where it lay until discovered in
1860 and restored by Canon Howman of Barnsley.

Inside the church is a very curious feature. The Pleydells lived at Ampney Park
for over 150 years, from 1561 until 1724. Their monuments record, as is perfectly
normal, the dates of their deaths — but then go one stage further and tell the
very hours!

The other Ampneys, too, have ancient crosses. Ampney St. Peter has a fourteenth-
century cross — and a fifteenth-century fertility carving north of its font. Down
Ampney has two stone memorial crosses, the oldest claiming to be the site of the
historic meeting with the British bishops to
which St. Augustine travelled in 603. The
rectory here is the birthplace of Ralph
Vaughan Williams, recorded for posterity in
his stirring hymn tune 'Down Ampney'.

Not to be outdone, the church of Ampney
St. Mary, wiped off the little brook by the
Black Death and isolated from its village, has
wall paintings dating from the twelfth to the
fifteenth century. That on the south wall, of
Christ injured by manual labour on Sundays,
includes details of medieval crafts — look for
the small figure of a wheelwright truing a
spoke by holding it to his eye. The carved
lintel over the north doorway shows a griffon
and a lion trampling two snakes with sinister
faces: this is a graphic ancient symbolisation
of good conquering evil.

POULTON

BETTY'S GRAVE

Location:	North of Poulton crossroads on the A417, five miles east of Cirencester. Sheet 163 10370206

More than one name from history exercises our imagination. One arm of a signpost west of Fairford is marked 'Betty's Grave', and close by is a well-marked grassy mound. But who was Betty and why was she buried here? A suicide? A poisoner? A witch who lies with a stake driven through her heart?

There are two legends about Betty. One is that she was a farmworker who took up a wager to reap an acre field of corn with her own sickle within a specified time. She completed the task successfully but was buried at the spot where she fell down dead from exhaustion at the end of the day's work. Another version is that she was a Poulton woman who poisoned herself, with her possibly illegitimate baby, and was buried at the nearest crossroads.

So who is Betty? Is she a hook-nosed hag huddled in black tatters with gnarled fingers clutching a knobbly stick, or a buxom wench, sun-bonnetted, with blistered hands from a well-worked scythe? Or a sad mother at the end of her tether, unable to withstand her neighbours' opprobrium or to see any future for herself and her child? The choice is yours.

Whichever is true — and the last seems the more likely — a crossroads was an irresistible invitation to witches who got up to all sorts of mischief.

READY TOKEN

A LAST RESTING PLACE

Location:	Five miles north-east of Cirencester, south of the A433. Sheet 163 10570463

Ready Token sits on the old Roman road of Akeman Street, and there are several explanations for its curious name. One is that cash not credit was demanded of stagecoach travellers; another is that it was the refuge of highwaymen who handed a token to the pub landlord to show they were not the law; yet another that thethe name derives from Old English 'rhydd'. Whichever is accepted, Ready Token certainly had a reputation for dark deeds. It was said that travellers who put up there would disappear overnight: when the inn was renovated recently, eight skeletons were found under the floor.

Not all inhabitants worried about its reputation, and some were reluctant to leave. The copse at Ready Token was chosen by its owner, together with his pet dogs, for their last resting place. The epitaph reads:

> *When I am dead my dearest*
> *Sing no sad songs for me*
> *Plant thou no roses at my head*
> *No shady cypress tree*
> *Be the green grass above me*
> *With showers and dewdrops wet*
> *And if thou wilt remember*
> *And if thou wilt forget.*

At nearby Barnsley, the village pub is called just that: The Village Pub. It is the only one in England formally so-called, and got its name to distinguish it from the Greyhound, which is now a farm — and carries a pub sign saying 'Greyhound Farm'.

A brass plaque in Barnsley church commemorates a young man who drowned where there is no more water than is found in a dew pond:

> *O Death how sudden was Thy stroke,*
> *The nearest Union Thou hast broke,*
> *Nor gave me time to take my leave*
> *Of my dear parents left to grieve;*
> *The watery wave which stopped my breath*
> *For want of help, soon caused my death.*

QUENINGTON

HEAVEN AND HELL IN STONE

> *Location:* St. Swithin's church, Quenington, three miles north of Fairford.
> Sheet 163 14570470

Quenington is a delightful village in the Coln valley. The fourteenth-century gatehouse of the Knights Hospitallers and the round dovecote, mentioned in documents of 1338 and retaining its potence, survive in the grounds of Quenington Court.

It is though the church of St. Swithin, near the river by a mill, which draws major interest because of its magnificent doorways and tympana. They stand as testimony not only to the skill of the craftsmen but to close relations between the secular and the sacred.

The north doorway is mid-twelfth century work of unusual richness and splendour. It has three orders with different kinds of chevrons and round mouldings, one with Norman limpet shells. The abaci and the capitals are carved, the latter with Jacks-in-the-Green. The tympanum is earlier and represents the Harrowing of Hell, with details taken from the spurious Gospel of Nicodemus:

Satan is bound, and one figure rises from the sea, another from Satan's mouth, a third from death. Christ pinions the Devil with the Cross, and with outstretched arms rescues the trapped souls. An unusual feature is the sundisk with a face, which represents God, a reference to the Gospel of Nicodemus which tells how the sun suddenly illuminated the depths of Hell to announce the arrival of Christ.

The south doorway is a finer composition still, as it is all of one piece, including the tympanum. The subject is the Coronation of the Virgin, its earliest representation in western European art. The Virgin and Christ are seated side-by-side as he crowns her. Next to the Virgin are seraphim and the symbols of SS. John Luke; next to Christ the symbols of SS. Matthew and Mark, and a little temple, probably the celestial Jerusalem. Around the border are representations of various animals — a fox, a hare or rabbit, and a horse can be identified. Are they symbolic of demons waiting to snatch the souls of those attending in an irreverent or thoughtless spirit, or were they to frighten away devils from this holy place?

Heaven and Hell may lose all their nebulosity when interpreted in stone, yet these richly decorated frames and vigorous carvings are as exactly executed as if embroidered rather than chipped out by mallet and chisel.

SOUTHROP

A UNIQUE FONT

> *Location:* Three miles north-east of Fairford, west of the A361.
> Sheet 163 03290348

First recorded in the Domesday census as 'Sudthropa', the southern independent farmstead, Southrop lies amid lush pastures in the Leach valley. The church of St. Peter, though small and situated in the farmyard of the Manor, is precious because of its age: but it has two other claims to fame, its association with John Keble, and its font.

John Keble, author of the 'Christian Year', was curate here for the years 1823–25, and in the rectory held the discussions which sowed the seeds of the Oxford Movement. He it was also who discovered, built into the south doorway, the richly carved font, hidden from the Puritans.

The font is unique. Carved c.1180, it has an arcade of eight trefoiled arches. On the east side is Moses with the tablets of the Law, flanked by Ecclesia (the Christian church) with chalice and pennoned cross, and Synagogue (the Jewish church) blinded by a broken staff. The remaining five arches hold figures of armoured and armed women representing the Virtues attacking their opposite Vices, shown as ugly, deformed creatures:

*Modestia (self-retraint)
is beheading Ebrietas
(drunkenness);
Patience (patience) is
whipping Ira (anger);
Misericordia (pity)
spears Invidia (envy);
Temperancia (sobriety)
stabs Luxuria (luxury);
Largitas (generosity)
tramples Avaricia (excess).*

The names of the Virtues are inscribed on the arches of the panels while those of the Vices are cut backwards on the panels themselves, possibly to lessen their power.

Though the sculptures may look lifeless, the figures are carved with far greater freedom and iconoclastic sophistication than any contemporary font.

There is much of interest outside the church, too. Almost under the belfry is a tabletomb which shows masons' tools, square, divider and hammer. Tradition holds that this is the tomb of a mason who broke his neck falling from the belfry and was buried where his body landed. There are also a number of tabletombs with the rare bale top and an even more curious one which has on its lid a stone coffin: was the occupant trying to confuse the devil by simulating a burial above ground?

In the barnyard next to the church is a small group of trees, a peaceful lawn around a large mill press. Each tree was planted in memoriam of a much-loved pony and buried beneath are Firebird, Smokey, Conker and Mystery.

FAIRFORD

WOOL, GLASS AND WOOD

Location: St. Mary's church, Fairford, on the A417, four miles west of Lechlade and eight miles east of Cirencester.   Sheet 163 15100120

Fairforde never florishid afore ye cuming of ye Tames unto it

wrote Leland, antiquary to Henry VIII, after his visit in the early 1540s. John Tame was a woolstapler and cloth merchant from Cirencester, who, like many of his colleagues in an age of different values, sought to use his enormous worldly wealth to erect a lasting sacred memorial. In the last decade of the fifteenth century he almost entirely rebuilt St. Mary's.

The church is full of treasures but it is for the twenty-eight medieval stained-glass windows covering an area of over 2,000 square feet that it is best known. Apart for safety during World War II they have never been removed, and are the only complete set of this period to survive in the whole of Britain.

Ones eyes are constantly drawn to the windows, and they are known as 'the poor man's bible' for they depict in glowing, jewel-like colours the pictorial story of the entire Catholic faith. The source of the subjects was the fifteenth-century Biblia Pauperum, the whole suite a moralising and instructional guide for those in the past without access to a printed copy of the Scriptures. Look, for example, at window fifteen, which conveys vividly the horrors of damnation for those who stray from the paths of righteousness. In the Last Judgment the application of colour is so symbolic: the earth glows red in the fires of the end of the world; angels and devils fight for the judged, and fallen souls are being hounded into the fires of Hell by hordes of luridly-coloured demons, one of whom, in blue with a beard, is taking an old man off to his doom in a wheelbarrow; Satan himself has a row of sharp teeth, staring eyes, and a green tail, a final warning to the impenitent.

As beautiful as the windows and with the same didactic intent are the quaint wood carvings of the fourteen misericords in the chancel. There are different scenes, many domestic, including a grotesque head (probably a green man), a woman dragging a youth by his long hair and beating him with a washing beetle, a man holding two dogs, two wyverns with entwined tails possibly representing the devil, a fox with geese it has just killed, a dog sniffing and raiding the cookpot whilst his mistress spins, a wheatsheaf and reapers, and a lovely carving of the battle between the sexes (with Woman winning) as a wife belabours her husband with a ladle.

The magnificent artistic work is carried outside St. Mary's, too. The parapets are enlivened with spirited sculpture often copied from the bestiaries. One particularly delightful human jester, on the south side, is looking down and dangling a leg as if considering whether to jump, and wearing a rather large head-dress.

In front of the porch stands a memorial to

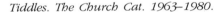

Tiddles. The Church Cat. 1963–1980.

It was in 1963 that the verger took pity on a stray, half-starved kitten he found in the churchyard. He fed it, cared for it, and named it Tiddles. The church remained Tiddles' home for seventeen years as she repaid his kindness by catching mice. She was always perfectly behaved, always clean, and during sermons would often curl on the lap of one or other of the congregation.

When she died in 1980 a local mason carved her memorial, and included a life-like portrait of her.

MEYSEY HAMPTON

A DOCTOR, HIS WIVES AND HIS PATIENT

> *Location:* St. Mary's church, Meysey Hampton, two miles west of Fairford, on the A417. Sheet 163 11800010

An enormous carved and painted stone memorial of 1626 almost fills a wall of the north transept of this church. It portrays local physician Dr. James Vaulx and his two wives: but it is so amusing to see how differently the wives are treated! One wonders whether Vaulx was happy to agree to the design of the monument — or was he past caring, by that time?

The good doctor's deceased first wife, Editha, is clearly idealised, slender and alert, wearing a stiff ruff and a small Tudor cap; her right hand rests on a skull and beneath her in a panel her twelve chidren crowd together, two tiny ones lying side by side on cushions. The living second wife, Philippa, is shown unflatteringly to have a double chin, fat face and lank hair, and wears the more simple clothes of Stuart times; she holds a book, and beneath her are her four children, one of whom lies down. The symbolism of the monument was contemporary: a skull denoted death, and children lying down signified that they had died before baptism.

Dr. Vaulx's claim to fame was that he almost, but not quite, became Royal Physician, for his reputation as 'practitioner of physick and surgery' had spread beyond this small village. King James I summoned the great man to his bedside and questioned him how he had gained his knowledge of healing, "by reading or by observation and practice". Vaulx evidently gave the wrong answer, saying it was by practice, whereupon the King declined to be practised on and dismissed him forthwith. No wonder the doctor looks depressed, resting his head on one hand, his elbow on a skull, while both his wives stare stonily ahead.

There is another very curious monument here, and is the only one of its kind in existence. The epitaph refers to Margaret Griswald who came to Meysey Hampton as a patient of Dr. Vaulx, and died one year before him. It took the great eighteenth-century antiquarian Samuel Rudder to decipher it, for all the letters are in both upper and lower case, superimposed on each other.

While outwardly insignificant, the church has other items of interest. A great rarity, an anchorite's Hagioscope (a hermit's squint) can be found at the back, while outside in a corner of the churchyard is a small building used as a watch house in those days when new graves had to be guarded against the activities of body-snatchers.

On the nearby village green is an intriguing pump. Raised high above the ground with a flight of stone steps leading up to it, it was used to fill casks carried on horse-drawn wagons.

SOUTH CERNEY AND OTHER PLACES
CURIOUS NAMES

> *Location:* At South Cerney, four miles south-east of Cirencester, south of the A419.
> Sheet 163 04819710

On the Cotswolds, one meets with many curious names. For some it it is possible to trace the derivation but others are beyond historical study and remain in folklore.

Agriculture has dwindled at South Cerney, but no-one has changed the name of a lovely old walk called 'Bow-wow'. Nearby is 'Upper-up' and 'Lower-up'.

It was from Painswick Beacon that Charles I watched his soldiers advance on Gloucester and to this spot, high on a wooded spur, the Royalists returned dejectedly some time later. The young Prince of Wales asked his father if they could go home. "My son," the weary King replied, "We have no home." Climbing down from the Beacon and taking refuge in the tiny hamlet deep in a wooded combe, the King is said to have exclaimed, "This is paradise." So Paradise it is (OS Sheet 162 86901150). The inn, formerly the Plough, on the sweeping road above Paradise, is appropriately named the 'Adam and Eve'. Belonging at one time to Godsell's Brewery prompted the local ditty:

> *The Adam and Eve Inn*
> *Paradise*
> *God sells beer!*

Whether or not acceptable cosmology, four miles due south of Paradise are The Heavens (OS Sheet 162 86900429) and the steepness of the valley in which the hamlet lies illustrates just how difficult it is to get there!

On the western shoulder of the hill between Rodborough and Minchinhampton Commons stands the curiously named hamlet of St. Chloe (OS Sheet 162 84300188) — but not named in remembrance of some venerable saint. The area first appears in a charter dating between 716 and 743 as 'Sentodleag' and in 896 as 'Sengetlege', a clearing made by burning, from the Old English 'senged' meaning singed or burnt.

Further south still is Knockdown (Sheet 162 83888844) — as it is on a crossroads of the busy A433 perhaps we don't have to research too deeply to discover how it acquired that name, nor how appropriate it is.

Then we find a railway name plate in a bus shelter

Yes, I remember Addlestrop,

wrote Edward Thomas, but lovers of his poem know it was the GWR sign — *only the name* — that captured his imagination when his train stopped here one summer afternoon. The station is no more and the plate is displayed in the bus shelter, with the poem on a plaque below.

DIDMARTON

AN UNCHANGED CHURCH

Location: St. Lawrence's church, Didmarton, five miles south-east of Tetbury, on the A433.   Sheet 173 82408730

Unlike most of its contemporaries on the Cotswolds, this church escaped Victorian 'restoration'; instead, the parishioners abandoned it and built another one. What survives today is a medieval church in its eighteenth-century condition, with Georgian interior arrangements, fittings and fixtures exactly as left.

In the south wall of the nave a towering 'three-decker' pulpit is positioned at the junction of the L-shaped church in order to see in both directions; it is given even greater authority by being placed centrally between two windows. There are fine, large box-pews on the south, still painted in the eighteenth century's favourite pale green. A Decalogue over the altar has been returned to its original place, brought back from a farm where it was abandoned over a hundred years ago.

BADMINTON

WHIMSICAL BUILDINGS

Location: In Badminton Park, Badminton.   Sheet 173 80508290

Badminton House and Park need no introduction to the visitor, though a search for curiosities will lead mainly to the grounds.

Perhaps best known for its sporting connections, particularly the three-day eventing which continues involvement with horses, for the 5th Duke of Beaufort is credited with introducing fox hunting into the Cotswolds in the 1760s, other activities took place at Badminton House: the game of badminton evolved and was first played in the entrance hall on the north front of the House and the modern court still uses these dimensions.

The present church at Great Badminton is generally of interest because of its funerary art, but has a curious feature: it is connected to the mansion by a corridor from the library to the 'tribune' — the Somerset family pew, a gallery at the back of the church containing a fireplace and comfortable armchairs.

In the grounds a number of fanciful park and farm buildings remain.

Swangrove is a maison de plaisance built c.1701 on the edge of the park. An elegant rendering of Cotswold tradition on a minute scale, it was originally a pavilion, though an upper panelled room, approached by outside steps, was added later in the eighteenth century. Alongside is a little castellated barn.

The Root House or Hermit's Cell, the largest surviving hermitage, is made entirely of logs of wood, an astonishing work by the mysterious Thomas Wright of Durham, architect and astronomer. It is wonderfully preserved, a fine room rather than a cell, of about twenty feet by fourteen, with a sloping thatched roof. The door frame is the upturned fork of a huge tree and four more big and particularly knotty trunks make the corner posts; the steep pediments each have sections of hollow trees as 'yeux de beouf'. Everywhere there is wild, jumbled infill of branches, roots and knots. Under the rear pediment is a branch bench with its ogee back lettered in nailheads:

HERE LOUNGERS LOITER and *HERE THE WEARY REST*

For a thatched building made of unworked roots and lumps of distressed trees still to be standing after 250 years is an outstanding achievement.

Other buildings, all unique, were erected between 1748 and 1756 when Wright was at the height of his powers. Ragged Castle, of c.1750 is a charming little rubble castle; the Slait Lodges have round towers at each corner and central chimneys, looking like pottery ornaments found on chimney pieces; Castle Barn has battlements and flanking towers.

This development of interesting buildings continued outside the park. On the road to Acton Turville are several Cottages Ornees with overhanging thatched roofs supported on rustic wooden posts, and with Gothic windows.

WARMLEY

HERE BE A GIANT

Location:	East of Bristol, on the A420. Sheet 172 67107350

Most of our giants are Neptunes — never Poseidon — and one giant Neptune has become a folly, now rather like an enormous garden ornament. Not only large, standing twenty-two feet tall, but very tough, once in the middle of a big lake, later solitary in the fields, now on the edge of a little wood, gazing in

wonder at the mobile homes which have sprung up in front of him. He is made of clinker, with a grotto of clinker behind him. We can see his cement-faced body, the armature of his left arm flung across his chest exposed, and the right arm gone, but the weathered, blind face is fierce and he remains an impressive and defiant figure.

He was part of a remarkable eighteenth-century industrial empire now almost overwhelmed by Warmley on the outskirts of Bristol. The Champions were a Quaker family whose spelter and brass works were established in Bristol by 1740. William Champion went to Holland to find more about the extraction of zinc and the manufacture of spelter and other alloys, and in 1749 he set up at Warmley large works for the production of zinc on a commercial scale, using ore mined on Mendip. By 1754, he had four furnaces for spelter, twelve for brass, fourteen for copper, and mills for making sheet metal, wire and pans — his huge brass pans for evaporating salt were called 'neptunes'. He had a pin factory, and exported large quantities of brassware to West Africa, including bars to make slave collars.

The empire flourished. He built a fine house looking down towards a large lake with Neptune in the middle and, beyond, a canal with a little eye-catcher boathouse at the end, which still stands. There was a bird sanctuary, and underground tunnels lined with slag, illuminated, and decorated with ferns. Some of the tall model cottages decorated with slag that he built for his workers remain, and so does the clock-tower with slag dressing and steel window-frames, which must be some of the earliest ever made.

The empire failed. He went bankrupt in 1768 with everything going wrong at once: he bought too much coal while orders were falling against foreign imports, and Parliament would not extend the patent for his process. A rival firm bought the works, and all that is left is what we can see. Neptune stands proud and fierceand defiant, though.

WOTTON-UNDER-EDGE

ANCIENT FARMING

Location: Nine miles west of Tetbury, off the B4060.   Sheet 162   75809400

If little is known about the extent and productivity of pastoral farming in Saxon times beyond that sheep grazing was important on ecclesiastical lands, almost nothing is known about arable farming. However, the ridge and furrow features found in some Cotswold parishes, resembling gentle waves on a calm sea or folds in heavy curtains, date from the Saxon period or even earlier. They were formed by the plough turning the cut sod to one side only and the ploughman moving up and down the field to create, as the soil gathers in one direction, a series of ridges and hollows. When this procedure was followed on sloping ground, the effect of running the plough across the hillside was to turn material downhill. If ploughing continued so that soil was heaped up at regular intervals, then features known as 'strip lynchets' emerged as deposited soil became banks separated by almost level terraces.

The Cotswold edge has nearly a hundred 'flights' of such lynchets, the majority on the steep slopes between North Nibley and Bath: many are visually spectacular. Just out of Wotton-under-Edge on the B4058 towards Nailsworth, near the village of Coombe, is a remarkable 'flight'. A local tradition has it that these lynchets, and elsewhere on the escarpment around Wotton, were used by the Cistercian monks of Kingswood abbey for their vineyards. There are further 'flights' on the slopes of Wotton Hill, off the B4060 towards North Nibley and Dursley.

For all that goods and people have been moving in and out of the Cotswolds for thousands of years, travel in the region by 1700 was neither quick nor easy. Important roads from earlier periods — the prehistoric Jurassic Way, the Roman roads or the medieval saltways and drovers' ways — were not always suitable for later needs. What distinguished development from the eighteenth century was the growth of toll or turnpike roads, a system which charged users a toll and, theoretically, drew sufficient funds from travellers for each parish to manitain its stretch of road. The companies which competed for custom for their roads during the eighteenth century took opportunity also to ensure their properties had individuality. Two tollhouses near Wotton are of very interesting designs. The one at the top of Rushmire Hill is built in ornate Gothic style, and is castellated. In partial contrast, Turnpike House, at Bushford Bridge is in the form of a round house, though again with castellations.

CHARFIELD

A RAILWAY DISASTER

Location: In the churchyard at Charfield, three miles south-west of Wotton-
under-Edge, on the B4058.   Sheet 162 72099220

Disasters always cause great sadness, and the
Cotswolds are no stranger to them. One of
the most curious is remembered at Charfield.

On the road to the hamlet of Churchend is
an old medieval church, now redundant. The
Charfield Railway Monument stands in a
remote corner of its churchyard, and recalls
the victims of a local railway accident in
1928, their names and their town of
residence. Twelve are named — but the
tablet also notes two unidentified children,
and the question of who they were remains
unanswered. Some talk about a woman in
black who used to visit the memorial; others
believe the two were not children at all, but
jockeys on their way to work. Whatever the
truth, there is no doubt that the Monument
is a record in stone of much personal grief.

Not far from this
churchyard, on
the road to
Wotton, is an
interestingly
designed
tollhouse, which
is round,
castellated and
now ivy-clad.

NORTH NIBLEY

GLOUCESTERSHIRE'S TALLEST TOWER.

Location:	At Nibley Knoll, two miles north-west of Wotton-under- Edge, on the B4060. Sheet 162 74239558

William Tyndale was one of those great controversial clerics who, collectively, spurred on the Reformation. While an undergraduate at Oxford he had formed advanced religious views, and argued them vociferously. After ordination in 1521 he became tutor to the children of Sir John Walsh at Little Sodbury Manor and under Walsh's roof thought out the future translation of the New Testament. It is in the Great Hall that Tyndale is said to have addressed words to an opponent which made him famous:

If God spare my life, ere many years I will cause a boy that driveth the plough shall know more of the scripture than thou doest!

Over the years Tyndale did translate the New Testament into English, an heretical act for which he had to flee the country. He continued his life of controversy, and in 1536 was strangled and burnt at the stake at Vilvorde in the Low Countries.

In a commanding position on Nibley Knoll, the Tyndale Monument was erected in 1866, a tapering stone belvedere tower with a pyramidal roof and a cross. It stands 111 feet high and has 141 stairs leading to the gallery. An inscription on the tower commemorates his tremendous achievement.

The inscription notes that Tyndale was 'born near this spot', though there is considerable doubt about that. There are several claimants to his birthplace: Tyndale Cottage in North Nibley is old but not necessarily correct; others hold out for Wotton, and still others for Hurst Farmhouse at Slimbridge. Biographical information in the sixteenth century being what it is, there is even a strong suspicion that the William Tyndale of North Nibley was not the same as the William Tyndale "born on the borders of Wales", who translated the Bible, in which case the monument is pure folly.

It is always interesting to speculate on the lives of families of men who made a mark on their times. Clearly Grace Smyth, was a long-suffering wife whose look of patient resignation on her effigy in St. Martin's church shows she learnt that virtue well. The meticulous recording of the length of her marriage

> . . .*for the space of Twelve Yeares and 35 Dayes*

suggests she found being the wife of John, steward to "the hundred and liberty of Berkeley", and antiquarian, a tedious business; his prolific compilations of the histories of the Berkeleys would have left little time for pleasant chit-chat with his spouse.

And what are we to make of the epitaph's final phrase about

> . . .*her voluntary leaving this life the IXth Day of Nov 1609.*

Was she really so relieved to be moving on? Where is her husband and why are they not portrayed together, as was the custom? Could they not even bear to share the same monument? The mystery deepens. Why is she the only link in this church with North Nibley's famous moment as the site of the last battle in England between private armies?

The major portion of the house shared by Grace and John Smyth has long disappeared from North Nibley, but an entrance survives and is inscribed:

NMMH SPNC ANNO DNI 1607

abbreviated from:

Nunc mei, mox hujus
Sed postea nescio cujus.

Freely translated, this becomes:

Today 'tis mine
Tomorrow, thine,
But whose next day
I cannot say.
In the year of Our Lord 1607.

HAWKESBURY

NOT ALL WELCOME

> *Location:* Four miles south of Wotton-under-Edge, west of the A46.
> Sheet 172 76818693

Modern churches go to considerable pains to make everyone welcome and standards of dress are not now seen as relevant. It was not always so, especially in the case of women. In rural areas dogs were vital to the task of animal husbandry, but in some churches they too were not welcome.

In the north porch St. Mary's church at Hawkesbury stood a painted board (not now in situ, but inside the church) requesting:

> *It is Desired That*
> *all Persons that come to*
> *this Church would be Careful*
> *to leave their Dogs at home and*
> *that the Women would not walk*
> *in with their Pattens on.*

To emphasise the request, and in case there was any confusion, a pair of pattens is displayed above the notice.

Though dogs were not welcome, and women had to be properly shod, we can be sure that this injunction was not extended to two famous people who are commemorated in this church, both of whom attained great importance in their day. In a mural tablet on the south wall is an inscription to Charles Jenkinson, 7th Baronet (1808) — a descendant of the Anthony Jenkinson who was a companion of the maritime explorer Sebastian Cabot — who became successively Lord of the Admiralty, Lord of the Treasury in 1767, and in 1778 Secretary of War under Lord North. In 1786 he was raised to the peerage of Baron Hawkesbury, and in 1796 was created Earl of Liverpool.

Against the north wall is a black and white tablet to the 2nd Earl (1828): on the assassination of Spencer Percival in 1812 he was appointed Prime Minister, an office he held for fifteen years. When in the area, look out for some interesting names. Near Hawkesbury is Starveall, the familiar name with which the Saxons dubbed every poor bit of land which didn't yield to their plough. Good land was deemed Fillhorn.

STINCHCOMBE

A ROMANTIC GARDEN

Location:	Stancombe Park, Stinchcombe, one mile west of Dursley, on the B4060. Sheet 162 73799740

The garden at Stancombe Park, Stinchcombe, is a romantic place with its hidden lake and secret twisting paths along which, unobserved from the house, clandestine meetings took place. However, the ghostly grottoes and shady trees did not afford the the complete anonymity the couple sought, for their names have been broadcast widely: the lass was a gypsy and her lover the local vicar.

In the mid-nineteenth century, Miss Purnell, who owned Stancombe Park, married the Revd. David Edwards, vicar of North Nibley. He set about laying a romantic

garden far from the house where, we are told, he could orchestrate assignations, without being observed, with the gypsy who was his one true love. In practice, it is difficult to see how he could have managed this, as the garden would have been filled constantly with workmen building all the impedimenta deemed essential to the creation of a mood. Without doubt, though, the mood he achieved was romantic in the extreme: any gypsy with fire in her blood would surely have capitulated immediately.

After years of neglect, the folly garden has been restored, and every ingredient of a romantic mood is here: water in the lake, (including the stone boar sitting on the island, a copy of one outside the Uffizi theatre in Venice, and named Cornelius locally), winding walks, fine trees, gloomy grottoes, mossy cascades, subterranean tunnels, pavilions of glass with conical fairy-tale roofs, and a temple. Could all these surprises, the choice of Egyptian and prehistoric themes for the exotic conceits, the transition from the romantic landscaped park to the formal flower garden near the house, really have been built because a vicar was love-torn?

Though not in the Revd. Edward's charge, the church at Stinchcombe is dedicated to the obscure St. Cyr, the infant son of fourth-century Christians. He is said to have boxed the ears of Alexander, the heathen governor of Seleucia, when he heard the name of Jesus blasphemed, and been stabbed to death in his mother's arms by the angry governor.

NYMPSFIELD

HETTY PEGLER'S TUMP

Location: Three miles west of Nailsworth, on the B4066. Sheet 162 79100010

Neolithic long barrows represent the state of the art means of disposing of the dead c.2,900BC. Each of the seventy or so long barrows which punctuate the Cotswold hills consists of chambers walled and roofed with massive slabs of local stone and enclosed by a cairn, a mound of stones now covered by vegetation. Variations in construction exist but the basic shape is roughly trapezoidal or rectangular in plan with a horned entrance in front of which was a forecourt, possibly serving a ceremonial function. Was it the latter which caused this barrow to be placed here? The village name of Nympsfield has been translated to mean 'tract of open country belonging to a place called Nymed', from the Welsh 'nyfed', a shrine or holy place. How sacred was this place?

The seventeenth century brought a new name to this most impressive of long barrows. Hetty Pegler's Tump is so-called after an Edith Pegler whose family owned the land on which it stands and who joined with her husband, Henry, in 1677 to sell that piece of open field. At that time it was known either just as 'The Barrow' or as Cold Harbour, a name generally given to a vagrant's refuge, but most possibly was given Hetty's name as the interest in antiquities developed nationally and locally during her lifetime.

The position of the Tump, high on the Cotswold edge, is symbolic. It belongs to an early part of the cultural tradition which lasted from c.3,000 to 1,800BC in Britain, and consists of a pear-shaped mound forty metres long, twenty-seven metres wide and three metres high, and the entrance portal is about a metre high. Internally, a passage leads to three chambers, a further two being sealed because of their dangerous state.

To the builders, the chambered mound represented the womb of the earth-goddess. Here, this concept received practical expression for the Tump was a communal burial mound and the rite of interment was inhumation of the unburnt

body. When first excavated in 1821, fifteen skeletons were found inside the mound, since when the remains of a further fifteen have been recovered from the gallery and chambers. But that was not all. An additional, later burial accompanied by three Roman coins has also been discovered: this barrow had remained a hallowed place through three millenia, being used for interment even during Roman times. The siting at Nympsfield was indeed symbolic.

WOODCHESTER

AN UNFINISHED MANSION

Location: Five miles south-west of Stroud, off the B4066.   Sheet 162 80950149

In the valley between Stroud and Nailsworth, the mills and houses reflect their cloth-making past. Here, Woodchester Park extends some two-and-a-half miles westwards along the Inchbrook stream, its five lakes stretching towards the Cotswold scarp. Though almost unknown and with incomplete interior, its Mansion must rank as one of the great achievements of nineteenth-century domestic architecture, a remarkable synthesis of French Gothic Revival and the local Cotswold tradition. If ever a house deserves to be called a folly, this is it.

William Leigh was an extremely wealthy man and a devout Roman Catholic. Acting on the advice of Pugin, the great Victorian architect, he bought and demolished Spring Park, Lord Ducie's house which had been under construction for six years, and of which only The Tower remains. Leigh then baulked at paying the price Pugin proposed for building a new house on a different site in the Park and instead employed a young, brilliant, local architect, Benjamin Bucknall. Work was begun in 1858 and for fourteen years the house slowly took shape. The reason for this leisurely rate of building is unclear but would appear to be linked to Leigh's parsimony. Inside, two dates have been incised in stone and wood, 1862 and 1866, recording the progress of construction; a datestone on the tower reads 1872, and shortly after that the work

stopped. After Leigh's death in 1873 his son, another William, returned from Australia but did nothing towards finishing his father's intended house — The Mansion has never been completed and stands to this day just as the craftsmen left it at the end of what was their final day's work, with partially-built staircases, floors never added, fan vaulting of the highest standard of masoncraft never finished and bearing the marks of the chisels ready to be smoothed, fireplaces of great quality in spaces high on the walls where rooms should have been.

Here is a true sleeping beauty, magnificently built in the style of Voillet-le-Duc, constructed almost entirely of solid golden limestone, even for the massive stone bath and shower room which have gargoyles instead of taps, for drainpipes and soilpipes, from the half-carved and abandoned gargoyle to the bats on the belfry and to the tracery of the rose window in the chapel.

It was all begun to accommodate a family and servants who never came.

NAILSWORTH

A HUGE KETTLE

Location: At Nailsworth, four miles south of Stroud, on the A46.
Sheet 162 85009950

*What is life, if full of care
We have no time to stand and stare?*

wrote the 'Tramp Poet', W.H. Davis, who made Nailsworth his last home and
died here in 1940. If we do his bidding and make "time to stand and stare",
there is much to delight the eye and stare the senses.

Nailsworth is an industrial town in a dramatically-incised valley. In places the hill
rising from the river, the Nailsworth Ladder, has a gradient of almost one-in-two.
In the centre of the industrialised valley are the gaunt, grey mills, their wheels
now stilled, but brought back to life with new enterprises. The original of John
Halifax's mill is said to be the Dunkirk, the largest mill building in the district.

Attached to a nineteenth-century building in George Street is a wrought-iron
bracket carrying, fifteen feet above the ground, an enormous copper kettle. In its
present position for over ninety-five years, it was the sign for the original 'Copper
Kettle Tea Shop', and one of the few reminders of early forms of advertising.
This one has a diameter of four-and-a-half feet, an estimated weight of over one
hundred-weight, and can hold eighty-two gallons of tea. Its great size is indicated
by the ordinary kettle perched on the knob of the lid of the monster.

KING'S STANLEY

THE FIRST FIRE-PROOFED BUILDING

> *Location:* At King's Stanley, three miles west of Stroud, south of the A419.
> Sheet 162 81350429

Cloth mills record the industrial archaeology of each of the five Stroudwater valleys. Each is a history in stone or brick, but one more interesting than most can be found here.

At the beginning of the nineteenth century, Stanley Mills were owned by the Marlings, one of the great Stroudwater mill-owning families of the past. They had constructed between 1812–13 one of the most remarkable buildings of the industrial revolution. The L-shaped five-storey mill was mainly of brick in classical style with Venetian windows. The date can be seen in several places on the ironwork, including the ornate fanlights.

What makes this mill different from all others is that it was the first fire-proofed building in England. To this end it was constructed entirely without wood. Doors and all the internal structure are of iron, with rows of classical-looking cast-iron Doric columns and trusses supporting cast-iron beams and stone-flag floors throughout. Another remarkable thing about this building is that it is still not known who designed it in the first place, more likely an engineer than an architect.

The Marlings lived at Selsley. Though no longer used as intended, the six-storey tower of Ebley Mill, Selsley, with its steep slate roof, has a companion piece in the tower of All Saints' church, also in Selsley. Both towers were built under the direction of Sir Samuel Stephens Marling who followed the style of a church he had seen at Marling in the Austrian alps, from where he believed the family had originated.

All Saints' has interest for another reason. In 1862 the architect, G.F. Bodley, gave his friend William Morris his first opportunity to execute ecclesiastical stained glass, and the windows are therefore the very earliest work produced by the firm of Morris and Co. Morris and his devotees — Philip Webb, Ford Madox Brown, Sir Edward Burne-Jones and Dante Gabriel Rosetti — all contributed to the glass, some of which is dramatic though distinctly secular in spirit.

Working in a public house must have been a dangerous business. In the church of St. George's, King's Stanley, is an epitaph to Ann Collins, a barmaid, who died in 1804:

> 'Twas as she tript from cask to cask,
> In at a bung hole quickly fell,
> Suffocation was her task,
> She had not time to say farewell.

RODBOROUGH

TOLLS

> *Location:* In Butterow, three-quarters of a mile east of Rodborough, south-west of the A419.   Sheet 162 85680428

For all that goods and people have been moving in and out of the Cotswolds for thousands of years, travel in the region by 1700 was neither quick nor easy. The eighteenth century saw the growth of toll or turnpike roads, a system which charged users a toll and, theoretically, drew sufficient funds from travellers for each parish to maintain its stretch of road.

In Butterow, on the hill from Bowbridge which is so exceedingly steep that one wonders how horses ever managed to pull their loads up it, an octagonal toll house, dated 1825, is in Gothic taste and almost uniquely retains its board giving the list of tolls in 'old' money.

BUTTER ROW GATE

Tolls authorised to be taken at this Gate	S.	d.
For every Horse or other Beast drawing any Coach, Stage Coach, Post Chaise Diligence, Van, Caravan, Sociable Berlin, Landau, Chariot, Vis-a-Vis Barouche, Phaenton, Chaise, Marine Calash, Curricle, Chair Gig, Whiskey Hearse, Litter or other such Carriage	0.	3
For every Horse or other Beast drawing such Waggon, Wain, Cart or other such Carriage not having the Fellies of the Wheels thereof the breadth of Four inches and a breadth of more than Six inches at the Bottom or soles thereof	0.	2½
For every Horse or other Beast drawing such Waggon, Wain, Cart or other such Carriage having the Vellies of the Wheels thereof of the breadth of Six inches or less at the bottom or soles thereof	0.	2
For every horse, Mule or Ass laden or ridden but not drawing the sum of	0.	1
For every drove of Oxen, Cows or other meat cattle per score, and so in proportion for a greater or less number	0.	3
For every drove of Calves, Hogs, Sheep or Lambs per score and so in proportion	0.	2½
For a greater or less number . . .		
For every Carriage drawn or propelled by mechanical machinery or Powerother than Animal Power for each	1.	0

By order of The Trustees, Wilberforce Heelas, Clerk

On the edge of Rodborough Common broods Rodborough Fort, not a country house at all, but an inhabited folly. It was first built by George Hawker, c.1761, "on common land granted by the Lord of the Manor", taken out of the Common. Although it was originally called Fort George, it was said later to have

. . . none of the medieval appearance of the present fort being low and squat . . . its only claim to the title was a bastion on which stood a battery of cannon placed there by Captain Hawker.

In fact the Fort was a single-storey, five-bay building with a canted centre and Gothick windows, recorded only in a painting attributed to R. Hawker and now in Stroud Museum.

The Fort passed through the hands of a number of prominent Stroud businessmen before being bought in 1868 by Alexander Holcombe. He had it rebuilt in 1869–70 as a rock-faced but otherwise picturesque Gothick toy fort; the lop-sided gateway which contributes so much to its appearance was added in 1873. More recently it has been vacated and left in disrepair but the air of neglect adds to its gloomy ambience.

MINCHINHAMPTON

WHAT IS TOM LONG DOING HERE?

> *Location:*   Three miles south of Stroud, between the A46 and A419.
> Sheet 162 85800130

Minchinhampton Common, west of the town, consists of 580 acres of exposed downland still grazed by sheep, cattle and horses. At the meeting point of six roads in the middle is a many-armed signpost bearing a plaque inscribed 'Tom Long's Post'. And here is a mystery, for just who was Tom Long? There are several popular beliefs. Some say he was a highwayman who was gibbetted here, or, alternatively, who committed suicide here to avoid capture. Others say he was not a highwayman at all but a local person who committed suicide and in accordance with the custom of the time was buried at the nearest crossroads.

No-one is certain and there is no written report of Tom Long's activities. Strange indeed, because records of similar activities exist. Certainly the lonely stretch of upland crossed by the Stroud-Cirencester turnpike road just east of Minchinhampton was one of the more popular 'robbing' places on the Cotswolds and can claim a written history of highway robberies dating back to 1371, when a group of robbers lay in wait for merchants using that route (Calendar of Patent Rolls, 1370–74, 378). For other areas, more recent records exist, for example of two highwayman brothers, Matthias and Henry Finnel, who in 1829 were caught at Trouble House, two miles north of Tetbury on the Tetbury-Cirencester road (now the A433).

For Tom Long there is nothing: so just who was he?

The area is proud of its history and hangs onto its past. In Minchinhampton, the Market House is supported on stone columns and dated 1698. Still displayed is the list of charges made for the hire of cubs (nothing to do with young foxes but

a local word for cattle pens) and other facilities for the traders: payment must also be made to the 'Town Cryer', though not more than 6d for each crying.

Still other activities took place. Mrs. Craik wrote her famous novel, 'John Halifax, Gentleman', whilst staying at Rose Cottage in nearby Amberley.

STROUD

A WINNER AND A LOSER

| Location: | At the junction of the A46 and A419. Sheet 162 85200535 |

Mincing Hampton, Painswick Proud,
Beggarly Bisley, Strutting Stroud.

The old jibe was intended to exacerbate rivalry between the villages, but little of Stroud can now be equated with the rhyme. Haphazardly built on steep slopes of a spur above the river Frome, it is a working town which

> *. . . holds naught that's pretty, wise or witty.*

But St. Lawrence's church has some very curious memorials. John Hollings had a disagreement with a former friend who announced publicly that he hoped to live long enough to see Hollings 'safe underground'. Hollings did die the first but, in order to thwart his adversary and deprive him of his pleasure, left instructions that his coffin should not be buried underground: it should be left on the surface and covered with a pile of stones. The stone tiers remain piled in the churchyard, and John Hollings is no doubt still chuckling from his coffin above ground — though there are no reports that he has been heard!

In the southwest corner of the same churchyard is the grave of one of the participants in the last duel to be fought on English soil. Lieutenant Joseph Francis Delmont, aged twenty-one, of the 82nd Regiment was killed by a brother officer in 1807 in the duel which took place in the grounds of The Grange, Folly Lane, close to the church. Inside the church a Jacobean gentleman kneels with wide-open, staring eyes: was it something on this earth or something extra-terrestrial which brought this expression to his face? Has he come upon John Hollings?

HAMPTON FIELDS

A STONE WITH MEDICAL POWERS

> *Location:* On Hampton Fields, one mile south-east of Minchinhampton and
> one-and-a-half miles north of Avening. Sheet 162 88509990

The Anglo-Saxons were converted to Christianity, outwardly at least, as early as
the sixth century, but common folk did not easily lose their faith in the power of
magic and charms. The practice of passing children through holes in specific
stones was widespread, in the belief that they would be cured of measles,
whooping cough and other infantile ailments. After all, why were these holes put
there in the first place?

The Long Stone stands
upright on Hampton
Fields where it has
evidently been set by
human enterprise, but
not shaped or tooled
in any way. Originally,
it may have protruded
from the larger end of
a long barrow, now
ruined, but its purpose
is unknown. It is
reputed to have
therapeutic powers,
being particularly
effective in the case
of rickets, and in
former days mothers
pushed their sick
children through the
largest of the holes to
cure them.

These particular holes
in the Long Stone
were used also for
betrothal ceremonies,
the boy and girl
holding hands
through the stone,
which may have been
a fertility rite.

NETHER LYPIATT

MASTER AND BEAST ARE BOTH REMEMBERED

> *Location:*   Nether Lypiatt Manor, two miles south-east of Stroud, north of the A419.   Sheet 162 86450382

Nether Lypiatt Manor lurks in folk memory as one of the places where the Gunpowder Plot was hatched. In 1712, Robert Atkyns described it as "a very neat new-built house", and in plan it is a perfect forty feet square. The rainwater heads bear the date 1712 and a crowing cock, the crest of the owner, Judge Charles Coxe, who in 1699 had inherited the estate from his father-in-law and then rebuilt the Manor.

Coxe was a man of distinction and held several posts of national importance. He was Judge Clerk of the Patent Office, Member of Parliament for Cirencester and later for Gloucester, and Justice of a Circuit. In history, though, he has been resolved into an arch-villain. Coxe is said to have reprieved an iron-smith from the death sentence on condition that he fashioned the beautiful gates and screen in front of the house, but because the poor smith did not make them exactly symmetrical Coxe had him hanged as soon as the work was completed. There is nothing but legend to support this charge, though there is visible proof of the Judge's tenderness. In a dell to the south of the house he raised an obelisk in memory of his horse, when it died in 1721. On a bronze plaque was inscribed:

> *My name is Wag who rolled the green*
> *The oldest horse that ever was seen*
> *My years they numbered forty-two*
> *I served my master just and true.*

As with his master, stories are told of Wag, who obviously made a great impression on the area. Equipped with panniers, he would descend by himself to Stroud, collect goods ordered at the shops, and when laden, return. He would also roll the lawns of the Manor without human guidance. There is though a more sinister side: Wag haunts the Manor. The clatter of his hoofs may be heard on Christmas Eve, and sometimes he is to be seen galloping soundlessly through the wood where he is buried. Wise people leave a coin at the base of his obelisk to avoid being disturbed by him.

PAINSWICK

A UNIQUE CHURCHYARD

Location: Three miles north of Stroud, on the A46.   Sheet 162 86700970

Painswick is a good example of how size has little to do with stature, for this old market town, built of the local silvery-grey stone and beautifully set between two steep valleys, has been pivotal to the economic and cultural life of the area for centuries.

The church of St. Mary was at the centre of fierce fighting in the Civil War, and cannon-ball and bullet marks pock the east and west walls of the tower. Parliamentarian soldiers were imprisoned inside and one of them, Richard Foot, to while away his boredom, carved a quotation from Spencer's *Faerie Queene:*

Be bold, be bold, but not too bold.

There is an odd item in the church. Fixed to the wall at the rear of the nave is a very fine model of Sir Francis Drake's flagship *Bonaventure.* It is large, about seven-feet long and was made by a local man in 1885. Why it is in the church at all is a mystery, because there does not seem to be any connection with either Drake or the sea.

Painswick is, though, that rare place where the church takes second place to the churchyard, about which legends abound.

Painswick maidens shall be true Till there grows the hundredth yew.

The clipped yews, planted c.1792, are one dominant feature of the churchyard, and centred round the impressive colonnades is the tradition that only ninety-nine will grow at any one time — plant another, and the Devil will kill it off. These yews are clipped each year on 19 September. The following Sunday the ceremony of Clypping the Church is performed. This has nothing to do with

shaping the trees but celebrates the patronal festival: the Clypping derives from the Old English 'clyppen' or 'yclaeppen', to embrace or encircle, and the church is encircled by the congregation signifying their love for Mother Church. It is possible that this is a descendant of some pagan rite, later christianised, during which the faithful encircled the object of worship.

The yew trees form an effective foil to the other dominant feature, the tabletombs, a collection which is beyond compare anywhere in England. They were designed and carved in the Renaissance tradition by the most expert masons including the local family, Joseph Bryan and his sons, John and Joseph. Their work was not confined to funerary art, for John designed also the north-east gateway, composed the fine classical stone reredos, and rebuilt the spire after it was struck by lightening in 1763. His own remarkable tomb, of 1787, which describes his genius simply as 'carver', is a pyramid, a miniature version of the tomb of Caius Cestius in Rome.

Apart from their artistic quality and range of design, the seventeenth- and eighteenth-century tabletombs, the cylindrical variety known locally as 'tea-caddies', give a roll-call of the wealthy clothiers and merchants connected with the town's past as a wool town. Amongst the more notable of the Bryans' tombs is an hexagonal one of 1727, with lettering and cherub heads on a copper plate, another characteristic because of the softness and poor weathering quality of Painswick stone, set into the side panels. Others include a headstone to Thomas Hamlett, "freemason", who died in 1733, with a comprehensive array of masons' tools displayed.

Though one tends to concentrate on the yews and the tabletombs, there is another feature of the churchyard which should not be missed. The lych-gate was built in 1901 with old belfry timbers and is decorated appropriately with bells carved on the barge-boards. Cut in plaster is the musical setting for "Rejoice in the Lord".

An Act of 1350 required all towns to provide stocks for the punishment of vagabonds and petty offenders. Those at Painswick, which date from the seventeenth century, are unique. These are made of iron and shaped like a pair of spectacles, and are referred to as 'the Squire's specs'. Sited near to the old Court House where the constable lived and could keep an eye on their occupants, they were last in use in 1840.

EDGE

A LONE MONUMENT

| *Location:* | On Cud Hill, Edge, two miles north of Painswick, west of the B4073. Sheet 162 85531251 |

Commanding spectacular views, westwards over the rolling Severn Vale to the Black Mountains, southwestwards to Harescombe Beacon, northwards to the Malverns, eastwards to Painswick Beacon, and southeastwards to the steep Painswick valley, at the highest point of Cud Hill, stands a monument. Of dressed local stone, twelve-feet square, with open arches on three sides though that to the north has been blocked, it is unroofed, open to the sky. The wind whistles through and the moon and the sun shine in and all is peace.

Just driving by, one would be excused for thinking it a folly. This is not the case. It was designed and created by Winifred Blow as a memorial to her husband, Detmar, a devotee of the Arts and Crafts Movement, disciple of William Morris, architect of considerable note, and founder of the Hilles estate. Commenced in

1939 but never completed because of the outbreak of war, the memorial was built following arts-and-crafts principles using only authentic materials and Cotswold craftmanship.

In the same field and just to the north of the monument, in a straight line, are buried Detmar and Winifred together with their two sons, Jonathon and Richard. There is also a dog, not a family pet of the Blows but buried by a local person who was obviously struck by both the serenity and the captivating view as a suitable last resting place for a faithful companion. Suitable indeed.

BISLEY

CELLS, WELLS AND FISHES

> *Location:*   At Bisley, four miles east of Stroud.   Sheet 163 90400600

At the top of George Street, Bisley, facing one wall of the church, is a unique detached, stone-built and Cotswold slated building, making what must be the prettiest village lock-up. Bearing the date 1824, it has two cells, possibly one for men and one for women, though that does raise the question of whether the existence of only two cells represented a lower crime rate than today. Under a pretty ogee gable and ball-finial, there are gridded lunettes over the doors. When in use the wives of offenders locked inside were allowed to fill a teapot with ale and poke the spout through the grill. Prison rules are different now.

Bisley has seven springs which flow out of the hill and issue from pools in a Gothic decorative stone well-head, at the base of the mound on which the church of All Saints is built. The traditional well-dressing ceremony which takes place at Ascensiontide is not of such antiquity, but was instituted in 1863 by the vicar, Thomas Keble.

There is another ornamental well-head but it is not included in the ceremony. In the churchyard of All Saints' is a remarkable hexagonal erection covering an ancient bore-hole. Sometimes called rocket-shaped, this lantern-like structure is a 'Poor Souls's Light', the only out-of-doors one in England, where candles were placed in the recesses while Mass was said for the poor and alms were left in the nook. It dates from the later part of the twelfth century, and is said to have been built in commemoration of a priest who fell down the shaft and drowned in the well one night on his way to comfort a dying parishioner. As punishment Bisley was excommunicated and the villagers were forced to bury their dead at Bibury, a journey which involved carrying the corpse across country for several miles; a corner of the churchyard there is still called "the Bisley piece".

There is yet another unique feature concerning water. The church contains an elaborately carved font, but while admiring the artistic work on the exterior visitors often miss its real curiosity because they fail to look inside the bowl: at the bottom two fishes are carved in relief as though swimming in water.

EDGEWORTH

A MIRACLE

> *Location:*   St. Mary's church, Edgeworth, five miles north-west of Cirencester, between the A417 and A419.   Sheet 163 94820600

The whole of Christendom was appalled at the murder of Thomas à Becket in 1170. The image of the Archbishop hacked to death at the altar of his own cathedral was enough to bring pilgrims from all over Europe while stories of miracles wrought by him grew plentiful. In St. Mary's church, Edgeworth, is a record of this village's particular miracle attributed to Thomas à Beckett, which contributed to his canonisation only two years after his murder. It was one of thirteen such happenings concerning people from Gloucestershire.

"Once there was a boy called Richard Sunieve, son of a poor woman, but herdsman of a well-to-do knight of Edgeworth, Sir Henry Fitzherbert . . ." The beginning of the contemporary chronicle by Benedict of Canterbury has a familiar ring but this is no fairy tale. In the course of his work Richard contracted leprosy which after eight years became so terrifying to the people of the village that he finally had to leave home and wander the countryside. His ageing mother, like all mothers before and since, would not desert him in his extreme need and followed him, ministering to him as best she could, even though his condition was so foul that she could give him food only at the end of a long stick, or place it where he could find it.

Eventually Richard came to Canterbury where, after drinking holy water mixed with one spot of the Saint's blood, and kissing the sepulchre, he was cured

completely. Eventually, he returned, overjoyed, to Edgeworth, where he was received with delight by his family and all the villagers.

Some 200 years after the miraculous healing of Richard Sunieve, the figure of an Archbishop was set in stained glass in the small north window of the chancel of St. Mary's — and the fact that it has survived at all is no small miracle in itself when so much medieval glass was broken at the time of the Reformation.

It is worth looking inside the fifteenth-century font at this church, because it contains a miniature copy, in carved stone, five-inches high. Note also the fifteenth-century pews with 'poppy-head' ends. 'Poppy' in this connection is a corruption of the French 'poupee', a doll, and indeed the carvings can be seen as a head and two arms, like a rag doll on a stick.

MISERDEN

A GOAT AND SHEEP

> *Location:*   The church of St. Andrew, Miserden, seven miles north-west of
> Cirencester, between the A417 and B4070.   Sheet 163 93600890

For several centuries it was customary, when designing effigies, to put at the feet
of important people some animal symbolic of characteristics of that particular
person — a lion for manly courage and
bravery, a dog for loyalty, a lamb for
gentleness and love of God. But there
is a curious motif in this church.

Sir William Sandys has at his feet a
gryphon attacking a falcon, while his lady,
Margaret, has a very vicious falcon,
looking both spiteful and elegant. At right
angles to them lies William Kingston, who
died in 1614, a member of the powerful
family who were lords of the manor. Here he lies on a tombchest, quite unnote-
worthy: but what is the significance that, at his feet is not a creature renowned for
noble characteristics, but a goat. And what is the goat doing? It is eating a cabbage!
What message was Kingston trying to portray when he briefed the designer,
Samuel Baldwin of Stroud? Is there a moral here which is now beyond us?

The bells in the churchtower also give messages to visitors. One, weighing a ton
and dated 1722, is inscribed laconically:

> *I to the church the living call and to the grave doe summon all.*

Those lying in the churchyard below were summoned by that bell. The epitaph
of Samuel Hurrell, a shepherd who died in 1807, emphasises the importance of
his work for the area:

> *From youth through life the sheep was all his care,*
> *And harmless as the Flock his manners were,*
> *On earth he held the faith to Christians given*
> *In hope to join the fold of Christ in heaven.*

Rebecca Gittins died later, in 1858, and the carving on her headstone reads:

> *My glass is run, my days are spent,*
> *My life is gone, it was only lent,*
> *As I am now so you must be*
> *Therefore prepare to follow me.*

HARESFIELD

THE TAILOR OF GLOUCESTER

> *Location:* St. Peter's church, Haresfield, five miles south-west of Gloucester,
> east of the B4008. Sheet 162 81041048

One of the most famous of all stories is that of *The Tailor of Gloucester*, which Beatrix Potter called "my own favourite amongst the little books" and was written as a Christmas present in 1901 for her young friend, Freda Moore. What is not generally appreciated though is that it was whilst visiting her cousins, Judge Crompton Hutton and his family at Harescombe Grange, that Beatrix Potter first heard the story from Miss Caroline Hutton, who heard it from Miss Lucy of Gloucester, who heard it from the tailor . . .

The tailor who was at the centre of the ladies' gossip at their tea party was then a very young man, John Pritchard of Gloucester. Beatrix Potter was fascinated, for she delighted in fairy stories, and she changed elements of the basic tale, the fairies to mice, the young and busy tailor to an old and poor man, and the civic occasion of the Root, Fruit and Grain Society to the mayor's wedding.

John Pritchard did not remain a tailor for much longer, but became a teacher and lived at Haresfield. He died there in 1934 and his tombstone records that he was indeed the Tailor of Gloucester.

Haresfield church has other curiosities. There is on display a tooth, believed to be 600 years old. And how many churches have an epitaph penned by the great Dryden, as this one to a little John?

The churchyard boasts a fine collection of tabletombs, highly decorated with skulls, crossed bones and seraphim, and are outstanding examples of the art. From Haresfield Beacon the most majestic prospect may be viewed. Beside Cliffwell Cottage near the Beacon stands a wellhead built in 1870, with the inscription:

> *Whoever the Bucketful upwindeth*
> *Let him bless God, who water findest,*
> *Yet water here but small availeth*
> *Go seek that well which never faileth.*

ELKSTONE

A FASCINATING CHURCH

> *Location:*   At Elkstone, eight miles north-west of Cirencester, between the A417
> and the A435.   Sheet 163 96751238

The Church, the chief owner of the new wealth from sheep following the
Conquest, built extensively on Cotswold, producing one of the most glorious
concentrations of Norman village church architecture in England. One of the most
outstanding and best preserved is St. John's at Elkstone, which was begun c.1160.
At 900 feet it is the highest on the Cotswolds, and has walls four feet thick. It
retains its original, aiseless, twelfth-century form in all essentials with the
exception of the fifteenth-century west tower.

The tympanum of the south door is the most notable in the county and an
example of the wealth of artistic quality in Cotswold parish churches. It shows
Christ in Majesty, with God's hand above, surrounded by the emblems of the
Evangelists and the Lamb of God. Such is its power that visitors neglect to look
closely at its framing by a row of witty beakheads, their sinister appearances
varied by a figure leaning backwards and clutching the snouts of his neighbours,
and relieved further by two ordinary human heads — are these portraits of the
donors of the church? Humour was a necessary feature of a mason's skill.

In fact, the carving is of wonderful quality throughout, the grotesques especially.
There are gargoyles on the embattled parapet and sculpture on the buttresses
with grotesques playing musical instruments, citole and recorder. On the nave
exterior is a full series of corbels of animals, birds and signs of the zodiac.

Inside, the Norman vault of the sanctuary is quadripartite with ribs and two
quarter-rolls left and right of a square band. They meet in a curious boss formed
of four grotesque heads buckled together as if by
a leather belt, each facing down a rib.

There is yet another curious and very rare feature:
over the chancel is a columbarium, a reminder of
the days when pigeons were a significant means
of ensuring supplies of fresh meat and eggs.

Such churches are reminders of the tremendous
artistic talent and working skill of the masons, but
also that this profusion of Norman sculpture is but
a fraction of what existed in these churches
before the religious controversies and iconoclasm
of the sixteenth and seventeenth centuries.

COBERLEY

RICHARD WHITTINGTON'S MOTHER AND HER FATHER-IN-LAW

> *Location:* At Coberley, three-quarters of a mile south of Seven Springs, west of the A435. Sheet 163 96601580

St. Giles' church at Coberley is rich in monuments. Two are unique.

The large effigies in the south chapel are probably of Sir Thomas de Berkeley and his Lady. In accordance with medieval custom he lies in the fashionable armour of his youth; his feet are crossed and rest on a lion, a sign of his manly courage. His wife, Joan, lies beside him in contemporary dress, a whimple, hood and gown: but what is she doing here at all, lying in stately stone? She was Sir Thomas' second wife and after his death married again. She moved to Pauntley, twenty-three miles across the Severn, and bore her new husband, Sir William Whittington, three sons, the youngest of whom, Richard, became three times Mayor of London and the Dick of pantomime fame.

So that part of the pantomime which says that Dick was brought up by his widowed mother is true, though in reality she lived in considerable comfort as Lady Whittington at Pauntley Court. Why then is her effigy here? Dare one postulate that in those days alink with noble status took precedence over death? Certainly according to the 'Inquisitions post mortem' Sir William Whittington was outlawed after the wedding, but this may have been a case of him marrying Sir Thomas' widow without the monarch's necessary permission: innocuous enough to our thinking perhaps but liable to heavy fines on the estate by royal command.

What happened to Sir Thomas' first wife: why is she not included here, also, which would have been accepted custom? Did Sir Thomas demand that his widow, who was later widowed again, should ultimately lie beside him? Even

though it was contemporary practice to have one's effigy made before one's death, Sir Thomas must have known that Joan, being young and vulnerable, had every likelihood of marrying again. And why did she agree to be included in the sculpture — did she, wife-like, not argue but made sure that after his passing she acquired another husband and possibly a last resting place elsewhere?

The mysteries of this monument continue. Who is the small child lying beside them, holding her glove and with her pet dog at her feet? Is she an unrecorded offspring? And the young man in the niche nearby, with vigorously curling hair — is he a son?

In the same church, in the Sanctuary, is the small monument of a Knight in chain armour. This is Sir Giles de Berkeley, who died in 1295, and was Sir Thomas' father. It shows only the bust of the Knight, but his mailed hands are clutching a heart, over a heater-shaped shield on his breast, and thus implies that Sir Giles' body lies elsewhere.

The significance of 'heart shrines' is that they originated during the Crusades when to return the whole remains of those who died far from home would have been a difficult and costly undertaking. So only the embalmed heart was sent to be deposited in the church wall, and the practice became customary through the Middle Ages and even survived the Reformation.

Sir Giles had been to the Holy Land with Edward I, with whom he became close friends, and later was a Member of Parliament and Justice of Assize. In 1294, whilst still in his early fifties, he realised that his health was failing and made a will leaving his peacocks and swans (indicating the size of his property) to his friend John Giffard of Brimpsfield. He also asked that his body be buried before the image of St. Giles in the church at Little Malvern, but that his heart be removed and deposited in the chancel of this St. Giles'. Less than a year later he was dead.

Sir Giles was obviously a man of considerable determination, for Coberley's third noteworthy monument, a slight swelling of the ground outside the chancel and near the heart-shrine, covers the grave of Sir Giles' charger, Lombard; only the thickness of the wall divides the horse from his master's heart. We can still marvel that even to ask at that time around 1290 to bury an animal in consecrated ground was a capital offence, and to see that it was done would have been unthinkable: here, legend says that it actually happened.

SHIPTON SOLERS

COWS, SHEEP AND SHIPS

Location: At Shipton Solers, five miles south-east of Cheltenham, just north of the A40.   Sheet 163 03531850

The pretty thirteenth-century church of St. Mary's at Shipton Solers stands high and proud from the road through the village, but it was not always so: for fifty years until 1930 it was in disrepair and was used as a farm store.

The derivation of its name is still a puzzle. It may derive from the Old English 'scypen' which later developed into 'shippon', a cattleshed, but just as probably was related to the sheep which walked around this area. The Solers' were an ancient family and lords of the manor. The stained glass in one of the windows has a most curious composition of a Cotswold house, sheaves of corn and a ship. This may be symbolic of Christianity sailing forth; if it was meant to be a rebus on the village name then the designer failed to understand the local dialect where 'ship' translates as 'sheep'.

Was time so very precious to those attending this church? Fixed in an elaborate frame to the wall by the seventeenth-century pulpit, and easily reached by the preacher, is an hour glass, used to time the sermons in the old days. Judging by the amount of sand and its rate of fall, the sermons must have been marathons.

LECKHAMPTON HILL

THE DEVIL'S CHIMNEY

> *Location:* Half a mile south of Cheltenham, off the B4070. Sheet 163 94591848

What is one to make of the Devil's Chimney? This pinnacle of rock juts high out of the scarp face at Leckhampton, at the extreme edge of Crickley Hill, on the natural grasslands which make up the 400-acre common. Leckhampton is a place of associations. It was the

November evenings! Damp and still
They used to cloak Leckhampton Hill

that tantalised the young James Flecker to write one of his last poems as he lay dying in Switzerland. Its atmosphere has fascinated others since, and before then it was a place of habitation and fortification for our distant ancestors.

Why is the Chimney here at all? In 1900, the geologist Buckman expounded the theory that it is the result of differential erosion over a period of many hundreds of years, but the legend is the only explanation which has stood the test of time.

The saying, "As sure as God's in Gloucestershire", derived from the large number of abbeys and churches in the medieval county. This so annoyed the old Devil that he hid on the edge of Leckhampton Hill and pulled out great rocks with his pitchfork to throw down on the monks and pilgrims who passed that way. His evil trick was reversed and the rocks fell on top of him, so he now lives deep down in the Cotswold limestone below Dead Man's Quarry, the Chimney marking the spot.

According to Ruff in his 'History of Cheltenham' in the early nineteenth century it was:

built by the devil, as the vulgar say. It was no doubt
built by shepherds in the frolic of an idle hour.

Which shepherd had 'the frolic of an idle hour', indeed? Are we to suppose that the rocks were chipped out by their crooks?

It has been suggested that the Chimney is "a quarrymen's joke made about 1780", but surely the work involved in constructing any such 'joke' must have been enormous. Is the real reason more prosaic? Is the Chimney merely a column left partly because it was inferior quality for building stone, even at the rate of 1d a ton delivered down the railway specially constructed in 1798 by Charles Brandon Tyre, and partly as a gimmick?

Interestingly, the reckless who climbed it always left a coin on the cap as a token to Old Nick. The record for people standing on the top at any one time was thirteen, but climbing the Chimney is now prohibited as erosion has threatened the danger of collapse. The cost for the Devil to have his Chimney repaired in 1985 was £25,000 — few mere mortals maintain such a costly chimney — but we will for a few more years be able to have our myth.

BIBLIOGRAPHY

English Church Monuments, K. Esdaile

The Gloucestershire Village Book, Gloucestershire Federation of Women's Institutes

The Cotswolds, M. Hall and E. Frankl

The Hidden Places of Gloucestershire, M and M Publishing

Scene Together, Aylwin Sampson

Tales of Old Gloucestershire, Betty Smith

The Cotswolds, Brian Smith

Timpson's Towns, John Timpson

Cotswold Churches, David Verey

The Cotswolds, G.N. Wright

Dragon on chancel arch, St. John's Church, Elkstone.

THE AUTHORS

Margaret Caine and Alan Gorton have lived in Gloucestershire for a combined total of over forty years. Individually, they have contributed to the study of Cotswold history, lore and culture, but have always been drawn to the unusual, eccentric, intriguing and curious. Thus they can bring to this, their first collaborative publication, a wealth of written and visual material, much of it never seen before.

In the course of extensive travelling over the Cotswolds, Margaret has taken every photograph in this book, here extracted from her unique library. For his part, Alan has brought the histories, myths and legends which give substance to this visual record.

The Living Cross, St. Lawrence's Church, Wyck Rissington.

INDEX

S.B. Publications publish a wide variety of local-interest books, including many other titles in the *Curiosites* series. For a full list please write (enclosing SAE) to: S.B. Publications, c/o 19 Grove Road, Seaford, East Sussex BN25 1TP.

Rails through Connemara

The Galway-Clifden Railway

by
Jonathan Beaumont

© Oakwood Press & Jonathan Beaumont 2021

Published by Oakwood Press, an imprint of Stenlake Publishing Ltd, 2021

British Library Cataloguing in Publication Data
A Record for this book is available from the British Library
ISBN 978 0 85361 759 4

Printed by Claro Print, Office 26, 27, 1 Spiersbridge Way, Thornliebank,
Glasgow G46 8NG

Dedication

To my family

Title page: On 16th July, 1934, 'J18' class No. 582 slows to walking pace as it enters Moycullen station with the 4.30 pm mixed train from Clifden to Galway. As can be seen, while it is probable that very few passengers are aboard, the train is conveying a substantial quantity of goods wagons. By now, the original Midland Great Western Railway (MGWR) cab has been replaced by a standard Inchicore design, the new owner's parentage also obvious by the standard pattern chimney and smokebox door. The leading carriage is a MGWR third class vehicle of 1892 vintage. The driver leans out ready to exchange the staff, which can be seen in his hand.   *H.C. Casserley*

Front cover: MGWR 'D' class 2-4-0 No. 40 *Lily* pauses at Ballynahinch around 1902. The train is in the colours of the company's recently-introduced but short-lived 'Tourist Express'. The locomotive was built in 1886 and used all over the MGWR system, being withdrawn in 1922.   *Painting by Sean Bolan, reproduced courtesy of The Lord O'Neill*

Rear cover: A poster produced by the Midland Great Western Railway to advertise all-in tours of the West of Ireland, including Clifden, in the early years of the 20th century.

Oakwood Press, 54-58 Mill Square, Catrine, KA5 6RD,
Tel: 01290 551122 *Website:* www.stenlake.co.uk

Contents

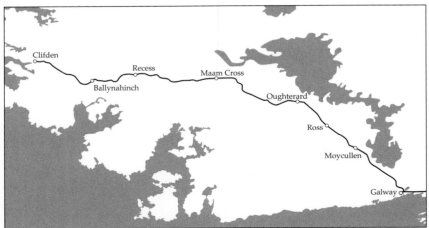

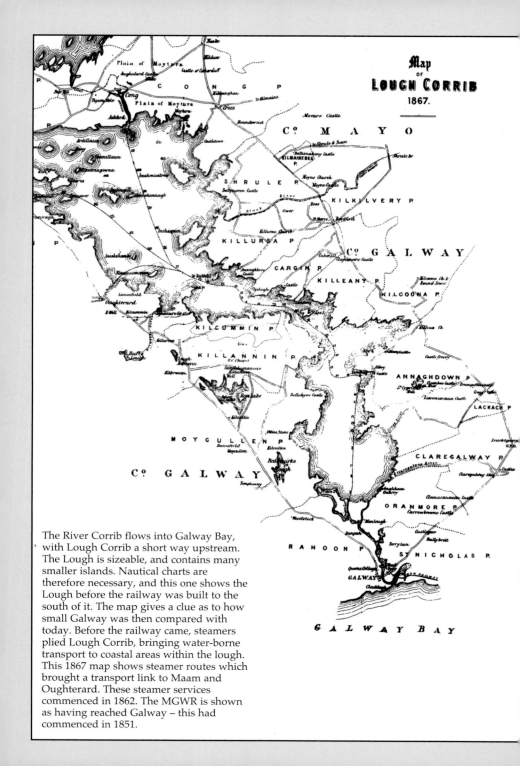

The River Corrib flows into Galway Bay, with Lough Corrib a short way upstream. The Lough is sizeable, and contains many smaller islands. Nautical charts are therefore necessary, and this one shows the Lough before the railway was built to the south of it. The map gives a clue as to how small Galway was then compared with today. Before the railway came, steamers plied Lough Corrib, bringing water-borne transport to coastal areas within the lough. This 1867 map shows steamer routes which brought a transport link to Maam and Oughterard. These steamer services commenced in 1862. The MGWR is shown as having reached Galway – this had commenced in 1851.

Chapter One

The setting:
Early plans and proposals

The remote Connemara region is one of Ireland's many great scenic delights. It encompasses mountains, lakes, wide skies and spectacularly unspoilt scenery which stretches across much of western Co. Galway to the Atlantic Ocean; the very edge of Europe. Much of the land is sparsely inhabited and wild. Few minerals exist in commercial quantities, apart from the famous Connemara Marble, near Ballynahinch. Instead, the local economy is primarily agricultural with sheep farming playing a major role, though fishing in coastal areas and of course, tourism, have all played their part in the past.

Connemara's remoteness has led to its being one of the main surviving bastions of the Irish language today. This has been due to less contact with the outside world prior to the coming of the railway, and a strong local pride in keeping the language alive. The area was badly affected by the Great Famine, with rapid population decline in many areas especially the Doolough Valley from the 1840s onwards. In the worst affected years, 1845-51, population loss was at its most severe but varying degrees of failure of the potato crop were to cause further depopulation over the next half-century and beyond.

At the eastern end of the Connemara region is the city of Galway, the capital of the western province of Connaught. The city's present day population is some 75,000 people, though this was considerably less in the past. At the region's western side lies the bustling market town of Clifden (An Clochán in Irish, meaning 'the stepping stones'), situated on the Owenglen River. It is a comparatively modern town by Irish standards, only having been established in 1809 by one John D'Arcy, whose vision was to develop the wool and fishing industries in the area. In 1822, D'Arcy received a Government grant to relieve poverty which existed in the area even before the famine. As a result he had the town's fishing quay built by 1831. By 1823, Clifden was a significant town in an area previously one of the remotest and most sparsely populated anywhere in Ireland. By the 1870s, with the worst depredations of the famine in the recent past, tourists began to be attracted by the recreational fishing and hunting opportunities, game shooting being particularly popular. Today, tourism is the major player in Connemara's economy.

Into this scenario came the earliest proposals for a railway to serve the district. The main line of the Midland Great Western of Ireland Railway Company (MGWR), to give it its full title, commenced operations between Dublin and Galway in August 1851.

From the earliest times, the main priority west of the city was to link Galway city with Clifden, though various routes between the two would be proposed over the next 30 years. As early as 1860 a public meeting in Clifden proposed a tramway to link the town with Galway. Such a proposal would probably have resulted in a coastal roadside route being taken which would have led to extremely long journey times. The earliest advent of road traffic would have killed it stone dead, even if it had approached viability in the first place. Despite a further meeting in Oughterard the following year, at which representatives of local mining interests were present, nothing came of the scheme. The proposal allowed for propulsion by 'animal or mechanical power'. A horse-drawn tramway over 49 miles (at least) would have been entirely impractical. An already slow passage would be slowed even further by several changes of horses, and loads would have been limited.

In November 1863 a Bill was presented to the Government* proposing a railway from Galway to Oughterard, a remote town in mid-Connemara, which would eventually become one of the stations on the route as built some 30 years later. This line, the West Galway Railway, was also stillborn as the owner of much of the land through which it would pass, the Law Life Company, objected.

In November 1871, the West Galway Railway proposal was revived. A survey was carried out by a civil engineer, J.J. Coughlan, who knew the area well. He referred to the potential traffic for the railway,

> On the road to Clifden, one is bound to meet half a score of carts and drays heavily laden with flour, barrels, crates, etc., droves of pigs etc. Thousands of cattle from fairs at Maam, Leenane, Letterfrack, Clifden, Roundstone, Oughterard, etc. Salmon and Lobster traffic, deep sea fishing off Boffin and Shark Islands, would all be greatly improved by a railway communication ... A 3ft gauge railway could be built for £200,000 including all the law, engineering and other expenses. As regards the terminus, the Old Clog factory could easily be adapted and would make a splendid one.

It was proposed to seek powers to purchase land compulsorily, build a railway and all associated works, and make the necessary arrangements for operation with one of the existing larger railway companies to the east of Galway city. The line was to have connected Galway with Clifden; the first proposal for a full specification railway linking the two places. What may be an early view of property speculation may be seen here - much of the land through which the line had to pass had been owned in recent times by the Law Life Co., but it was noted at a meeting of the shareholders of the Midland Great Western Railway at this time that 'a large property in Co. Galway held by the Law Life Company had now passed into other hands, and the gentlemen who were the owners of it were about promoting the line'. These new owners were not destined to make as quick a profit as they possibly expected, as the scheme foundered, and was noted as having been withdrawn in March 1872. They had presumably believed that they might sell the land at an inflated price to the Midland Great Western Railway. This newly proposed railway would commence near the western end of the Lough Atalia bridge just east of the MGWR's Galway station and its western terminus would be in 'the townland of Tullyvoheen adjoining the Workhouse'. A branch line off the main route would terminate at Rosroe Point in Bertraghboy Bay. This, presumably, was intended to facilitate the local fishing industry.

---

* Throughout this book, 'Government' and 'Parliament' refer to the British Government in relation to events prior to Ireland's independence in 1921. Descriptions of 'Government' in the period since December 1921 refer to the Irish Government.

Several months later, mention was made at the Midland Great Western Railway's half-yearly meeting of a proposal for a line running from their own Galway terminus through Oughterard to Clifden. A Bill was being prepared by the promoters for submission to Parliament at the time and the MGWR's Board noted that the only implication for them at that stage was that they were sanctioned to enter into a working agreement if the line was completed. This Galway, Oughterard & Clifden Railway (GO&CR) was proposed as standard 1600 mm (5 ft 3 in.) gauge, although by December the act had been amended to allow it to be built to the narrow 914 mm (3 ft) gauge. Financial calculations showed considerable savings in construction costs to be possible this way.

By September 1872 the Act of Parliament had been obtained for the GO&CR and at the autumn half-yearly meeting of the company, the proposal was described as a 'line from Galway to Clifden which would pass through the Property of Englishmen who had Purchased the estates of the Law Life Company'. Doubtless a suitable profit, after all, was expected by these landowners. Their property speculation looked as if it would pay off.

Over the winter of 1872/73, the lasting effects of the Great Famine were continuing to take their toll in the general area. Frustration was expressed with the seeming lack of any form of progress with building any railway at all, following the delays caused to ships carrying food relief supplies to Clifden by bad weather.

By May 1875, Parliamentary approval for the construction of the line had been approved in London. However, by December 1876 it was clear that very little private capital would be subscribed towards the railway. Some £13,560 had been subscribed from the Clifden area, but only £880 had been raised from all other sources. By today's standards this total sum would approximate to about one million euros; hardly enough to build a 75 km railway! Moreover, the landowners through whose lands the railway would run were not prepared to fully co-operate with the proposals. A meeting of influential landowners was held in Clifden at which it was resolved that in view of this, the railway line as proposed was not a practical option to pursue. However, it was felt that a railway would still benefit the town so another more economical proposal was put forward. This involved the construction of a 3 ft (914 mm) gauge line from Galway via a coastal route to Clifden. This line would have left Galway city's Claddagh district and run via Salthill, Barna, Costello, Screeb, Inver, Gowla, Bertraghboy Bay, Cashel and Ballynahinch,† reaching Clifden by the Roundstone Road. The cost would have been some £150,000 - or over 10 times the amount subscribed for the previous scheme, despite being narrow gauge. This coastal route would have been of much greater use to the community as much of the region's economic activity at the time revolved around the coastal fishing industry. In addition, and on account of this, these villages contained a much great population than the largely uninhabited regions through which a direct interior route would pass. However, by using this coastal route the

---

* The spelling 'Ballinahinch' is often used nowadays, but throughout this book the older spelling of 'Ballynahinch' is used, as this is how the railway companies inevitably referred to the place.

overall distance between Galway and Clifden would have been considerably longer, and with a narrower track gauge and doubtless sharper curves and heavier gradients in the area to be traversed, journey times would have easily exceeded three or possibly four hours. It was proposed that it be put to the Midland Great Western's Board that the receipts from traffic on the line could be divided between themselves and the Connemara company on the basis of 15 per cent to the Connemara company, and 85 per cent to the MGWR. This would be in exchange for the Midland working the line, if the Connemara company built it.

Another proposal put to the MGWR was that if they constructed the line to full 5 ft 3 in. gauge, an assurance would be sought that they would receive an annual subsidy from the Baronies in the area for 20 years. The subsidy would be on an annually reducing basis. Thereafter the line would belong to the MGWR in its entirety. The only condition to be made was that the company would be required to operate at least two trains per weekday in each direction, with one on Sundays at ordinary rates and fares. For the time being, they refrained from getting involved.

Records of these proposals and relevant discussions give the impression that it took some time for the full scale of this project to sink into the minds of those proposing the line. Given some time to mull over it all, the promoters may have realised the commercial futility of such a roundabout narrow gauge route, and now a change of tack saw them approaching the MGWR to 'invite' them to construct the line themselves, and to the standard 5 ft 3 in. (1600mm) gauge! The MGWR had at this stage been approached by many deputations, in many districts, making the same sort of proposals and offers, but hardly surprisingly they declined them all. The Midland Great Western was, after all, a private company whose first responsibility was to its shareholders, and whose aim was therefore to stay solvent and trade profitably. Had there been a strong commercial case in favour of building any such rural lines, they would doubtless have already done this themselves!

Nonetheless, by December surveys had been almost completed for this route, and levels had been taken by engineers from a Dublin firm headed by William Lewis, former Chief Engineer of the 3 ft gauge Ballymena & Larne Railway in Co. Antrim. Not all was going according to plan, though, as during 1880 despite a favourable report from the Board of Works, Galway's County Grand Jury had thrown the proposals out due to some missing documentation.

By April 1881, the route of the railway was finalised. It would commence in Galway at the intersection of Eglinton Street and Williamsgate Street, following the former to Wood Quay Street, over the New Bridge, Beggar's Bridge and Canal Bridge. It would proceed along the Newcastle Road and Mailcoach Road, ending eventually at Oughterard outside the Ross Hotel. There, a second phase of construction would bring the railway on to Clifden, following the mail coach road to a terminus in the town opposite Mullarkey's Hotel. Again, the scheme looked to be going somewhere, with some comfort being taken by the fact that it had been 'taken in hand by the well known energy and perseverance of Mr H.C. Drinkwater, who is no ordinary man - he has reclaimed some 9,000 acres of land on the River Fergus in County Clare'. A month later, Drinkwater (who was one of the main proposers of this scheme) had managed to have the whole thing approved by a special session of the Galway Grand Jury. The MGWR were now taking notice, and expressed approval by offering to co-operate with whatever exchange facilities would be necessary in Galway station.

By 1883 no actual progress had been made with building anything. The MGWR as a commercial undertaking was not inclined to invest in a new line with little chance of recouping its money, let alone operating a profitable railway. The Grand Juries in the area were equally unenthusiastic about committing ratepayers' money to any of the various schemes proposed. But no less a personality than the Prime Minister, William Gladstone, expressed an opinion that a railway, as opposed to some sort of tramway, would be preferable. The implication here is that the political establishment was realising that the concept of a railway in the area was a sound one. All that was required was to find somebody to pay for it.

Perhaps spurred on by Gladstone, on 7th August, 1883 the Tramways and Public Companies Act was passed, giving the Baronies powers to guarantee up to 5 per cent annual dividend on the capital of a new railway, also to actually operate or subsidise the operation of lines which failed to be financially self-sufficient. By September, several schemes had been proposed, as follows:

West of Ireland Steam Tramway Co.
Alongside the Galway-Clifden road, or close to it. Cross River Corrib by swing bridge in Galway, then stopping places every two miles, stations at Moycullen, Maam Cross, Recess, Ballynahinch & Clifden. Built to narrow (3ft) gauge. Galway terminus near 'New Dock.
Cost – £121,715
Engineer – A.D. Johnstone
Name of line – Menlo Line

Galway, Oughterard & Clifden Tramway & Light Railway Co.
Connected in Galway to the Galway-Salthill tramway (3 ft gauge), following this line as far as Eglington Street. From Galway ('New Docks'), alongside Lough Atalia in the city-Ballinafoyle-Terryland-Menlo; crosses river near Friar's Cut. A branch line to Roundstone was to be included.
Cost – £172,793
Engineers – J. Price & Price Williams
Name of the line – Winby Line (after the name of the main promoter)

Guaranteed* Light Railways & Tramways of Ireland Co.
Tramway from Galway to Newcastle and light railway from there to Clifden.
Cost – £260,213
Engineers – Nimmo & Townsend
Name of line – The Tram

* By Baronial guarantee

None of the above made it as far as the Spring Assizes of 1884, in all cases because the Town Jury would only be prepared to guarantee, under the Baronial guarantee scheme, a quarter of the necessary public money. Following various meetings to examine the viability of each of the above schemes, and their rejection, the 1883 Act itself began to be examined. In reality, it had inadequate provisions to protect the poorer Baronies from the financial burden likely to arise should a built line require Baronial funding. The implication may be taken that those concerned accepted that this was more of a probability than a possibility.

The meeting resolved that whether or not the MGWR would become involved, and irrespective of the gauge eventually used, the landowners present were to be asked to donate the land over which the line would pass to the promoters. A committee was established to proceed with plans for a suitable line, consisting of Henry Hodgson (Junior) of Oughterard; Sir Charles Osborne, Baronet of Inver; Marcus Lynch of Barna; Major Archer Daly of Furbough [sic]; Henry Pearse: Michael Hennessy; Major John Lynch; Capt. Blake Forster and James Campbell, all of Galway; Isidore Lynch of Spiddal; and John Gill of Salthill. By 1884, these schemes described above had been abandoned in their existing form, as sufficient capital could not be raised either by the Grand Juries or private investors. The Grand Jury of Galway was only prepared to guarantee six pence in the pound in local rates, but four times that was needed. By 1885, the Judicial Committee of the Irish Privy Council had rejected the idea of a light railway between Galway and Clifden with branches to Maam and Roundstone.

The Ballynahinch & Roundstone Railway would operate to the 3 ft gauge and would run from Ballynahinch, where it would connect with the Galway-Clifden line, to Roundstone. The terminus would be 'in the garden of Fort House, 30 yards south of the southwest corner of the said house...' Like the Clifden schemes, not enough money was forthcoming from potential subscribers.

However, the schemes might be dead, but the idea was not. Drinkwater now promoted the West of Ireland Steam Tramway Company, one of whose Directors was John Jameson, of the famous whiskey distilling family. Another scheme followed; the two followed minor variations of the same route. Further schemes were promoted, and public meetings held during 1885/86. The MGWR sat back and waited. Again, nothing came of these schemes.

The promoters were over optimistic about the generosity of the Baronies. A subsequent meeting heard that three of these strenuously opposed the scheme which had settled on the coastal route, with branch lines to Roundstone and Maam – the latter probably the least feasible of all. On 7th February, 1885, the Judicial Committee of the Irish Privy Council rejected the proposed railway in its entirety. The committee had heard long arguments about the benefits the railway would bring to the area, with one submission claiming that the line was of national importance. However, other arguments to the effect that the estimates of potential traffic were unrealistically optimistic won the day. In 1887, the next proposal was the Galway, Clifden & Roundstone Light Railway. This would commence in the district of Townparks by a junction with the city tramway line near the Irish Church Mission School at Taylor's Hill. It would terminate in Clifden's Market Square. A branch line would leave this line in the townland of Ballinafad, and terminate at the 'new pier' at Roundstone. By 1888, The Galway & Mayo Light Railway proposed to build a line from the city to serve Headford, Cong, Maam, Leenane, Letterfrack, and Clifden, with another line to Claremorris and Ballinrobe. This route to Clifden would have been very roundabout - and thus slow.

As we can see, the lack of enthusiasm by local authorities in committing money to railways, and the caution of investors, was in marked contrast to the optimism and enthusiasm for the various schemes proposed. While most new railways would have certainly assisted life in the areas served, partly by creating employment, and partly by making travel much easier, the other side of the coin was that in an economically deprived and sparsely populated area, any railways built would be hard to justify as financially viable concerns.

The unavoidable reality was that any direct route would of necessity avoid just about any place in the area with any population to speak of, while a scheme linking the majority of Connemara's communities would take an unrealistically lengthy meandering route. Neither was entirely satisfactory; therein lay the problem.

This appears to have been the end of the proposed narrow gauge coastal route, with its branch lines. However, the MGWR now noted at a shareholders' meeting the following month that a direct broad gauge route, connecting with their own Galway terminus, was worthy of 'every assistance' from the company.

In January 1887, following amendments to the Act which served to improve its usefulness in the west of Ireland, two new schemes were proposed:

1. Galway & Clifden Light Railway - direct route via Moycullen. Oughterard and Recess. A branch to Roundstone from somewhere in the vicinity of Ballynahinch station was included as a possible addition.
2. A revival of the 1883 tramway concept, the West of Ireland Light Railway & Tramway Company, whose route would reach Clifden via Headford, Cong and Leenane. The same company also suggested a direct route as an option.

Again, both were rejected by the relevant Grand Juries.

In October 1888, the *Railway Times* reported that these two plans for alternative routes had been deposited for consideration. The first route would have required less engineering works and would cost a little over half of the £325,000 cost of the Headford route, despite having a branch line to Roundstone added. The *Railway Times* reported some Government observations about this scheme, principally that they did not consider the Roundstone branch to be necessary. It was also added that the towns of Headford and Cong would probably be better served by a railway from Tuam, on the Athenry-Claremorris line, and that the Headford-Cong section, if built, would be the most expensive stretch to construct due to the nature of the ground. It was noted that a line to Clifden would benefit the quarries of the famous Connemara Marble, though the construction of a quay line at Clifden would prove very difficult and costly. However, the potential for tourist access was already being recognised and it was felt that any railway to Clifden would carry large numbers of passengers in the summer. The deposited plans included a junction with the MGWR's line near Galway station, rather than a separate terminus, this being the scheme also favoured (if not insisted upon) by the MGWR.

At this stage it was also proposed that a branch from Recess to Killary Bay be made, to cater for tourist and fishing traffic. The branch to Roundstone was also considered as an option. Despite passing through an extremely sparsely populated area en route, with absolutely no centres of population. Killary Bay is a natural fjord and is one of Ireland's most beautifully scenic locations. While such a line would have given the traveller a spectacular journey, even the most optimistic estimate for this line, of £40,000, was hopelessly unrealistic given the likely demand for its use.

Nothing further would happen for the next 18 months, despite various other proposals being made, generally variations of the same themes. One further proposal suggested a railway directly from Clifden to Ballinrobe, Co. Mayo - again, such a line, while scenic, would have passed through desolate and sparsely inhabited countryside.

This might have been the end of it. All over Ireland, and in most other developing countries, myriads of proposals were made throughout the 19th century for railways which would never see the light of day. Some were sensible enough, but the necessary capital could not be raised; most were not. However, in the 1880s, after the major construction period of main routes had all but covered the principal centres of population, the attention of the British Government had turned towards offering assistance towards the creation of infrastructure in areas where a need could be established, but commercial viability was unlikely without it. It was perfectly clear to all that railways would bring benefits of all sorts to rural areas – whether economically deprived or not - but who would pay for them to be built, or subsidise their operation if they were not strictly commercially viable?

Thus, in 1889, the Light Railways (Ireland) Act was passed. This enabled construction of railways with Government grants where they served districts which would not otherwise attract them as commercial propositions. The idea was to use the railway to assist in the regeneration of these areas and attract inward investment. Several lines in different parts of Ireland – mostly western districts – were built as a result of this Act, and were known as 'Balfour lines', after Lord Balfour, who introduced the legislation. A railway to Clifden seemed to be tailor-made for this Act, and when Balfour visited the area in 1890 he spoke of the railway bringing benefits of employment, and opportunities for trade outside the area.

By the end of 1889, four updated schemes were now proposed, others having been withdrawn or rejected over the previous years. In some cases, proposals were still being made despite previous or initial rejection.

1. The Menlo Line, Galway-Oughterard-Clifden (passed by the Grand Jury in 1884, but rejected by the Privy Council).
2. Direct route through Bohermore, Terryland and Dangan, and on to Clifden.
3. Galway, Inver & Clifden Light Railway - via the coast.
4. Connemara Coast Railway - via the coast.

The British Government appointed a commission to investigate which route might be the best. Despite most habitation being along the coastal area, it was simply too long a roundabout route, and the direct route through the middle of Connemara was favoured. As it would turn out, the Clifden line would be the longest of all of the 'Balfour' lines, most of which were narrow gauge and of shorter length.

During 1890, the Grand Jury of Galway, as well as local clergy, attempted to advance the case both for Government support for the construction of the railway, and for the MGWR to enter into an operating agreement. This time, all parties were satisfied that Clifden would benefit from the railway, and while the Government saw an additional benefit in the provision of work for local people in building the line, the promoters managed to persuade the railway company that they could meet its requirements. The Secretary to the Treasury, a Mr Jackson, promised to use every influence he had to start the project without delay. By 20th September, an agreement was finally concluded between the Government and the MGWR - no middle men this time. The agreement not only covered the Galway-Clifden line by the direct route, but also an extension of the Manulla Junction to Ballina line in Co. Mayo, as far as Killala. This line served a district somewhat smaller, but with similar physical and economic characteristics. Under the agreement, the Grand Jury of Galway was to contribute £30,000 towards the railway, and the British Government would pay £244,000. The funds were to be paid to the MGWR, who would employ the contractors and others necessary. A week later, the MGWR's Chairman met Mr Jackson to finalise details for the construction of the line. After some discussion, a planned branch line from Recess to 'Killeries' (Killary Harbour / Leenane) was dropped from the plan, as was a quay siding at Clifden. The plans for the Killala line, and a line proposed under another agreement, from Westport to Achill, were also approved. Meantime, as the potato crop had failed again, in order to expedite construction, the Treasury agreed to pay the full amount, including the £30,000 which had been due to be paid by the Grand Jury.

However, other proposals and other routes were still being considered. One particularly bizarre one, the Ulster & Connaught Light Railway, would have connected Clifden and Galway, on separate branch lines, to a lengthy meandering narrow gauge route across Ireland to the east coast at Greenore. This proposal, of which a line to Clifden was just one detail, is described in *Appendix Seven*.

It is worth mentioning that when the line did eventually open in 1895, a proposal was put forward for a large deep water transatlantic port in Galway city. Had this been proceeded with, a branch line to serve it would have left the Clifden branch on the western side of the city in the vicinity of Newcastle, initially following the route of the later Shantalla Quarry line, described in *Appendix Three*.

The scene was now set for the construction of the line by the direct route, some 30 years after the earliest proposals had been made.

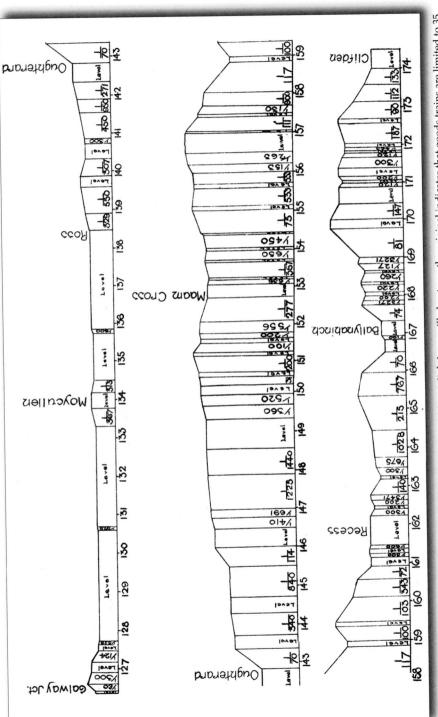

Gradient profile of the line, as included in the MGWR's gradient tables. A lightly pencilled note on the original indicates that goods trains are limited to 35 vehicles between Galway and Oughterard, but only 30 between there and Clifden. It will be seen that the steepest gradients on the line, both of 1 in 70, were of just under half a mile west of Oughterard station, and a similar distance east of Ballynahinch. Further gradients of 1 in 75 and 1 in 72 were to be found between Maam Cross and Recess. The distinction between the fairly level line east of Oughterard, and the more undulating nature of the line west of there

Author's Collection

Chapter Two

Construction and opening of the railway

Having now agreed to construct the line, the MGWR immediately appointed John Henry Ryan and Edward Townsend of Galway as civil engineers to prepare the contract plans, undertake costings and survey the route. Ryan wrote an account of the work for the Journal of the Institute of Civil Engineers some years later, observing that the MGWR had given him very little time to undertake his work satisfactorily, and to make matters worse, he and Townsend had encountered very bad weather while surveying. It is therefore to their credit that the work was accomplished on time. It was planned that construction work would begin at Christmas 1890. Accordingly, the first earth was turned on 4th December, 1890 near Maam Cross, and in Galway. Since the Government had advanced considerable funding to enable construction on the basis that it would provide relief to the locality, the Royal Irish Constabulary were to provide weekly updates to Dublin Castle on the numbers of men employed, what they were being paid, and their views on the overall effectiveness of the railway construction as a means of relief. On 6th December a group of 200 men were brought to Galway from Loughrea, where they had just been released from the construction of the line from there to Attymon Junction. These men were engaged on drainage work; along the route of the entire railway. This was the necessary initial preparation as a firm track bed had to be formed across what was frequently soggy, undrained land. Where the railway was planned to cross streams or small rivers, an ingenious method was used to enable the bridge or culvert to be constructed without interference from the flowing water. The culvert would be created to one side of the stream, and once complete, the water was diverted to flow under it. This left the original route as dead water, and it could be filled in to provide a basis for the embankment on one side of the new course. An example of this, at Knockbane, is shown below.

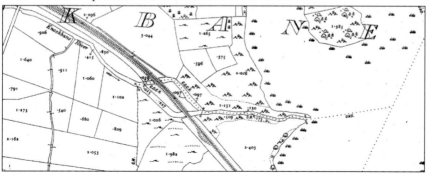

Map of line at Knockbane, between Moycullen and Oughterard. The Knockbane River flows under the railway at two points. One is the original route of the river. Before the bridge can be built, the river has been diverted to a new bridge. This particular example has had both culverts retained, but others would only have one.

Robert Worthington, a prolific builder of railways at the time, was quickly appointed as contractor to carry out the construction. The MGWR was familiar with Worthington as he was also engaged in work relating to the Westport-Achill line. Work started on schedule but quickly ran into trouble. The effects of the Great Famine had affected this part of Ireland particularly severely over 45 years earlier, and the local population and economy were still suffering considerable hardship. The autumn of 1890 had produced another partial failure of the potato crop - this happened on numerous occasions in the 19th century, not just in the famine years of 1845-51. Construction workers therefore depended very heavily on their wages for their survival. They felt that despite the large grant given to the MGWR by the Government, they were still underpaid. In February 1891, after just a few weeks at work, the labourers went on strike for 15 shillings. instead of 12s. Carters refused 30s., and work ceased. At this stage, 100 men were employed at Clifden, with 500 working elsewhere on the line. Local people objected to the fact that many of the construction workers had been brought into the district from elsewhere by the MGWR. Their objections were based on the facts that (a) the construction work was supposed to provide relief for local people, and (b) because these outside workers were said to include 'undesirable people'. These 'imported' workers had a reputation for drunkenness, theft and fighting. Whether this was entirely deserved is difficult to say!

As a result of the strike, Worthington laid off 60 men, even though he had promised to double the workforce if the engineers would hand over their plans to him. The reason for this resulted from frequent misunderstandings, arguments over money, and general friction between Worthington and the MGWR's engineers on the Achill line, which was being built at the same time. It is clear from lengthy correspondence between the two that there was no love lost - Worthington did not trust the MGWR at all, and the feeling appears to have been mutual. After Worthington threatened to reduce his workforce on account of not having the plans given to him, the MGWR responded by cancelling the contract and appointing an English firm, Messrs Braddock & Matthews of Lancashire, to complete the work for £18,715 17s. However, the Corrib viaduct was omitted from this quotation, giving rise to some dispute later on between the MGWR and the new contractor. Braddock assured all concerned that Irish labour would be employed, and within two weeks had employed almost 900. Matters were looking good, and Braddock received much praise when he introduced a voluntary insurance scheme for the men employed. According to their pay, men agreed to have deductions made each week of either one or two pennies. Three local doctors in Galway, Oughterard and Clifden each agreed to act as assessors of any injuries received in cases of accidents.

However, labour relations were still not what they might be as a further strike ensued in August 1891, when 200 men demanded an extra two shillings each per week, plus extra payments for wet days, which it has to be said are not unusual in Connemara, and this had been an especially wet season. Despite the poor conditions, the ground preparation and drainage had been completed by this stage, so that work could continue. Like Robert Worthington before him,

Braddock was now becoming embroiled in local labour issues. He too was widely accused of employing too few local people and bringing in 'undesirable' workers from elsewhere. However, a local priest had reported to the Chief Secretary for Ireland that only nine members of his parish had answered Braddock's invitation to work on the railway construction - and, according to the priest, five were generally too drunk to carry out any work! The other four left as they considered the working conditions to be unsatisfactory.

Looking at it from a different perspective the result was that in these circumstances, Braddock had little choice but to bring in outsiders, whether 'undesirable' or not! Perhaps this explains the demands for higher wages from another point of view; living away from home for these men would have possibly involved them in expense not encountered closer to their homes. Such extra expense would not be readily affordable by people reeling from the effects of the famine and associated hardships.

On 17th June. 1891, the *Galway Vindicator* newspaper reported,

> So far as we have heard, a very absurd strike has taken place on the Recess section of the works. Some pick-hammers and barrows were broken wantonly or maliciously, and the ganger Mr Maloney, to cover the loss to the contractor, stopped 6*d*. from pay. Maloney was in the employment of Mr Worthington and was retained by Mr Braddock, so he is an experienced ganger. The men are in good employment and should be most careful of the general property of the contractor.

This gives us a clue to the realities on the ground.

The impression may be given that the workforce were ungrateful for the assistance given by Government grants and the offer of secure work for several years. The conclusion might even be drawn that they were irresponsible for turning such opportunities away, especially in the light of the extreme poverty and hardship in the area. However, the reality was that in comparison with elsewhere, wages were indeed poor, and working conditions extremely onerous, with long hours in the harsh and unforgiving Connemara weather. Local people had their pride, their self-respect, in spite of decades - for many their entire lifetime - of severe deprivation, and saw themselves as being taken advantage of. Given the dire poverty in many parts of Connemara, the decision to take any form of industrial action would not have been taken lightly by the workmen. Perhaps both Worthington and Braddock assumed that they might expect their employees to tolerate harsher conditions than elsewhere, given the lack of much alternative employment?

Shortly after contracts had been signed, the MGWR's Manager, Joseph Tatlow, and his locomotive engineer, Martin Atock, visited the new works to decide on the exact sites for the new stations.

Braddock's relationship with the labour force had been found wanting, but now that with the railway company was also beginning to show signs of strain. On 2nd December, 1891, he informed the MGWR that he had spent £12,000 more than he had been paid, and he wanted an up-to-date assessment of work undertaken by the engineers, with attendant valuation. Should this not be forthcoming, he threatened withdrawal from the contract. The reality appears to have been that he had underpriced the work. He also requested funding for

These illustrations show the Corrib viaduct in Galway under construction and just after completion.
NUIG, Galway

The tunnel at Prospect Hill under construction in 1893.

track materials for a five-mile stretch of the line; this caused some query, as the MGWR's engineers had stated that 'none of the line is ready to receive permanent way, and not likely to be...' The MGWR, in consequence, followed this advice and refused to comply with Braddock's request.

At the village of Ballinafad a provisions store was opened by the contractor during the period of the construction work. It proved its worth not only to railway workers, but to local people too. However, the construction work also attracted the attention of unscrupulous individuals who made and sold poítín (illegal 'moonshine' - a highly potent spirit derived from potatoes) in rough 'shebeens', adding to an already growing problem of drunkenness among the construction workers. The railway contractors, aided by the local clergy, tried to have these places shut down from time to time, but without success. This did not endear the construction workers to local people, but the problem persisted until the railway had been opened and the construction workers had left the area.

The main obstacle to the progression of the railway out of Galway was the wide stretch of water of the River Corrib. The MGWR sought tenders for the construction of a large viaduct to carry the railway across it, this structure being by far the major engineering feature on the whole line. Four contractors tendered for this, the highest being from Robert Worthington, despite his ongoing difficulties with the MGWR over works elsewhere, and his forced disengagement from the Clifden line. Possibly he thought that in case of arguments while the work was in progress, should he be awarded it, he would quote on the high side to ensure he covered his costs. By extension, we can assume that he may have taken the view than if the MGWR was going to try to negotiate a lower price, it wasn't worth his while. Worthington's quotation was £231,804. Braddock, by contrast, quoted £204,800 and was awarded the contract. However, negotiations had not been concluded between the MGWR and the navigational authorities, and some last minute amendments to the plans had to be made. Thus, a delay of four months was to follow before Braddock was re-awarded the contract, one clause of which stipulated that the viaduct must be completed within 15 months. It had three spans of some 150 ft each. One span was designed to lift to allow passing boats through. This had a lifting span of 21 ft. The construction of the viaduct was a complicated task, dealt with in *Appendix Two*.

By February 1892 some 2,000 men were at work on three lines then being built: Galway to Clifden, Westport to Mallaranny (on the Westport-Achill line) and the Ballina-Killala line. Of these, 950 were engaged on the Clifden line. Eight miles of track had now been laid, and work was progressing well. However, Braddock was beginning to encounter some of the same problems that Worthington had experienced through souring relations with the MGWR. The Corrib viaduct had not yet been started and work on the Prospect Hill tunnel nearby had ceased because the contractor had run out of bricks with which to line the wall.

In the summer of 1892 Braddock had left the workmen for four weeks without wages, as a result of which, hardly surprisingly, they went on strike. Naturally, this delayed the work again. The MGWR was beginning to realise that Braddock & Matthews were more of a liability than an asset when it emerged that they had accumulated various unpaid debts all over Galway city.

Their lack of bricks to line the tunnel may have arisen from a supplier refusing to provide any more materials until payment was forthcoming for previously incurred debts. More recent research suggests, as mentioned before, that among other things, he underpriced the contract initially, and that this contributed to the matters described as Braddock attempted to cut his own costs.

Workers increasingly complained of non-payment of wages, with some making the journey from Moycullen into Galway city to demand payment on several occasions. Some workers at Oughterard attempted to sue Braddock, and a strike of other workers took place in May 1892. The actual number of men employed was, according to a report by the engineers, too few anyway. Therefore the engineers asked the MGWR what it intended to do about the strikes of construction workers. Despite the seriousness of this issue, they had to repeat their question a month later and observing that their earlier correspondence on the matter had been ignored. Braddock, meanwhile, had been blaming the engineers for lack of instructions. In hindsight, one may draw the conclusion that Braddock was, in the circumstances, simply trying to shift the focus of blame elsewhere.

As an unfortunate aside, on 18th June, 1892 a fatality occurred when a young boy named Joyce was struck by a loaded wagon while attempting to stop it with a wooden block under a moving wheel. The child was aged about 10 or 12, but was actually an employee. Boys as young as that would regularly have been employed on works like this. If the age of the child is not enough of an indicator of the wretched working conditions of the day, the circumstances in which he met his death was worse. What we now call health and safety regulation was, by today's standards, poor to non-existent on large construction projects. The unfortunate child received such a blow that he died within half an hour.

On 7th July, 1892, the MGWR served Braddock - in person - with a notice terminating the contract at his Liverpool offices. In addition, the MGWR confiscated their horses, locomotives and tools on the line. The following day, Braddock's agents in Galway and Oughterard were served with the same notice and the engineers, Ryan and Townsend, posted notices to the effect at various locations along the course of the line.

Braddock had gone the same way as Worthington, and the MGWR was now left with the prospect of completing the line itself.

The contractor responded by suing the MGWR in the Court of Chancery for seizing their equipment, but the judge dismissed the case. A protracted court case followed, with Braddock claiming for what he said was work not paid for, while the MGWR invoked a list of costs related to employing a clerk of works during Braddock's contract, and expenses concerned with seizing his equipment (largely legal costs). As late as May 1896, after the line had been completed and opened to traffic, Braddock presented a bill to the MGWR for £558 19s. 6d. He claimed that this was for rails, sleepers, planks and plant which he had supplied to make temporary track during the construction, and that it should have been compensated for when seized. He threatened to sue. As might be expected, the MGWR ignored his correspondence entirely, and nothing more was heard.

The MGWR's half-yearly report in August 1892 stated: '...we have got into considerable difficulty with that line. The Contractor is in Default and we have terminated his contract and taken possession of all plant on the line'.

Into the clamour, another new proposal surfaced for a connecting line from Ross to Headford! Naturally, nothing came of this either.

With Braddock out of the way, the MGWR continued the construction itself. The company's own estimate for the opening of the line was to have been the end of 1893, but this was now realised to be impossible due to the various delays. It installed its own engineers to oversee the work until a new contractor could be found. It paid the men the amounts owing to them in full, and work resumed. By September, the MGWR had appointed Travers H. Falkiner, a contractor who they already had working on the Killala branch, to continue the work. For the MGWR, another sting in the tail was the growing realisation that it would have to contribute over £140,000 further itself to see the project through. On the ground, a landowner, Lord Stratheden, and his tenant, Campbell, wanted a higher price for the part of their land through which the railway ran, plus a one-off £500 compensation; a significant sum in those days. The money was intended to pay for a new gate lodge and access road to his property.

By late summer 1893 fourteen miles of track were down, almost a third of the route. This had brought the railway through Moycullen and Rosscahill to Oughterard, where the worst gradient on the line (1:70) would be encountered. The new track was of flat-bottom rail weighing 65 lb. per yard (about 0.5 kg per metre). It was laid on soleplates on half-round sleepers, attached with spikes. Track of similar specification was used on the Westport - Mallaranny - Achill and Killala lines. Rails were 30 ft (just under 10 m) in length. This was to be the standard for the whole line except for the track across a stretch of bog near Clifden, where 79 lb. rail was to be used to avoid buckling should the trackbed subside. All bridges from Oughterard onwards to Clifden now had their foundations laid and it may be taken that the right of way was completed, with track laying continuing. Ryan and Townsend, the civil engineers, reported that in several locations the railway had to be 'floated' over the bogland by placing large quantities of brushwood over the bog, followed by a layer of dried out turf. This created a cushion over which a light embankment could be added to carry the track. However, this method was used as a last resort due to the scarcity of timber or shrubs in the area. When solid foundations were needed for an embankment, materials would be taken from elsewhere on the line where blasting had occurred. At Rineen, some 15 km from Galway, a large quantity of rock was blasted out for use elsewhere on the line. Between Oughterard and Clifden, several rock cuttings proved to be difficult to blast out, owing to the presence of several different types of rock and unexpected drainage problems.

By autumn 1893, plans for the stations at Moycullen, Ross and Oughterard were approved, and the Post Office had advised their costs for erecting telegraph poles the length of the line and installing telegraph equipment at all necessary locations. This was estimated at £1,150. It would appear that all major earthworks for the railway had been completed at this stage. Messrs Ross & Walpole were contracted to supply the water towers at Clifden and Recess stations, and the Oughterard footbridge for £88, while Cowans, Sheldon & Co. won the contract for the turntable at Clifden, to cost £265. A hint of the desperate straits encountered by local people at the time is a mention that the

Oughterard Union, who ran the workhouse there, asked the railway company to place an 'iron railing' between the railway and their adjacent premises; this was agreed to.

For protection of level crossings, 18 gate houses were constructed along the line, described as having 'all the rooms built on one floor ... and built in superior manner'. It might be added that grand as this sounds, 'all' the rooms generally meant two or possibly three of them! The design of these gate houses was virtually standard across most of the entire MGWR network.

With so many construction workers in the general area, the Congested District Board wrote to the MGWR requesting assistance from the work gangs with the completion of the road through the Doolough Valley. Naturally, the MGWR refused; it had already suffered from as many delays in building the railway as it was prepared to accept.

Meanwhile, the route of the railway was now public knowledge. The Ballynahinch landowner, Richard Berridge, who had been so generous in donating almost half of the land needed for the whole route, pointed out that several cottages that the railway was to build for him in compensation for the removal of others in the line of the railway, were 'unsatisfactory'. Some correspondence was exchanged between Berridge and the MGWR's Company Secretary, which when not to Berridge's satisfaction was inclined to result in a somewhat terse exchange. The impression is given that the MGWR wanted to stick with its own plans, not taking into account Berridge's earlier generosity. Berridge, for his part, was clearly irritated by this, at one stage demanding compensation, but compromise was eventually reached.

Next, Berridge complained that 'the proposed siting of Ballynahinch Station is most objectionable...' (while viewed from the castle). He also insisted on

Here we see the methods used for construction of cuttings, often through solid rock. This view is near Recess.   *NUIG, Galway*

ornamental gates where the drive up to the castle crossed the railway adjacent to the entrance out onto the main road, as well as a gatehouse there. The MGWR acceded, and these stand to this day, as do many mature trees which Berridge had planted to obstruct the view of the station from the castle. He was not finished, however, with raising issues which concerned him. He told the company that he had heard that they intended to build a hotel in the vicinity of Recess and wanted to know if this was correct. He pointed out that if so, this might be detrimental to the business interests of a hotel already in the locality, owned by himself and a Mr Tweedie. Unfortunately, this was indeed the company's intention, though their main concern for the moment was to get the railway finished. Berridge accepted things as they were eventually, though various correspondence was to ensue where other minor matters were to be clarified.

The line's station buildings were substantial, being built very much to main line standards, and contrasting sharply with the generally poorer structures in the area in general. Stations were built on concrete foundations and the engineers described them as 'very permanent structures'. Most railway buildings on the line were of cut stone - this was limestone from quarries in Galway and Oughterard. In some cases, Clifden and Ballynahinch station houses being examples, attractive red brick was used. The MGWR used this elsewhere; Ballyvary and Mallaranny in Co. Mayo being examples. Platforms were of concrete with brick facings, and edged in cast slabs of concrete. While the line's original plans appear to have allowed trains to cross only at Moycullen, new Board of Trade regulations now dictated that passing facilities must also be provided at Oughterard, Maam Cross and Recess. Most stations had accommodation for the station master in the station building, that at Clifden being particularly commodious.

By the end of 1893, the number of people employed on the construction of the line was some 1,500.

Good planning had ensured that gradients and curves on the line were easy. Where a reverse curve was necessary, the Midland Great Western had stipulated that a short straight section must be placed between them. Sometimes it was necessary to remove material from one site, and take it to another to fill in a hollow or bog. On one occasion the company was subjected to a writ issued by Lord Fingall 'and others' to prevent them taking sand and gravel from Knockshanbally, in the Danesfied estate adjacent to the line outside Galway. However, the situation was ultimately resolved, as the MGWR was eventually offered the quarrying site by the owner, a Mr Redington. Many railway companies used one or two large quarries adjacent to their lines to obtain ballast for the track, but the MGWR had many small ones also. This particular site was one of several small pits along the route of the line. Traces of these and others like them on different lines are not always evident; some were not only small, but extremely short lived. Geological and topographical circumstances would dictate such things, rather than whims of Directors or railway company policy.

As the official opening of the first stretch approached, Maam Cross and Ballynahinch stations were not yet complete, but would be opened a few weeks

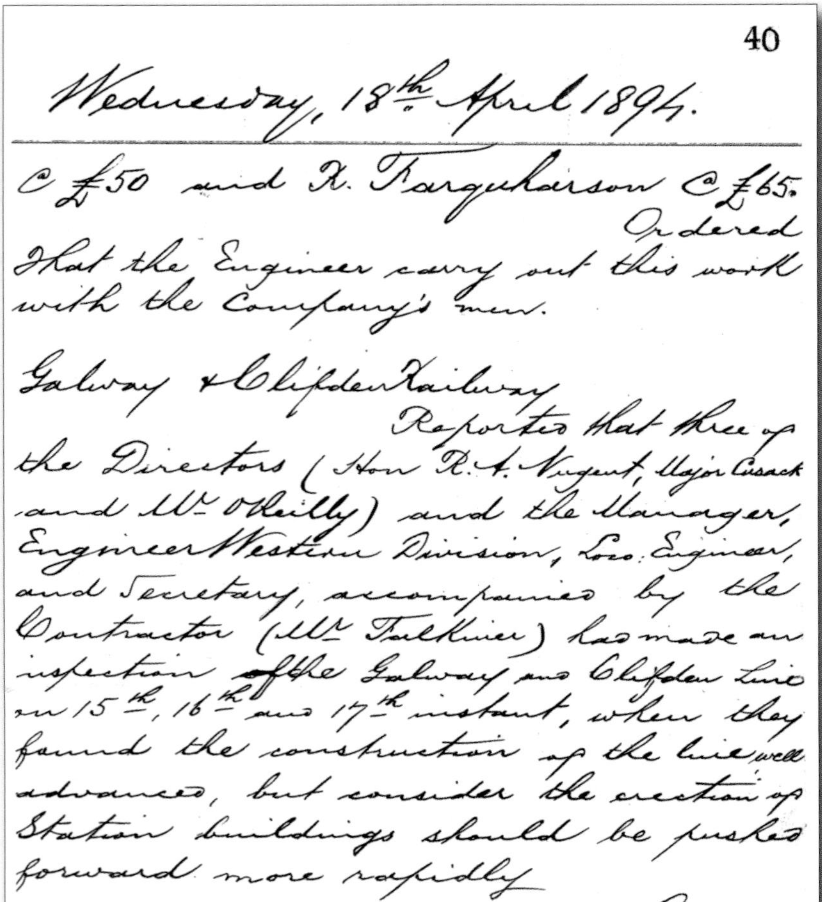

Wednesday, 18th April 1894.

C £50 and R. Farquharson C £65.

Ordered

That the Engineer carry out this work with the Company's men.

Galway & Clifden Railway

Reported that three of the Directors (Hon R. A. Nugent, Major Cusack and Mr O'Reilly) and the Manager, Engineer Western Division, Loco. Engineer, and Secretary, accompanied by the Contractor (Mr Faulkner) has made an inspection of the Galway and Clifden Line on 15th, 16th and 17th instant, when they found the construction of the line well advanced, but consider the erection of Station buildings should be pushed forward more rapidly

Ordered

That Mr O'Neill's attention be called to this, and directed to take necessary measures to expedite Station buildings &c, and if he requires additional temporary office assistance to apply for same at once.

In the Manager's reports —

Ordered

That with regard to Lock up enclosure recommended to be provided

Extract from MGWR company's minute books, dated 18th April 1894.   *CIE Archive*

later. The station at Rosscahill (always simply called 'Ross' by the railway) had yet to be started - though it had been announced publicly that it would be. Trains could now cross at all stations except Ballynahinch, though a passing loop and second platform were added there later. Further siding accommodation was provided in the form of a quantity of rails which had been initially laid on the as-yet unopened Westport-Achill line, where they were deemed to be too light. These tracks, as sidings in various stations on the Clifden line, would remain in their new home for most or all of the line's life. Since it was now expected that the initial opening of the line would only be as far as Oughterard, a locomotive turntable would be required there. In August 1894 a tender from Messrs Ross & Walpole was accepted, at a cost of £238. This firm had provided water towers at various other locations on the MGWR, including the Clifden line. While it may seem somewhat extravagant to provide a turntable at what would only be a very temporary terminus, it must be remembered that it was always the intention that tender locomotives would be used, and in any event it was expected that on fair days special cattle trains would terminate there. As will be seen later on, short Galway-Oughterard trains were to be a feature of the passenger train service as well, at different times in the history of the railway.

A group of construction workers take a break at Maam Cross station during construction of the station. It will be noted that while the station building, goods shed and signal cabin are structurally complete, the water tank has yet to be placed on the water tower in the centre background. It would appear that the track has not been fully finished off.

CLIFDEN. Co. GALWAY. 852. W.L.

An overview of Clifden from the south, showing the railway station in the centre, not long after the line opened. Several goods wagons await unloading at the goods platform which is twice the length of the passenger platform. This proved to very adequate, as freight consignments always made up the bulk of the railway's revenue. Sadly, at no stage in the life of the line did passenger usage regularly come close to what could be deemed economically viable, with

By September 1894 the railway was essentially complete, with track now having reached Clifden. The MGWR had given notice on 22nd August of its intention to open the line as far as Oughterard as soon as possible. Consequently an inspection train consisting of a locomotive and carriage conveyed the MGWR's traffic manager and several other company Directors the whole way to Clifden on 25th September. This is the first through working of a train, other than the contractor's own operations, the whole way. By 10th October, the Board of Trade Inspectors arrived in the form of Major Hutchinson, the civil engineers Ryan and Townsend, and Falkiner and Jackson, the contractors. Bridges were tested by coupling two of the MGWR's heaviest engines and running them over them - these were, of course, engines which would not normally be allowed over the line at all. A few days later, the MGWR's Directors and the civil engineers and contractors travelled out again as far as Recess, with a locomotive and carriages of the types that would be intended to make up ordinary trains - plus, of course, the Director's special first class coach. Most matters were deemed to be satisfactory, though some work remained to be done to several of the station buildings. A repeat inspection was organised for 15th December, by which time all was in order. The Board of Trade replied on 26th December that public trains could commence straight away as far as Oughterard.

Even as these final preparations were being made, the British Government wrote to the MGWR asking when the line would be ready to go to Clifden. They were anxious to assist with the provision of relief from 'distress' locally - the potato crop had partially failed again in recent times. Meanwhile, boat owners and various other traders in Galway complained to the company about the disruption they had suffered during construction. Perhaps they were testing the water regarding compensation, but nothing came of it. And finally, Mr Travers H. Falkiner, the contractor, asked the MGWR what they wanted him to do with 13 of Braddock's horses which he no longer needed. These were some of the horses which the MGWR had seized from Braddock in lieu of debt. The way was therefore now clear for the opening of the first stretch of the line.

When the line was first opened, the MGWR used 'half round' sleepers with the rails directly spiked to them. A small slot was cut in the top of these for the rail to sit into. On a main line they would be somewhat closer together than shown here, which was in a siding. By the early years of the 20th century, conventional heavier sleepers were used, but the 'half-round' type with spiked rails could still be found in obscure nooks and crannies as late as 1960, when this photograph was taken in Ballaghaderreen, Co. Roscommon.   *Courtesy H. Stacpoole, C.L. Fry Collection*

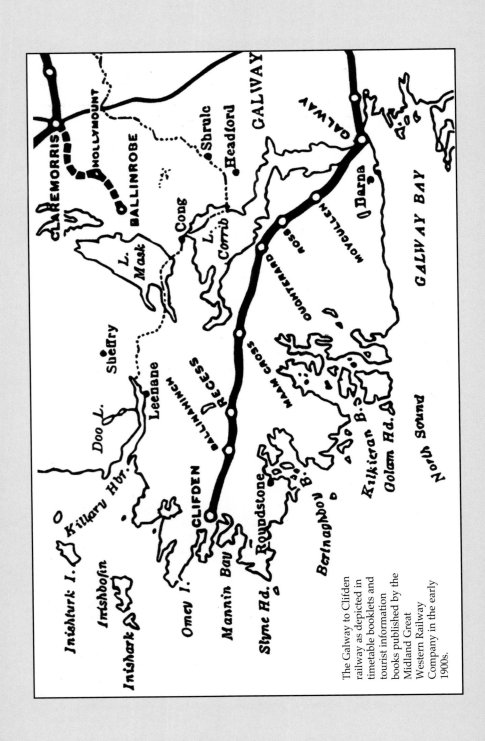

The Galway to Clifden railway as depicted in timetable booklets and tourist information books published by the Midland Great Western Railway Company in the early 1900s.

Chapter Three

Description of the route

Upon leaving Galway, as mentioned before, the train would reverse out of the platforms towards the Lough Atalia bridge, before pulling forward and passing to the right-hand side of the station past the locomotive shed and turntable. After passing under a bridge, a short climb brought the railway to a four-span bridge over Forster Street. There followed a short tunnel which despite being designated as such by the MGWR, was described by the engineer as a 'cut and cover'. This tunnel was very short and carried the Prospect Hill Road over it. It was close to the town reservoir and the lining wall of it doubled as the reservoir's retaining wall. Almost immediately, the line crossed the Headford Road on a bridge of 28ft span before arriving at the edge of the River Corrib. This was crossed by the major engineering feature of the line, the Corrib viaduct. *Appendix Two* with details of bridges will be found at the end of the book.

The line continued across open countryside, initially passing through where the campus of University College, Galway is currently situated. Today this area is very much within the western Galway city suburbs. It was described as passing 'deserted mansions, breweries and factories', with the ruined De Burgos castellated mansion and the picturesque Menlo Castle to be seen from the train. Now, from the right-hand windows, the passenger would see Lough Corrib as the train skirted its western shore and as it picked up speed to a sedate 35 miles per hour or so. Lough Corrib is Ireland's second largest inland fresh water lake. Shortly, the train passed through woodlands before slowing to enter Moycullen station.

Our traveller would now hear the bustle and commotion on the platform, the local people and traders speaking in Irish - now, they were in Connemara! Moycullen, or Maigh Cuillinn, means 'the plain or field of holly'. At Moycullen, the station was a short walk downhill from the village main street. A substantial stone station building and goods shed were provided. From here the countryside became more remote with lake and woodland scenery to each side of the railway as it travelled westward. As the Galway-Clifden road now came into view, the next station reached was Ross, serving the village of Rosscahill. The railway crossed the Galway-Clifden road on a level crossing before entering the station. The station house here, built just after the line opened, was again of substantial stone construction. The station was built primarily to serve the Martin family of Ross House, as the village was then (as now) very small. The line continued through similar countryside for a while, though becoming ever more sparsely populated, before arriving at Oughterard (Uachtar Ard; the 'upper height'). On entering Oughterard station, the line passed the town workhouse on the right before entering the station, a substantial stone-built structure. Oughterard was the largest intermediate town along the route, and would have been the terminus of one of the earlier proposed routes. To the right of the station building, our traveller would see several sidings for loading cattle wagons, as sheep and cattle traffic could be very busy here on fair days. The cattle platform was built to an unusual style with arches under it, and can still be seen. The station building was on the

Galway city and surrounds about 1896. The station goods yard contains a wagon turntable; this was later removed, and further sidings were laid in this area. The newly-opened Clifden line may be seen curving round the north side of the city, though there is no sign of the Shantalla siding. It had not yet been built. The route of the city tramway line may be seen. It commences in Forster Street, curves round Eyre Square, and follows William Street, Shop Street, Mainguard Street and Bridge Street before heading over the bridge, along Lower Dominick street, and out to Salthill.

Right: The route of the railway leaving Galway *circa* 1896. Shantalla siding is not shown as it had yet to be built. It would leave the main line at Newcastle, just south of the ruined distillery, skirting the boundary of Newcastle Lodge, and continuing west past the stream named Sruffaunacashlaun on the map. Queen's College is now University College Galway.

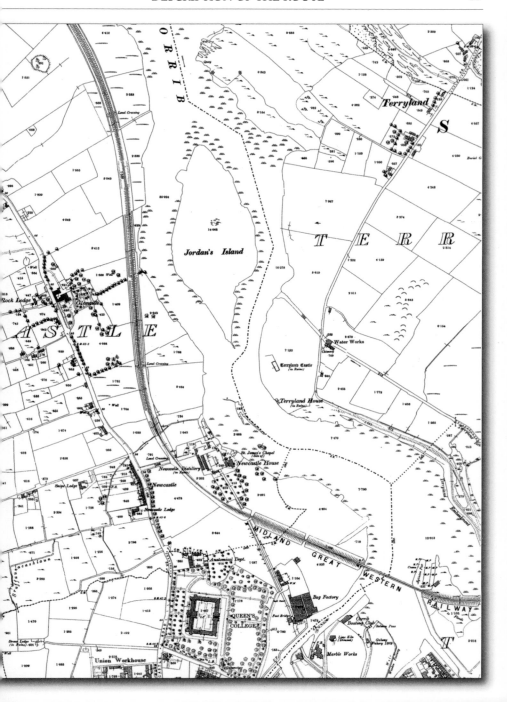

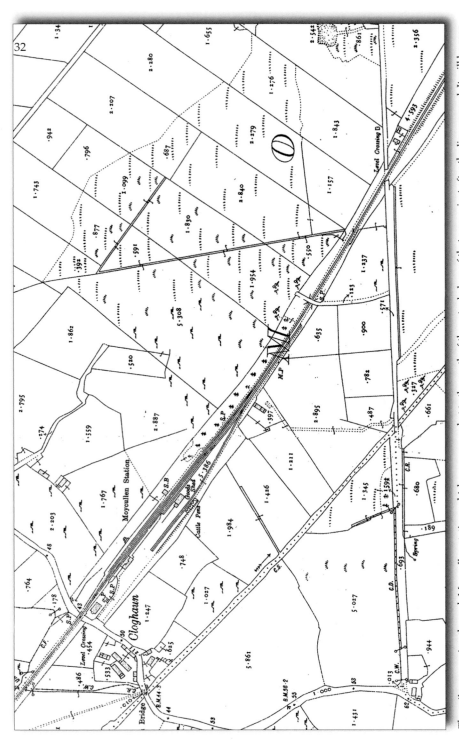

The railway passing through Moycullen station, which was somewhat to the north of the actual place of that name, just after the line opened. It will be seen that the local settlement, called Cloghaun, consisted in those days of little more than a few thatched cabins and small houses adjacent to the line. The size of the station seems entirely disproportionate to the size of the village, but this would have reflected the fact that it served a wide area and people would travel

right, and a goods shed and water tower for locomotives completed the picture. On the accompanying map, the locomotive turntable may be seen on the south side of the station. This was used for turning locomotives shortly after the line opened, as the service initially did not go further. Latterly, the only use for it was for occasional fair day cattle trains and other short workings.

In Oughterard village there was an establishment named the 'Railway Hotel'. It should be noted that like the erstwhile 'Railway Hotel' in Clifden, it never had any connection whatever with the railway. It was commonplace for hotel proprietors to name establishments thus, as it would imply proximity to the main means of transport.

After leaving Oughterard, the line crossed a minor road and ascended a gentle uphill gradient towards the west. Views of lake and mountain now gave way to distant mountains, as moorland birds, hares and rabbits abounded – this was the real Connemara. The line skirted the lakes of Boffin, Inieran, Arderry and Shintilla. At this stage the countryside was remote indeed, only the road some distance to the left giving any idea of civilisation at all. Everywhere else the countryside was pristine, unspoilt. A short deep rock cutting followed, after which the train arrived at Maam Cross station. 'Maam' means a mountain pass or gap, and the village of this name lies some miles to the north of this cross roads. It is situated at the edge of the Maamturk, or Maumturk mountains, the 'pass of the wild boar'. It is in the heart of 'Joyce Country' ('Duiche Sheoigheach'), a central Connemara region named after the Joyce family, who were one of the 14 Anglo-Norman merchant 'tribes' who settled in the area many centuries ago. The road junction itself was, and is, the major meeting place in Connemara, where roads from the remoter north, south, east and west of the region converge. The cross roads is in the townland of Shindilla, and the locality is known in Irish as 'An teach dóite' (the burned house). The origin of this name is uncertain. On account of this central location, for many centuries there has been a monthly market here for cattle and general goods. Once the railway was established, large amounts of cattle began to be handled by rail. The station had the usual facilities, with the main station on the right and goods shed and loading bank on the left from the point of view of those approaching from Galway. There was a long platform for loading cattle trains.

Immediately beyond the station was a level crossing, and the line continued past ever wilder bogland punctuated by small lakes, bare grey rocks and mountain scenery on all sides. The views were wide, wild, pristine, beautiful, unspoilt; they still are. Entering the valley of the Recess River, the line now reached Recess station, on the shore of Glendollagh Lough, or Glendalough Lake. The local name of this place, An Sraith Saileach, translates as 'the stream of the willow tree'; like many Irish place names it is as picturesque and descriptive as the place it refers to. However, the lake name translates as the 'Glen of the two loughs', possibly a reference to the two halves of this body of water.

It was here that the MGWR would build its tourist hotel after a few years. Beyond the station, a small river bridge and immediately afterwards a level crossing over the Clifden Road led the railway into the area known as 'Joyce's Country' and shortly the line passed alongside the beautiful Derryclare Lake (Loch Dhoire an Chláire = 'the lake of the oak grove on the plain'). This is still a popular scenic photographic stop on any tour in the area. More lakes came into view: Athry

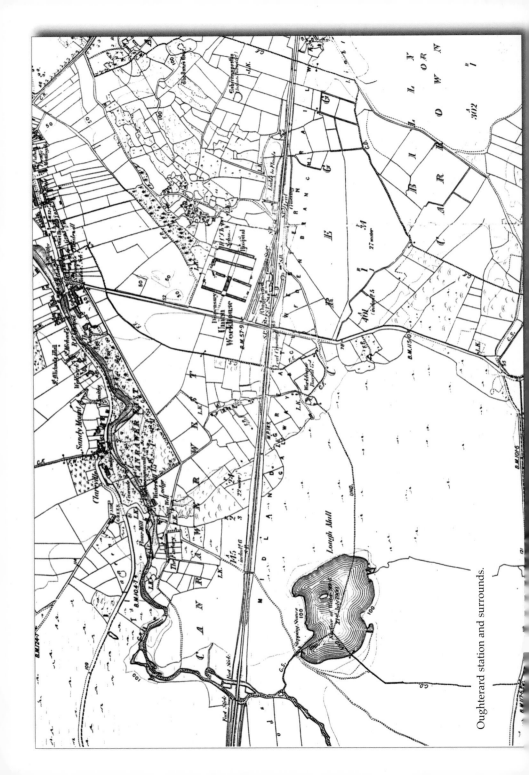

Oughterard station and surrounds.

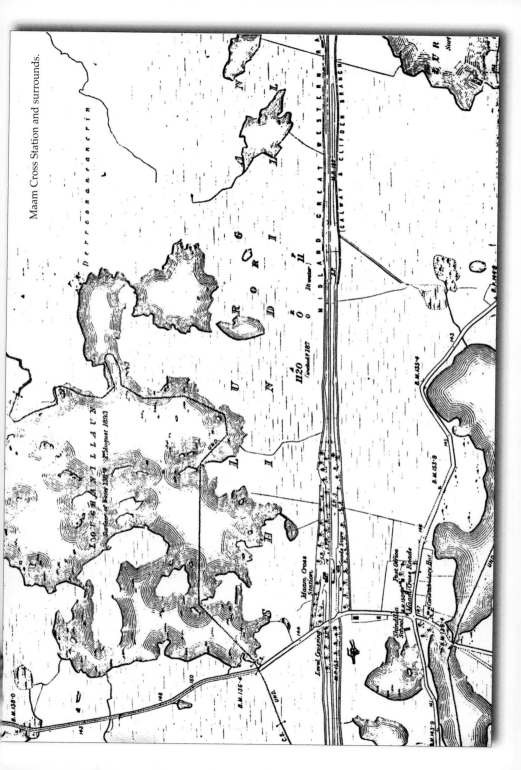

Maam Cross Station and surrounds.

An idea of the vast remoteness and wild beauty of Connemara can be gained from this view across Glendollagh Lake of Recess station, shortly after the railway opened. It appears to have been taken from the approach road to Glendollagh House, on the south side of the lake. In the centre background the station can be seen, with the goods shed on the right. The hotel was just out of sight to the right of the picture. Lissoughter Hill and the Maumturk Mountains brood silently in the background.   *Lawrence Collection/National Library of Ireland*

Recess station shortly after the line opened, looking towards Galway. The water tower for locomotives is on the right-hand side of the track, with the signal cabin beyond it and the neat white picket fencing, seen at many stations on the line, is evident behind the passenger platform.
                    Lawrence Collection/National Library of Ireland

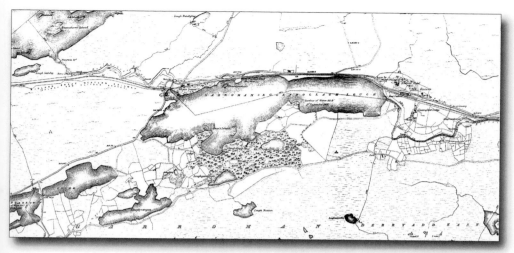

Recess area, showing the station in its picturesque setting on the shore of Glendollagh Lough, also referred to on the map as Garroman Lough. To the eastern side of it, adjacent to Lissoughter Lodge, was the unfortunately short-lived Railway Hotel, near which was the all-important Post Office. Recess station itself may be seen at the west end of the lough, and the hotel halt platform on the right of it (both are shown enlarged below). This would date this map to be just after 1902.

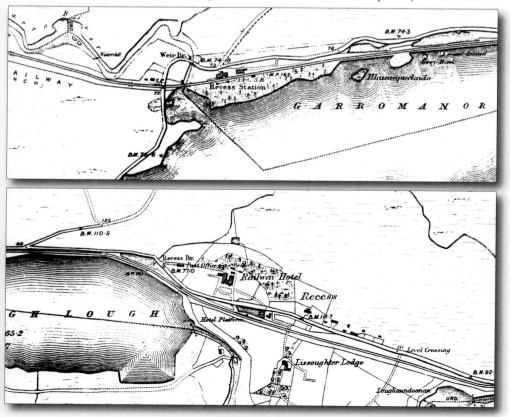

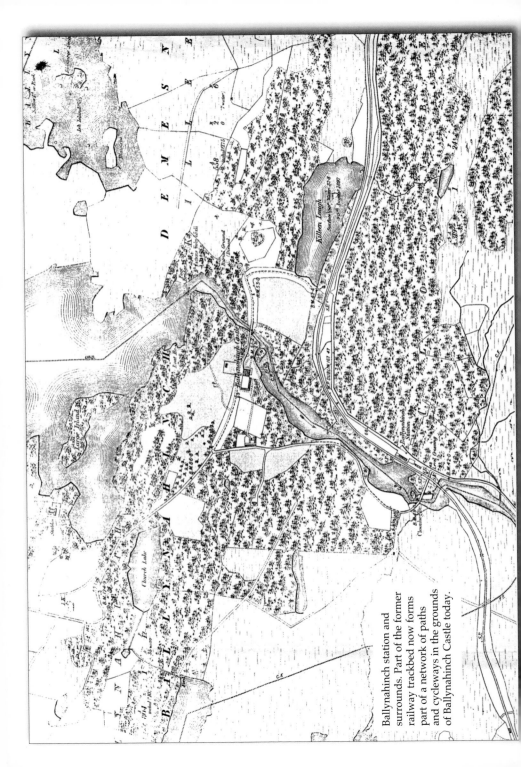

Ballynahinch station and surrounds. Part of the former railway trackbed now forms part of a network of paths and cycleways in the grounds of Ballynahinch Castle today.

Lough, Ballynahinch Lake, Lough Nabrucka, and Killeen Lake glimmered serenely under the Connemara sky as the train passed. Now the train approached the remote township of Ballynahinch, where was situated the magnificent Ballynahinch Castle, now a hotel. The name refers to numerous local lakes with small islands in them: Ballynahinch means the 'townland of the islands (or river meadows)' (Baile na hInse). At the time the railway was built, the hotel was owned by Richard Berridge who had donated the land through his estates over which the line would run. This covered some 20 miles - almost half the entire route of the line - Berridge was a major landowner in the area. The donation of this land was doubtless of major importance in determining that the route chosen would be the inland one, not the coastal one. From Ballynahinch station a road ran some five miles to the village of Roundstone, the subject of earlier plans to build a branch line there. Had this eventually been built, this would have been the junction station. Ballynahinch station house was of red brick construction, more reminiscent of those at Ballyvary and Mallaranny in Co. Mayo, than the more common cut stone designs seen elsewhere on the MGWR system. The goods shed was of stone, and while initially only one passenger platform was provided, another was added later to enable trains to cross at this location. On account of the restricted site at the lakeside, the second (up) platform was situated slightly to the east of the main (down) one. The setting of this station must be one of the most scenic in Ireland. Today, the station may be seen still, as it has been beautifully kept by its successive private owners since closure, over 80 years ago.

Beyond Ballynahinch the railway entered its remotest stretch yet - an area of unspoilt lake and bogland with spectacular views of Connemara's wide-skied scenic splendours. Some six miles (9 km) were to pass through this still almost uninhabited wilderness before the line approached the town of Clifden on a long low embankment. As mentioned earlier, this town was only established some 75 years before the railway came – the original name for the area is An Clochán ('the stones' or 'the stone steps'). Given the rocky nature of the area, this makes sense to anybody casting a glance around the town's hinterland.

The station here was substantial with a well-finished red brick station building (now part of the Station House Hotel), and goods and engine sheds of cut stone. The locomotive shed had two roads. Nearby, of course, were the locomotive turntable, water tower and coaling stage, both still extant. The railway station lay above the harbour, though no siding ever ran down there as it would have been far too steep. This, of course, limited the railway's potential for serving the fishing industry.

The town of Clifden lay a short walk beyond the station, the bustling end of a long journey for a tourist from Dublin, but home to those who used the railway on a daily basis.

Throughout the life of the line, little changed. A passenger on the first train in 1895 would have seen much the same as one on the last train 40 years later, as little expansion had taken place in any of the places served. No alterations of any substance had been made to any part of the railway infrastructure either.

In the early years of the 20th century, an English railway enthusiast named Thomas R. Perkins, a Methodist preacher from Henley-in-Arden, Warwickshire, England, set himself the task of travelling over every railway line in both Great Britain and Ireland which was open to passenger traffic. He was a chemist by

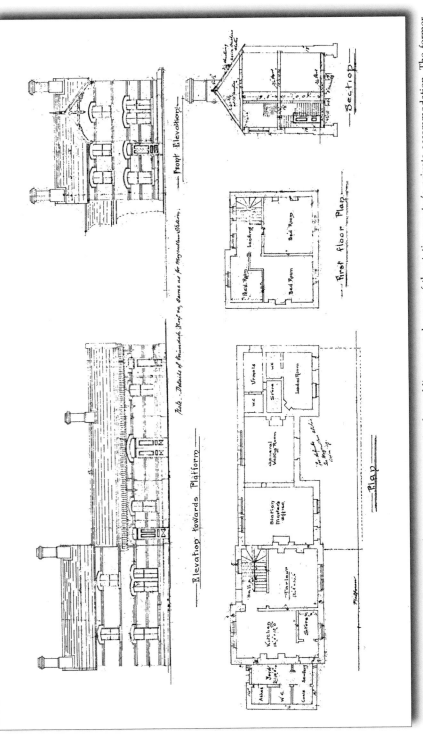

Original plans, Ballynahinch Station. The lower storey contained a public area, and some of the station master's private accommodation. The former included a station master's office which was directly accessible from his own accommodation, a general waiting room for passengers, and Ladies and Gentlemen's toilets. The latter consisted of an entrance hall, kitchen and parlour along with stores for personal effects. A staircase led from this area upstairs to the station master's three bedrooms. There was no bathroom – it was customary in those days to carry out such functions with a tin bath filled with hot water from kettles or pots boiling over the cooker.

Ballynahinch station, looking east, shortly after the line opened (*above*). The castle may be seen in the distance. It is obscured in the lower picture (probably *circa* 1900-1905) by the trees planted at the insistence of the owner of the castle in order to shield the view of the railway from there. In the upper picture there is just the one platform on the down side, by the time the lower view was taken the up platform and passing loop on the left had been added. Space available on the left led to the new platform being further away from the photographer in the upper picture, and connected by a barrow crossing visible in the foreground.

(Both) Lawrence Collection/National Library of Ireland

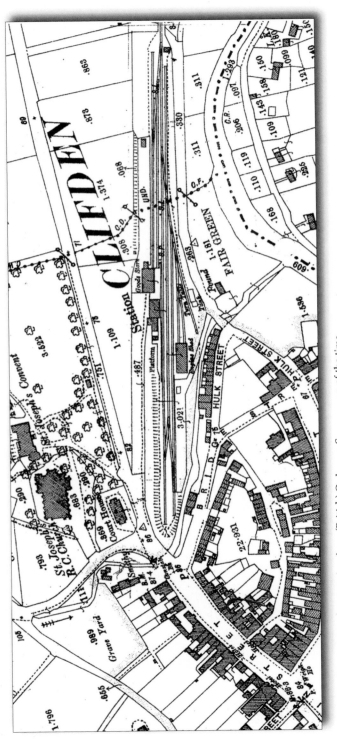

Plan of Clifden station after opening from (British) Ordnance Survey map of the time.

New Bridge, outside Clifden. The railway track on the right is now replaced by the modern road, but here the solid rock foundation can be clearly seen, along with the original type of track and sleepers. *Lawrence Collection/National Library of Ireland*

trade, and he and his wife operated a pharmacy between them. This meant that they almost always took separate holidays, so that Perkins could freely indulge his interest in railway travel. He exploited this advantage to the maximum and achieved his aim after some years in June 1932, upon arrival at Athboy, Co. Meath, his final newly-covered line. This involved clocking up a considerable mileage, and naturally, this included the Galway-Clifden line. As a Methodist lay preacher, Perkins always ensured that as far as possible he attended morning service in a suitable church while travelling, such was his devotion. No other distraction, of course, was allowed to get in his way. As far as can be gathered, he took few photographs on the line - he was more of a traveller than a photographer, but he did maintain meticulous diaries, most of which have survived. The whereabouts of his photographs of the Clifden line is uncertain.

Thus, we join Mr Perkins on a fine June day in 1932, as he enters Galway station from Athlone, where he had spent the previous night after covering the Attymon Junction-Loughrea line the previous day. The following is the extract from his diary. Notes appended are by the author.

Before Galway is reached the sea becomes visible from the train: the station, which is a terminus, has 2 platforms and an all-over roof.

The Connemara Train was standing at the opposite platform;* when I had taken my seat I was surprised to see a gentleman whom I knew, who lives near Stratford-on-Avon and had left home only the previous evening. He was going to Lough Corrib to fish, and our meeting was a mutual surprise. We travelled together to Oughterard, where he alighted.

The Clifden branch diverges from the main line before Galway station is reached, so we were drawn out by a tank engine† to the junction, where No. 583,# an 0-6-0, was attached to the other end of the train and took charge. For the first few miles, the scenery, though rather good, was not particularly striking; soon, however, as we touched Lough Corrib and other smaller lakes, it steadily increased in beauty. A feature of the district one could not fail to notice was the number of large mushroom-shaped stones scattered about - a geological curiosity peculiar to that locality, I believe.§ Passing

---

* The 'opposite platform' no longer exists. † 'E' class (GSR 'J26' class) tank engines tended to be used for this purpose. # No. 583 was one of the standard 'J18' class used on all trains by this time. § These rocks are glacially deposited material dating back to the last Ice Age.

Clifden station soon after the opening of the line. The train consists of what would be the standard type of formation for most of the life of the line; a composite first/second class composite coach, a third class coach (in the middle, in this instance), and a guard's/brake van at the rear. The middle of these three coaches is of interest here, as it is what even then was an old vehicle dating from the 1869-76 period. The MGWR was phasing these out even as the

National Library of Ireland

Moycullen the hills began to close in, and Ross station was beautifully situated in a pine-clothed gorge. After Oughterard the railway leaves Lough Corrib and plunges into the heart of the mountains, each mile being grander than the last, and reminding one of parts of the West Highland line in Scotland. On every hand rose the giant peaks of Connemara, seeming in places to present a solid wall along the horizon, while our course wound along the shores of beautiful little lakes or tumbling mountain streams.

Our train was 'mixed' and at several of the stations considerable shunting took place, so that I was able to get out and admire the scenery.* At Maam Cross several small pigs were put out onto the platform, tied up in a sack, and it was amusing to watch as its occupants wriggled about inside. The scenery here was overpoweringly grand, and the journey onwards to Recess baffles all description, as we steamed along the valley with the great mountains above us and the wood-fringed banks of the lake, in which at one point I counted nine black cattle standing. Climbing through a rock cutting to bare moorland, we soon descended into another lovely wooded valley, noticing on our right the pathetic ruins of the railway company's fine hotel, burnt out for pure 'cussedness'† during the Civil War.

At Recess station our engine went off for the usual 'shunting' – I snapped it while so engaged, and I also secured pictures of the quaint old saloon which headed our train; this was still in MGW livery and bore the crest and initials of the old company.# Although now fitted with electric light, the old 'saucepans' which covered the former oil lamps can still be noted on the roof.

Both guard and driver had apparently noticed my interest in the scenery, and it was amusing to see how at the stations they would both come up to me to advise me about coming 'tit-bits'. The guard actually wanted to find me a compartment to myself; while at one point, at which the driver had advised me to be on the look-out, I noticed, on putting my head out of the window, that he was leaning out of the cab and pointing towards the object which he wished me not to miss.

It is easy to understand why the MGWR selected Recess as the site for a tourist hotel; not only is the scenery magnificent, but the climate is wonderfully mild, palms and other semi-tropical plants growing here in abundance, while the rhododendron blossom added another touch of loveliness at the time of my visit. For some distance onwards we had on our right a couple of beautiful tree-fringed lakes, with a wonderful background of mountain peaks, and at Ballynahinch I noted its modern§ castle nestling amid the woods at the lake side.

Now we were climbing out of the valley to the bare uplands, where beauty gave place to stern and rugged grandeur, and a few minutes later we ran down to our terminus, Clifden, a beautifully situated seaside town 49 miles from our start at Galway.

And now ensued an experience both pleasant and painful; in order to reach the Achill branch at Mallaranny I had to travel 60 miles by 'motor coach', which in this case proved to be an Irish Omnibus Co.'s bus, with myself as the sole passenger!

Perkins continued to describe 'bumping and bouncing' along the rough and narrow roads which he describes as 'atrocious', though commenting in highly favourable terms about the scenery. As the Holy Mountain of Croagh Patrick in Co. Mayo came into view, Perkins quaintly describes it as being sacred to 'Irish Romanists'; it is thus tempting to imagine the content of some of his sermons! He continued via Westport to Achill Island, where he remained for the weekend before venturing elsewhere.

---

* This would also have served as a comfort stop, as the elderly carriages used had no toilets.
† Our traveller's understanding of the Irish political situation was clearly nowhere near as detailed as his railway knowledge! # This is likely to have been an old first class vehicle; the fate of his photographs is unfortunately unknown § In its present form, most of the castle was built in 1813 on the site of an earlier building.

The 'Tourist Express' about to leave Clifden. This photograph shows a typical train consist for this servic[e] in place of the normal trio of six-wheeled vehicles catering for all three classes and the guard – but devoi[d] of through corridors, toilets or catering facilities. The locomotive is No. 33 *Arrow*, one of 17 of the 'D' clas[s] This example had a long life, being built in 1876, rebuilt in the 1890s and lasting until 1961, long after th[e] Clifden line had closed. It will be in the standard MGWR lined green livery here, and was probably th[e] regular branch locomotive when the photograph was taken. Behind it, in the newly-introduced dark blu[e] and white livery for this train, we have the following vehicles, in order: 6-wheeled first class coach, [6-] wheeled second class coach, bogie coach, configuration unclear, dining car No. 3, then new (built 1904[?]) This carriage was converted to a third class coach and 6-wheeled brake/luggage van in 1915 . *NU[...]*

The locomotive has a wooden platform to house camera equipment and a photographer. The film-maker was London-born cinematic pioneer Norman Whitten. He ran the General Film Supply Co., responsible for periodic newsreels on Irish affairs. In 1914 or thereabouts, it was arranged that this crew would travel over the line. This picture appears to be taken outside the locomotive shed at Galway. Clearly, some of the people shown are locomotive crew members, while others are in smart civilian clothes. It is likely that Whitten is one of them. The film sequences apparently appeared in a short film called *Irish Events 1917-1920*. One wonders whether the images secured have survived.
Author's Collection

Chapter Four

The MGWR Years 1895-1925

The Midland Great Western Railway's main line was that from Dublin to Galway, which had been opened in stages during the late 1840s, enabling the first train to arrive in Galway in August 1851. From the outset, the Clifden branch was worked by locomotives based in Galway and Clifden, and this remained the case throughout the life of the line, with both locomotives and crews changing at Galway in each direction even on through trains like the 'Tourist Express'.

Following the opening of the first section of the Clifden line to Oughterard on 1st January, 1895, an initial train service of two trains per day in each direction was provided. One train carried passengers only, and the other carried both passengers and general goods. Such trains were always known as 'mixed trains'. In these days before refrigerated transport was available, livestock tended to be exported from rural areas to Britain, or sent to slaughterhouses in Belfast or Dublin. Thus, cattle traffic was an important part of the line's business, and while special livestock trains tended to operate on fair days, such wagons could also be hitched onto the back of a mixed train if necessary.

The first public train operated with little fanfare, though the MGWR's Chairman, Joseph Tatlow, and some local dignitaries were on board a special train, leaving first at 8 am. The train crossed the Corrib, heading out past Menlo Abbey and Newcastle to Moycullen, and on to Oughterard, which was initially to be the terminus pending minor completion work beyond there. This portion of the line was the first of three separate sections during construction, each having its own engineer in charge. The special train reached Oughterard at 9.15, and the locomotive took on water and prepared to return as the 9.25 public train; the line was now open to the public, at last. However, it was to be an unexpectedly slow start, as only 12 passengers boarded! 1st January was a religious holiday, and many people either stayed at home, or waited until the later train, which would carry a respectable crowd.

On their return on the first train, Tatlow and his friends adjourned for copious refreshments in the Railway Hotel in Eyre Square, Galway. The service had now started, without much ceremony, as far as Oughterard.

With construction now complete west of Oughterard, the other two sections were almost ready to open. On 3rd May, a train carrying a party of the MGWR Directors reached Clifden for the first time. Following their inspection, which was favourable, the line itself was deemed to be suitable to be opened throughout. However, the station buildings were 'nowhere near ready', and the contractors were told to employ more men if necessary as the company wanted to open the line fully on 1st July. Some attention was also necessary to improve drainage in some boglands adjacent to the railway. A few weeks later, contracts were awarded for the supply of a water tower at Maam Cross at a cost of £84. Thirteen other matters relating mainly to the completion of Ballynahinch and Maam Cross stations were attended to. By 26th June, Ross station was complete and its use had been authorised by the Board of Trade. Towards the end of October 1895 all of the more trivial outstanding matters had been completed at Ballynahinch station and it duly opened fully.

Within months of the opening of the railway, the inhabitants of the Leam district had requested a 'flag stop' or small halt, beside the line nearby. The MGWR refused this and no more was heard of such a proposal.

Consequently, on 1st July, 1895, the people of Clifden turned out in force to welcome the first public train to their town. The full Galway to Clifden railway was finally open. The line had cost, all told, some £9,000 per mile, most of which came from the British Government under the provisions of the Balfour Act. At this time, the cost was, per mile, between twice and three times what might normally be expected for a light railway of this length. However, the cost had been greatly inflated by difficulties with the contractors, bad weather, the wild terrain through which the line passed, and the costs associated with the Corrib viaduct. It must be added that like many similar railways it was built to a very high standard, as it was built to last for ever.

The entire route was just over 49 miles (79 km) from Galway station, with intermediate stations initially at Moycullen, Oughterard and Recess. In Galway, access to the station was provided by the unusual means of trains reversing into and out of the platform. A westbound train had to reverse out of the station, across the Lough Atalia bridge, then pull forward to the north side of the main station, before heading out to Clifden via the north of the city. Similarly, an incoming train had to approach the station, passing it and stopping on the bridge, from where it reversed back into the platform. This was due to the position of Galway station, originally built as terminus, at the edge of Eyre Square, in the city centre.

Tourism had been an increasingly important aspect of the local economy in the years since the worst ravages of the famine, and the potential of the new railway in attracting visitors to the area was realised at an early stage. For some 40 years, other areas in Ireland had developed significant tourist economies once the railways had arrived, and Connemara was an ideal place for this to happen too. Consequently, in the railway's first summer, summer tourist coach services were started to connect Clifden with Westport. On 24th July, 1895, the line saw its first special train - an excursion from Galway to Clifden and back. This train left Galway at 9.00 am, arriving in Clifden at 11.30. Return was at 7.00 pm, arriving back at 9.30. By summer 1895, not only had the Clifden line commenced operations, but so had the Westport-Achill line, very much a Mayo equivalent of the Clifden line. Thus, the traveller could take the train to Clifden, spend a few days there, and then continue by the tourist coach to Westport, from where he might take a trip out to Achill Island by train. The coach left Clifden at 9.00 am daily between June and September, and was operated itself by the MGWR. Arrival in Westport was at 5.30 pm. A corresponding service operated in the other direction, and both travelled via Letterfrack and Leenane. This service was prominently advertised from the outset in railway literature and timetables. It was destined to be successful, to such an extent that despite the comparatively short tourist season, the MGWR would eventually build hotels at Mallaranny, on the Achill line, and Recess, on the Clifden line. From 1903, a special 'Tourist train' was operated for some years, as will be seen later.

From the outset, cheap tickets were offered for such events as market days, day excursions and other tourism initiatives. By 1896, market tickets had been offered to or from Maam Cross, Oughterard and Clifden stations. Race days also attracted cheap fares, for example on 17th August, 1896 half-fare tickets were offered from all stations to the Oughterard races. Once the 'Tourist train' started operating, special tickets were offered combining rail travel and hotel accommodation at Recess or Galway, where the MGWR had its own hotel adjacent to the railway station.

Despite the line now being open and operating, issues relating to adjoining landowners were not all fully resolved. The Galway workhouse wanted a new fence where their property ran alongside the railway. Richard Berridge, who had donated almost half of the line's route, had raised the matter of compensation for several fishing lodges he had in the Ballynahinch area. Much correspondence flowed between him and the railway Directors, and his letters show an increasing level of frustration with what he saw as inexcusable delays and obfuscation on the part of the MGWR. Their Directors, on the other hand, appear to have taken that view that Berridge had already been more than adequately compensated, despite not having had to pay what doubtless would have been a substantial sum to him for the lands through the grounds of Ballynahinch Castle. In March 1895, Berridge had still not decided on what type of replacements he wanted, so he agreed that the company would pay a settlement sum of £500 instead. This was to cover everything to do with his fishing lodges, gates, sites and fencing. He was also paid £320 to build a fishing lodge himself. This was not the last of the correspondence between the two parties. Berridge had an interest in a local hotel at Recess and he objected to the MGWR's plans to build its own one there. In April 1895 he wrote to the MGWR enclosing a 'petition' signed by various people in the area, which he claimed had been given to him to support his refusal to sell a suitable site for another hotel.

Berridge was not the only person seeking compensation of some sort from the MGWR. On 26th June, a farmer claimed compensation for a donkey which had been killed by a train between Ross and Oughterard. Since the railway fences were intact, it was clear that the owner had been negligent in not preventing the unfortunate beast to wander onto the track. Liability was declined. Meanwhile, in the townland of Caher, near Recess, a Mr Festus Joyce claimed that due to the proximity of his house to the railway line, his thatched roof might catch fire. He asked the MGWR for the price of a slate roof. However, the same man had yielded some of his land for the railway, and was therefore told that the compensation he got for that, plus a new gate, was all that he would get. However, it can be established that in 1901 the house was not slated, but that by 1911 it was. It may therefore be assumed that as a precaution, Mr Joyce had this work carried out himself. In Clifden, a local haulier, Patrick Downey, was claimed by local people to have been put out of business by the new railway, and they asked for compensation for him. It need hardly be added that requests such as this were ignored by the railway company!

The impression may be had that, in keeping with other railway schemes elsewhere, the 'big company' (in this case the MGWR) was seen as fair game for any compensation claims. Throughout the ages, human nature doesn't change;

Broadstone station, Dublin in the 1930s. The arrival platform on the left was taken out of use in 1929, leaving only the departure platform, under the roof on the right, to serve both arrivals and departures. It is from here that the journey from Dublin to Galway, and onwards to Clifden, would begin. All remaining passengers services diverted to Amiens Street and Westland Row termini in the city in 1937, some 18 months after the Clifden line closed. The left-hand (arrivals) section was enclosed after the 1929 rationalisation, and then used to stable and service the GSR's bus fleet. Today it retains this role, though it encompasses the entire station area now, as the main maintenance facility and administrative headquarters for Bus Éireann.   *Irish Railway Record Society*

A train for the West leaves Dublin (Broadstone) about 1905. It may be the 'Tourist Express' as the two visible carriages are in the special dark blue and white livery which was first used on this train. The locomotive is 'K' class No. 32 *Ariel* built by the MGWR at Broadstone in 1898. It was retired by CIE in 1959, as No. 668 and classified as 'G2' class. An unusual feature on MGWR trains was the external communication cord system seen here leaving the driver's cab and stretching towards the carriages by means of a holder mounted on the tender. Carriages had small loops attached to the sides just under roof level to enable this cable to be carried along to the end of the passenger section of the train. The system was outlawed soon afterwards although many carriages of MGWR origin retained the hooks until withdrawal in the early 1960s.   *Author's Collection*

having said that, rightly or wrongly, the people concerned had suffered, or might suffer genuine loss.

The MGWR were keen to continue engagement with Richard Berridge on account of the hotel proposals for Recess. On 21st August, 1895 four senior Directors travelled from Dublin to Clifden to inspect the railway as it was now operating fully. Berridge travelled into Clifden and they met mainly on the basis of a social call; the MGWR's Directors appear to have wanted to be hospitable! In the same month, we get clues as to the workings of the earliest tourist excursions over the line in the form of an accident report. Driver P.J. Lambe ran over two sheep at milepost 150¾ 'while working an excursion from Athlone to Clifden'. By the following month, return tickets were being offered at single fare from all stations to Clifden, in connection with the races there. On the 18th September, this scheme was applied to the Moycullen races also, with single fare return tickets to that station for the day.

A Board of Trade re-inspection of the line on 21st January, 1896 led to a recommendation that platform shelters be provided on the up platform at Moycullen, and the down platforms at Recess and Maam Cross. Awaiting a train in such locations without any shelter would not have been for the faint hearted on a stormy day. It was also recommended that initial temporary speed restrictions could now be lifted.

Another legacy issue from the construction years was the thorny issue of the contractor Braddock's indebtedness, both to the company and to local workmen whose wages he had not paid. Two newspapers carried reports on arrears of wages, which the MGWR was asked to cover following Braddock's withdrawal from the building contract. The MGWR denied liability. However, following protracted claims and counter claims made by both Braddock and the company, the MGWR ended up paying Braddock £1,250 in September 1895. This was done on the basis of a 'gentlemen's agreement', and all seemed amicable. However, Braddock was to reappear in November, seeking further recompense for his own sub-contractors who were now seeking repayment of retention monies from him! Hardly surprisingly, the MGWR refused, making reference to the full and final payment in September.

Next on the list was a Mrs Peacocke, from Maam Cross, who requested funds to assist setting up a fair at the cross roads adjacent to the station. While the railway refused, the Peacocke family went ahead, and to this day Peacocke's hotel, café and souvenir shop is a prominent and pleasant stop on the road to Clifden. The author has enjoyed many a coffee or meal there en route through the scenic splendour of the area.

Another request was made to the MGWR by Canon Lynskey, the parish priest at Clifden, in January 1895, within a week of the first portion of the railway opening to Oughterard; he wanted an annual free pass for travel over the whole line when it opened, on account of his 'interest in the (railway) system and the staff'. The company declined!

Regarding the company's plans for a hotel at Recess, matters were progressing. An offer was made to a Colonel Whittle by the company to buy his hotel there, to which he agreed. By February 1896 this had been approved and the funds paid. The existing manager, a Miss Mullarkey, was offered the same position for the first season. However, after consideration she declined, saying she would finish the season with Whittle, then leave. Exchanges of some correspondence at the time, and various newspaper articles, suggest that in the Recess area there were mixed feelings about the railway becoming involved in hotel keeping. While some saw new secure employment opportunities, others saw a threat to the status quo. It is tempting to think of the old adage of 'glass half empty or glass half full' in this regard!

Now Richard Berridge resurfaced to complain that he had not been given the keys for gates across the railway from one part of his land to another. The MGWR responded by saying that apart from the fact that Berridge 'repeatedly left them open', inviting trespass, and had allowed his cattle to wander along the line at various times, the gates themselves were not up to standard. On 5th February an engineer was dispatched by the MGWR to inspect them and arrange what repairs might be necessary.

A separate siding off the line was planned in 1897. This would have left the main line on the outskirts of Galway at Newcastle to serve the nearby Perse's Distillery. The point at which it was to leave the main line was where the Shantalla Quarry siding eventually did so, therefore had it been built it might have had the quarry line joined onto it instead of the main route. Cost estimates for the distillery siding varied from £220 to £440. It appears that the distillery was not prepared to pay for it, so the proposal was dropped.

From 1898 a separate halt platform was opened just east of Recess station to serve the newly built hotel. All trains stopped here by request, even if there was no timetabled stop, to facilitate hotel visitors and allow their luggage (generally copious in those days) to be more easily transferred to the hotel. Staff and hotel supplies, arrivals were also able to make use of this facility.

As the railway operation consolidated, it became a central part of life in the area, as travel to Clifden or Galway from the remote townships in between became a great deal easier. Soon, the railway was carrying healthy levels of both goods and passenger traffic. Analysis of early traffic returns indicate that the goods traffic was made up of fish, livestock and general merchandise. Businesses in Moycullen, Oughterard and Clifden were ordering in significant quantities of supplies for local sale. Local people and tourists mingled in the passenger trains, though it is likely that the former predominantly occupied the third class carriages, and tourists in first or second! Tourism in the 19th century, we must remember, was for the well-off; an ordinary working man might hope for a day trip to the seaside once or twice a year at most. Given that many tourists in these times were from Britain, and Connemara was (and remains) a largely Irish-speaking area, a language barrier to normal conversation would have existed anyway. We may imagine the soft Connemara accents and the lilt of the old Irish tongue contrasting with the Victorian English of the well heeled and well educated as they awaited their train on the platforms.

In April 1896 a Henry Redman unsuccessfully asked the MGWR for a subsidy to operate a long car during the tourist season between Ballynahinch and Roundstone. Long cars were a phenomenon of rural Ireland in the days before the railways, when these horse-drawn vehicles connected communities in outlying areas by carrying both passengers, light goods and mail. The company

'K' class 2-4-0 No. 19 *Spencer* hurries away from Recess with the mid-morning train in July 1915. The train is typical of the time, not just on the Clifden branch, but on most MGWR branch lines. It consists of three six-wheeled coaches and a passenger brake van (directly behind the locomotive in this case, though more usually at the end). The locomotive was built in 1894 and lasted until the end of steam traction on CIE in 1963, almost 30 years after the Clifden line closed. *Author's Collection*

presumably took the view that whatever arrangements were already in place were adequate, and in any event there was no advantage to the railway in doing so. At the same time, the company declined an offer by Mr J.H. Pye to sell land and property in Clifden for the purpose of building a railway hotel.

By June 1898, however, complaints were beginning to be made by traders in Clifden that they did not have enough time to do business in Galway, and tourists coming to the town only had an hour before the connecting coaches took them away to Leenane. The townspeople wanted the timetable altered to compensate for these shortcomings, to which the MGWR responded by saying that they were happy to alter the timetable by having the 1.40 pm goods train leaving Clifden at 3.00 instead, and adding passenger accommodation to it, but this was during the summer months only. They declined to alter the tourist car service, probably because a later departure from Clifden would have resulted in an unacceptably late arrival that evening in Westport.

As we have seen, various proposals had been made to have Roundstone connected to the railway network via a branch line off whatever railway would eventually be built. However, where the railway passed through the district of Ballynahinch, the proximity of the railway to the modest amount of traffic on offer there was to prove to be sufficient. Consequently, Ballynahinch station began to handle fish traffic from Roundstone pier. In 1900, extra siding accommodation was installed at the station to cater for this.

Each year, the senior management of the MGWR visited every station on the line on their annual inspection. In 1904, they alighted at Moycullen and Recess while on the Clifden line and examined them in detail. Nothing untoward was found, but such inspections tend to seek something to report! As far as Recess was concerned, the only observation they made was a lack of pictures on the hotel walls and postcards for sale to tourists. At Moycullen they carried out an audit of the station books, finding all in order. Tatlow, the General Manager, turned his attention to some goods wagons awaiting transit. He looked under the tarpaulins on three, finding grounds to complain at last - one was so badly loaded the contents were falling about and would become damaged in transit, and the other two were only partly loaded. A more efficient procedure would be to try to put everything into one, retaining the other in the siding for future use. The station signage was also found lacking and it was ordered that this was to be improved.

For the first 10 years, train timetables provided two to three services per day. Over the years, times varied, but generally there was a departure from Clifden early in the morning, another around midday, and another mid-afternoon. Connections were made at Galway with trains to Dublin and elsewhere, but one service per day ran straight through. From the outset the line was simply known as the Galway-Clifden branch of the Midland Great Western of Ireland Railway. Trains were met by horse-drawn cars at Clifden station, and in March 1899 the Clifden Union complained to the MGWR that 'the car service at train arrivals is injurious to the interests of Clifden'. Clearly, traffic congestion had become an issue even then. The company responded by rather curtly reminding them that all was arranged for the benefit of the travelling public.

One of the more unusual loads transported over the line was in 1905, when the Italian scientist and engineer, Guglielmo Marconi planned to build a 'Wireless Telegraph station' outside Clifden. The boilers for the steam generating station adjacent to this were transported by rail to Clifden. There was a light railway at this site which is described in *Appendix Eight*.

While the period of Government control of railways during World War I (1914-18) had some effect on lines elsewhere, services proceeded as normal in the area. However, coincidentally, during the same period, Ireland's struggle for independence from Britain was in full swing, and much disruption took place within Connemara. Initially, Irish Republican forces played cat and mouse with British troops, and the dreaded 'Black and Tans';* this is referred to in *Chapter Seven*.

On 5th January, 1918, it was suddenly announced that Ballynahinch station was to be renamed 'Roundstone' with effect from 1st February. However, after just two days, and before the change was due to take effect, this was rescinded so that the name never actually changed.

By the late 1910s, the combined effects of the war, economic decline and the deteriorating political situation had taken their toll on the railways nationwide. Inflation was beginning to cause wages to rise without corresponding increases in revenue. In addition, the fledgling advent of motor vehicles was beginning to take some traffic away from the railway as hauliers sought cheaper and more flexible methods of transport. As a result the financial position of many of the railway companies was declining. This situation would soon be addressed.

In 1921 the Government of Ireland Act resulted in the division of the country into two political entities. The initial idea was that the north-easterly six counties and the remaining 26 would form two separate parts of the British Commonwealth, but the way it eventually played out was that while the six remained aligned to London, the 26 became a separate entity, initially named the Irish Free State. Later, though following the closure of the Clifden line, the 'Free State' would become the Republic of Ireland. Soon after the new state

---

* The Black & Tans were constables recruited into the Royal Irish Constabulary as reinforcements during the Irish War of Independence.

began to function, the issue of railway efficiency and solvency was addressed by the Government. In mainland Europe, the problem of railway companies becoming financially insolvent as road competition increased was generally solved by nationalisation of some or all of a country's railways. In Britain and the USA, myriads of small local companies would amalgamate voluntarily into much bigger concerns to achieve economies of scale with standardisation of resources. Nationalisation was considered in the Free State, but decided against. However, it was becoming clear that national cohesion of railway services would be best served by having all railways under the control of a single administration. This resulted in the amalgamation from 1st January, 1925 of all railway companies whose lines lay wholly within the Irish Free State as the Great Southern Railways (GSR).

Railway companies whose lines crossed the border into Northern Ireland were exempt. As one might expect, this primarily meant continued independence for the main line from Dublin to Belfast and a considerable mileage of routes in the areas where the border lay; this was the territory of the MGWR's neighbour, the Great Northern Railway. Several other companies, particularly in Donegal, maintained most of their route mileage in the Free State, but on account of short stretches in the North, remained outside the GSR. (As an aside, it is interesting to speculate how Co. Donegal's 200 miles of narrow gauge lines would have fared under the GSR.)

Thus, the independent existence of the MGWR came to an end, though many of their senior management gained places in the new GSR Board instead, alongside others from other constituent companies. As the new GSR attempted to improve overall efficiency by economies of scale, they would continue an unaltered service on the Clifden line - for the time being.

Station staff group at Oughterard station at an unknown date prior to 1925.

View of Galway station prior to the opening of the Clifden line, as it was in the 1880s/early 1890s. The large wall would soon be removed, and the new line would sweep in from the right. Other alterations would also take place to the platform length and track layout of the locomotive yard. Compare this with the picture on page 149, some 130 years later.

Irish Railway Record Society

Galway station as it was when the Clifden line was in operation. On the left, wagons may be seen in the goods yard, now part of the car park in the station. In the background (*left*) is the train shed with an unidentified locomotive shunting - it is from in behind this locomotive that Clifden trains arrived and departed. Today, the main platform extends far out from the right of this roof, towards the photographer. In the right background is the locomotive shed, with a locomotive being prepared. On the right-hand side, the line to Clifden can be seen curving away sharply.

Irish Railway Record Society

Chapter Five

Under Great Southern Railways management 1925-1935

From the start, the GSR's focus was on standardisation - as far as was possible - and cost cutting. By degrees, changes took place. Heavy locomotive maintenance gradually became more centred on Inchicore Works in Dublin, with the MGWR's old Broadstone Works concentrating on more minor tasks. Inchicore had been the major works of Ireland's previously largest railway company, the Great Southern & Western Railway. However, out in Connemara the only noticeable change was new numbering and liveries on the actual trains. The MGWR locomotives lost their shiny lined green or black liveries and picturesque locomotive names, in favour of the all-encompassing GSR dark grey, which covered the locomotives inside and out, above and below, almost as if they had been sheep-dipped in it. The livery was drab, though eye witnesses reported that it looked surprisingly smart when brand new. (The only relief was red paint on the buffer beams.) The GSR renumbered the locomotives of all its constituent companies, and standard cast GSR numberplates began to appear on their cab sides. Even these were painted over in grey, with numerals picked out either in polished metal, or pale yellow paint. No lining, coats or arms or other decorations whatsoever were added, though the locomotive number was also carried on the front buffer beams. The passenger carriages had been a mid-brown for most of the MGWR period, though the company had changed to a very deep burgundy colour about 1918. Since the GSR initially adopted a similar colour, dark maroon remained on carriages for some years, though now with the GSR coat of arms, rather than the MGWR one. It is likely, indeed, that existing stocks of MGWR maroon paint were used up before the GSWR shade was applied. The exterior woodwork on station buildings became dark green and cream instead of the MGWR's bright brick red and a light cream colour.

While ex-MGWR locomotives and coaches remained the norm on the line until closure, goods wagons originating from other companies became gradually mixed up with former MGWR stock. It is possible that locomotives and coaches from other lines might occasionally have visited Clifden after 1925, especially on excursions from far afield, but it must be added that no evidence of this exists. In contrast, photographs taken on the similar Achill line in Co. Mayo show occasional visitors. While ex-MGWR stock was of course the norm there, one ex-GSWR locomotive at least visited that line just before it closed, and one photograph exists showing a GSWR-origin passenger brake van in a train of otherwise MGWR stock the same as those on the Clifden line.

The period from 1915-1925 can be taken as the line's heyday. Traffic patterns and train services were now well established and while road competition had made its mark, it was yet to become a threat so serious as to warrant discussions on the line's actual future. However, the clouds would soon gather; the locomotives, rolling stock and track were beginning to show their age. Typical stock used on passenger trains in 1925 was between 40 and 50 years old; not only had this stock never been upgraded for the line, it never would be. While

On 16th July, 1934, during the line's last summer, the well-known photographer H.C. Casserley visited the line. Here the 1.15pm from Clifden arrives in Galway and heads out across the Lough Atalia bridge. Shortly, it will reverse back into the Clifden platform on the track in the extreme bottom right-hand corner of the picture. The locomotive is 'J18' No. 583, built at Broadstone in 1892, and in use with the GSR and CIE until 1963. It was formerly MGWR No. 82 *Clonbrock*. The leading carriage is a standard MGWR six-wheeled third class vehicle, with ventilators for gas lighting still visible on the roof. *H.C. Casserley*

On the same day we see No. 583 after it had reversed into the branch platform in Galway (*left*); while on the right 'D5' class 4-4-0 No. 550 waits to leave with the 3.30 pm mail train to Dublin. This locomotive was one of six built at Broadstone in 1905, at the time being the largest and most powerful 4-4-0s in Ireland. Originally 'A' class No. 124 *Mercuric*, it was renumbered and re-designated in 1925 by the GSR. This locomotive differed somewhat from its sisters, having been extensively rebuilt in 1924 following damage sustained in a derailment during the Irish Civil war at Streamstown in 1923. The vehicle directly behind it is a mail van. *H.C. Casserley*

Another view of Galway station on 16th July, 1934, showing (*right to left*) the main train described above about to leave, No. 583 having reversed the Clifden train in, and a row of open wagons being unloaded at the adjacent loading bank. The first two wagons bear the large 'G S' of the Great Southern Railways, but on the one behind them the faded initials of the MGWR may be made out.

H.C. Casserley

The stub of the Clifden line remained for many years after the line closed, and in fact the section seen here on the right is still in place, albeit disconnected from the rest of the tracks in the station in recent years. This view shows it fully intact on 10th June, 1964, nearly 30 years after closure. In this picture, carriage stock is stabled on the left in the bay platform. A silver-liveried 'tin van' and a black and tan painted 'Park Royal' standard class coach await next duty, with Crossley-engined 'A' class locomotive No. A16 in attendance outside the locomotive shed. This has seen its last steam engine, other than preserved special trains in later years. The turntable is still connected – it is hidden from view behind the pile of old rails in the centre of the photograph.

H.C. Casserley

A deserted Moycullen station in the early 1930s. As may be seen, a train has just departed into the distance.   *Courtesy Stations UK*

The end - the mid-day Clifden-Galway train pauses at Ross on what is believed to be the last day of operation, 29th April, 1935. The locomotive is 'J18' class 0-6-0 No. 576 of 1891, and the train consists of a first class coach, a third, and a brake van. This locomotive out-lived the line, being in service with CIE until 1957. It would therefore seem that this was the penultimate train ever to leave Clifden for Galway.   *Courtesy Stations UK*

the MGWR had abolished second class travel some years before, as already noted, other constituent companies of the new GSR had retained it. The GSR did not re-introduce this where it had previously been abolished, or had never existed. Indeed, they would abolish all but first and third class everywhere else on their system in 1930.

Like many, or most, rural Irish railways the first and last trains on the Clifden branch were to utilise the same locomotives and carriages. Money was scarce within the GSR from the outset and Ireland as a whole was in the midst of a period of underdevelopment. In short, the GSR was facing financial pressure from all sides. As the 1920s wore on and became the 1930s, the heyday of the railways was over. Road transport was increasingly seen as a viable alternative, especially where only a sparse train service was provided, and the GSR took over the Irish Omnibus Company in 1929. Due to the GSR's origins, it had inherited a large and motley collection of equipment, the majority of which was outdated and had seen better days. It is a great testament to the craftsmen of Inchicore Works that they managed to keep the whole system functioning as efficiently as they did, usually on a shoestring budget. Standardisation had been the exception rather than the rule, but the new company was struggling to reverse this. With over 400 locomotives, apart from the former Great Southern & Western Railway's '101' ('J15') class, few classes of locomotive had more than a dozen members; carriages were of all shapes and sizes, with more than a few built by the old companies as one-offs. Once the GSR management evaluated all possible ways of making economies, unremunerative rural branch lines would clearly be high on the list for close examination. The company was aware of the impending end of the Baronial guarantees of lines constructed under the 1889 legislation, and had an eye on the financial side of lines which in reality had never been financially viable on their own.

By 1927/28 it was clear that major track renewals would be necessary if the Clifden line was to survive. However, detailed analysis of traffic returns and operating costs made it perfectly clear that the losses incurred in operating the line, which had never made a profit, were rapidly increasing. It was considered that even if the necessary sum of £20,000 was spent to rectify arrears of track maintenance, it would not put the line back on an economic basis. It would simply prolong the number of years that the line would continue to eat into the GSR's increasingly depleted finances. The engineers in charge of track renewals asked if a petrol vehicle like that on the Achill line a few years earlier could be used, as it would cause less wear and tear, but the answer was no. The Achill car had not been a success, and in any event could only cope with very small amounts of traffic - just a fraction of the already hopelessly unremunerative quantities offering. In any event, the Clifden line was almost double the length of the Achill line and would be quite unsuitable for such a light vehicle.

However, even now not all was bad news. The elderly coaching stock they had inherited from the constituent companies could not all be replaced overnight (and in fact, much would not be within the GSR's entire 20-year existence), but some improvements could be made. In February 1924, 45 'old coaches' and 50 of less ancient construction were to be refurbished. From April 1930, all of the older third class coaches gradually began to have upholstery on the seats, which previously were of solid wood.

By 1926, the Shantalla Quarry siding had been out of use for many years, the MGWR management having questioned why it was still extant in 1921, despite the quarry having closed some years earlier. It would appear that no traffic had traversed the siding since about 1914. It was finally disconnected and lifted in July/August 1926, despite rumours that the new Irish Government was considering the reopening of the quarry. The rumours had not been correct and the land it occupied was sold off. Similarly, the GSR removed the siding and sold the land which it had occupied. The site of both quarry and siding were redeveloped and no traces of them exist today.

By the late 1920s the GSR was actively seeking to make economies all over the railway system. The main Dublin-Galway line had been converted from double to single track, and in many locations roofs were removed from locomotive and carriage sheds in order to avoid paying rates on the buildings. In 1930, a report was compiled detailing a number of lines proposed for closure. The Cork & Muskerry narrow gauge system of lines from that city to Blarney, Coachford and Donoughmore, the line from Kinsale Junction to Kinsale in west Cork, the Westport-Achill and Ballina-Killala lines in Co. Mayo, were all listed thus - along with the Galway-Clifden line. Closure was eventually proposed for 31st December, 1934, though the Kinsale line closed earlier, and others later. Investigations continued, and statistics were gathered to prove what the GSR already knew - that receipts were not covering expenses despite any economies being made.

The GSR continued to strive to make as many economies as it could. Staffing was rearranged in some cases, but more seriously, track maintenance and renewals was scaled down and put off, with speed restrictions appearing instead. Slowing the service, and reducing the number of trains, simply made the railway less attractive to the travelling public. Increasingly, lorries and cars were becoming available, enabling deliveries of people and goods to their doors. Receipts continued to fall, and by 1934 some trains were running with low single numbers of passengers, or none at all. Tonnages of goods carried had declined dramatically too. In October 1934 the GSR was informed by Galway County Council that the road, hitherto considered unfit for lorries and buses in any numbers, would be improved for this traffic by March 1935, therefore plans for closure could proceed.

Now, the GSR prepared costings for the replacement of train services by buses and lorries, not only for the Clifden line, but also for the following sections of railway: Westport-Achill, Co. Mayo; Ballina-Killala, Co. Mayo; Castlegregory Junction-Castlegregory* (branch line off the Tralee & Dingle Railway), Co. Kerry; Cork-Coachford-Blarney-Donoughmore* (Cork & Muskerry Railway system), Co. Cork.

In order to assist with the costings, plans were made to operate a bus service as an experiment to see how the costs would work out. The costs associated with the Clifden line showed a slight profit to be made in dismantling and selling the railway tracks, premises and scrap materials, as set against the costs of setting up road services and buying appropriate buses and lorries. It is interesting to peruse some of the endless amount of tables and statistics amassed by the GSR in considering the viability of the line. The following gives some idea of the significant amount of traffic still carried on the day of the monthly Clifden cattle and sheep fair:

* Narrow gauge (3 ft/914 mm)

Date	No. of wagons loaded
21st March, 1934	6
24th May, 1934	7
25th June, 1934	4
13th August, 1934	1
1st September, 1934	3
15th October, 1934	10
1st November, 1934	7
17th December, 1934	9
14th January, 1935	7
12th March, 1935	3
23rd April, 1935	5

Valuable as the railway was on these fair days, and busy though the station may have been on them, this was not enough to justify continuing the service. The following estimates were prepared to show the cost of demolition of the railway vis-à-vis the cost of establishing the road services.

1934	£
Estimated rail receipts (excluding mails)	11,146
Estimated rail service annual expenses	13,273
Estimated capital cost of establishing special fair units*	–
Estimated road service annual expenses	11,510
Total estimated cost for establishing road services (purchase of buses, lorries, premises where required)	9,480
Gain or loss; annual road service expenses compared with annual rail service expenses	+1,763
Estimated lump sum compensation to displaced railway employees	225
Estimated pensions payable to displaced railway employees	735
Total estimated expenditure on establishment of road services [£9,480+£225]	9,705
Net gain or loss; annual road service expenses compared with annual rail service expenses [£1,763-£735]	+1,028
Gross estimated value of recoverable materials	
(a) Re-usable materials	9,408
(b) Scrap materials	11,512
Total estimated gross value of recoverable materials	20,920
Estimated expenditure over next five years† to put permanent way as a whole into good working order	90,315
Proportion of this expenditure due to be incurred in the first year (1934)	37,104
Estimated cost of lifting track	
(a) Re-usable materials	2,005
(b) Scrap materials	8,359
Total estimated cost of lifting track	10,364

* This cost related to the provision of cattle lorries, which had to be specially built. In those days, the cargo-carrying part of a road lorry would generally have been timber built, and locally. The GSR bought in lorry cabs and chassis, and provided their own bodies built by Inchicore Works. For the five lines considered in this study (for which the figures are only shown above for Clifden), all but one were deemed not to require extra expenditure, as lorries already built for cattle transport elsewhere in the locality could be used without the need to build more. The exception, for the record, was the Muskerry system in Co. Cork, which would require considerable expenditure of this nature, as it served a cattle farming hinterland more so than the other lines, Clifden included.

† This would have covered the period 1934-39, had the railway survived.

W. H. MORTON,
General Manager.

GENERAL MANAGER'S OFFICE,

KINGSBRIDGE STATION,

DUBLIN, W.6, ___15th June___1934.

E.11042/5   COPY.

Dear Sir,

CLOSING OF UNREMUNERATIVE BRANCH LINES.
Ballina/Killala;
Galway/Clifden;
Westport/Achill;
Cork/Coachford/Donoughmore.

I send for your information copy of a communication
dated 14th instant received from the Department of Industry
and Commerce intimating that orders authorising the dis-
continuance of train services on the Cork/Coachford/Donough-
more, Galway/Clifden, Ballina/Killala and Westport/Achill
Sections are in the course of preparation and that the issue
of Public Notices by this Company may now be proceeded with.

Already a Public Notice has been issued in respect of
the closing of the Ballina/Killala Section as on and from
2nd July next, and Notices will shortly appear of the
Company's intention to close the :

Galway/Clifden	on	27th August, 1934;
Westport/Achill	on	3rd September, 1934;
Cork/Coachford/D'more	on	24th September, 1934.

Will you therefore please arrange so far as your
Department is concerned, letting me know what steps you
propose to take in regard to the personnel and material of
the respective Branches and/or the institution of the
adequate substitute road services which the Company undertook to provide.

General Board Order 3517 of 8/3/'34 authorised the
necessary expenditure for the provision of vehicles and
accommodation for the substitute road services required for
the above with a proviso that such was not to be incurred
until the Minister's order sanctioning the closing had been

GREAT SOUTHERN RAILWAYS.

M

GENERAL MANAGER'S OFFICE.

W. H. MORTON,
General Manager.

KINGSBRIDGE STATION,

E.11042/5

DUBLIN, w.6,   15th June   193 4.

(2)

first obtained.   This letter may be taken as advising you
that the necessary order has been granted by the Minister,
and that you will be in order in proceeding as directed
above.

Yours faithfully,
W H. MORTON

To/ Messrs.Hartnell Smith, Bretland, Harty, Nicholson,
     Meadows, Griffith and R. Stewart.

Initial proposals for closure of the Clifden line were circulated amongst nine members of the
GSR's senior management on 15th June, 1934. Closure was proposed for the end of August; this
would have given little time for preparations had the decision not been postponed until the
following year.   *Author's Collection*

On an unspecified date about 1930, 'J18' No. 576 calls at Oughterard with the mid-day Clifden-Galway service. A few people gather on the platform; how many are actually travelling?
Courtesy Stations UK

The above train leaves Oughterard for Galway. It will arrive in time to provide a connection to the up evening mail from Galway to Dublin. On the down platform, a few parcels await onward transmission to Clifden by the last westward train of the day.   *Courtesy Stations UK*

A few years later, on 16th July, 1934, H.C. Casserley took this shot out of the window of the westbound Clifden train. This had departed from Galway at 11.15 am, having taken a connection from the 7.20 ex-Dublin; an early start for the photographer and probable reason why photographs of the line in action are comparatively rare. The significant gradient beyond the station may be seen, the line would be far from level from here onwards.   *H.C. Casserley*

Maam Cross about 1930, looking towards Galway. The station building on the left remained intact until demolished in the late 1960s. The shelter on the opposite platform and the signal cabin in the distance were already gone by then. The water tower on the right and the goods shed, which is to the right out of the picture, survive to this day and form part of the Connemara Railway project, which aims to recreate a working railway museum with vintage trains operating on a stretch of track towards Galway (looking ahead in this photograph). To this end, a temporary track was relaid on the site in 2020, enabling the first train, albeit a narrow gauge one, to operate anywhere on the Clifden line since it had been closed in 1935. Due to pandemic restrictions, this event had to take place without public access.   *Courtesy Stations UK*

A view from the mid-day Galway-Clifden train at Maam Cross, 16th July, 1934. The picture is taken looking backwards in the Galway direction. By this stage the track is showing signs of wear and tear with a light scattering of weeds evident. The signal cabin is of standard MGWR design.   *H.C. Casserley*

A close up of the station sign. The boards were wooden with black backgrounds with cast iron letters screwed on and painted white. The sign is supported by what looks like old sections or rail, painted dark green. These were the standard 'house' colours of the GSR, and were used on woodwork on buildings and other station installations as well. Things had been brighter in MGWR days, with red featuring which later would be green; ironwork, doors and window frames.   *H.C. Casserley*

Recess station, looking towards the Hotel platform Halt and Galway, 1929/30. What looks like a cow on the platform is actually somebody bending over and attending to their luggage!

Stations UK

On 16th July, 1934, a view out of the carriage window (in the Galway direction) to show Recess station building. It is about 1.40pm. The train was, however, heading in the other direction towards Clifden. A few people await the Galway train on the other platform. The station building remains in existence as a private residence.   *H.C. Casserley*

No. 576 approaches the up platform at Ballynahinch on a summer day about 1930. The platforms here were staggered rather than opposite, as may be seen by comparing this and the following photograph. As built the station only had the down platform, the other being added later. The reason for the two not being opposite was that had the up platform been situated directly opposite the main building, the foundations would have been more costly to make due to boggy ground. Therefore, instead of being connected by the usual footbridge, they were connected by a barrow crossing where their two ends met. This was a highly unusual arrangement for crossing platforms on the 5 ft 3 in. gauge, though another example was at Mallaranny on the Achill line. Close inspection of the track suggests that the sleepers are past their best, track maintenance arrears were building up by now.   *Stations UK*

The same train about to depart (*see also page 39*).   *Stations UK*

On 18th February, 1935, GSR officials met to plan the impending closure of the railway. First of all, they had to answer queries from the Post Office as to how mail might be conveyed efficiently in the absence of the railway, and taking into account complaints already being made by the public. These discussions resulted in, among other things, a decision that the last trains would operate on Saturday 27th April, with the line officially closed on and from Monday 29th.

Some thought was given to making Clifden locomotive shed into a bus garage, as was happening at Achill station. This would cost £115. In the meantime, it was thought that for Moycullen, the former Co-operative Wholesale premises, later a cinema, might make a suitable bus garage. However, they eventually decided that no garage was necessary there. Representations by the GSR's bus department favoured larger buses than initially planned, 32-seaters instead of 20-seaters. They argued that the cost would be much the same for greater seating capacity, but the Galway County Council's surveyor ruled this out on account of undue wear and tear on the lightly laid roads.

Accordingly, with as little fanfare as accompanied the line's opening, notices were published in the local newspapers informing the public of the line's closure, along with details of replacement GSR bus and road transport services. On Saturday 27th April, 1935, the Saturdays-only 7.20 am passenger train left Clifden for Galway. At 8.59 it passed its counterpart travelling out to Clifden at Oughterard. The railway's last day had started. Arrival in Galway gave the train crew time to rest, and at 11.15 am they started back to Clifden with their train, now adding whatever goods there was on the last day, as this working was a mixed train. At 2.32 pm, their day, and their last ever journey, was over. The other trains that day ran as normal, with the 4.35 pm mixed from Clifden being the very last train to leave the town. The station master, Michael Grogan, and the station foreman, Edward Stankard, stood on the platform to see it off. Stankard was also a local businessman with a shop in Market Street, and had very probably been a good customer of the railway. Farewells were said as local people turned out to see the last trains off, travel on them, or just reminisce; many had not used the railway for years. This was the Clifden line's Indian Summer, as the stations hadn't been as busy for a long time. The 4.35 pm collected wagons from all stations along the line which had been left by previous trains to be unloaded along with the last ever laden wagons to leave the area. Thus, it was a sizeable train which would arrive in Galway at 7.42 pm.

At 7.14 pm the otherwise quiet Moycullen station witnessed the last crossing of trains ever, as the last train to leave Clifden passed the last one to arrive there. This was the final train forever, the 6.50 pm from Galway to Clifden.

Detonators were set at the stations and level crossings along the line when the 6.50 pm departure from Galway was preparing to leave. Those travelling from Dublin to Clifden that day were few in number. They had boarded the down train in Dublin at Broadstone station at 2.40 pm. Doubtless, they reflected as they traversed the central plains of Ireland, crossed the River Shannon at Athlone and made their way through the remote lands of eastern Co. Galway, on what way they would plan their journey in future. Arrival in Galway

Clifden station on 17th July, 1934. No. 589 is preparing to depart for Galway. The train awaits at the platform with two passenger carriages and a ventilated van and a passenger brake van of more modern (and main line) provenance than the passenger stock attached to it. Sadly, little evidence of public demand for a service is now apparent, with the driver being the only person visible. The seating capacity of the train is equivalent to just a couple of average-sized buses, though contemporary traffic statistics suggest that it will depart with perhaps a dozen passengers in total.   *H.C. Casserley*

allowed a 20 minute break before the Clifden train was due to leave. Now, a few local people joined them for the last trip, their soft Galway accents evident as some reminisced about taking a journey just 40 years earlier when the line opened. Some spoke in English, some in Irish - this was Connemara; many older women would still wear their traditional black shawls.

At 6.50 pm, the last train crept out of Galway station to the Lough Atalia bridge, paused to switch the locomotive to the front, and awaited the signal. As it lowered, the driver sounded the whistle, and the train slowly crossed over the points to the familiar line at the back of the station, through the short tunnel, and out towards the Corrib bridge. Those on board watched as the coal smoke drifted through a few open windows, and the train made its resounding way across; nobody would be travelling by train over it ever again. At this time of evening there remained but one incoming train to pass at Moycullen. Now out in the wilds of Connemara, it slowly continued through the now wilder mountain scenery to Recess. After that, the train hurried by the remote moorland and lakes, with just one more stop at Ballynahinch. At 9 pm, the train slowly pulled out of Ballynahinch, now (like Moycullen) reduced to the status of a halt, for the short but leisurely run into Clifden. As the town bore into view,

Two views at Clifden station on 17th July, 1934 with the 1.15 pm (arrive Galway 3.30 pm). A few years earlier, this journey would have taken 1 hour and 50 minutes, now it was taking 2¼ hours. This was due to severe speed restrictions over much of the line, track maintenance arrears were taking their toll. Maximum speed was not to exceed 25 mph in many places. Replacement bus services would average just over two hours. The only other train of the day at this time was the evening mixed train, departing Clifden at 4.35 pm and taking an excruciating 3 hours 7 minutes to cover the 49 miles, averaging only 17 mph. The train is headed by No. 589, built in 1885 as the MGWR's 'L' class No. 59. This was one of the longest-lived of these locomotives, lasting until CIE finished with steam traction in 1963, by which time it was almost 80 years old. This engine was a regular performer on the Clifden line in its later years, and is shown here with standard GSR chimney and cab design in place of the originals. The leading coach is No. 15M, a standard 50-seat 6-wheeled third class vehicle dating from 1894, followed by a first class coach of similar age, a ventilated van, and a passenger brake van of *circa* 1900-1905 vintage.   *(Both) H.C. Casserley*

the driver shut off steam, and the train slowly drifted up to the platform. It was almost 9.30 pm.

Local people came up to speak to the crew, and others mingled on the platform for a while, gradually drifting off into the evening and night. The locomotive crew unhitched the engine, and slowly shunted it to the locomotive shed. It was all over – the final whistle had blown.

It was Saturday night; many who had witnessed the last wisps of steam and coal smoke would doubtless go off into the evening to reflect on the day's proceedings. No trains were due to operate the following day, Sunday.

After a working career of just over 40 years, the Galway-Clifden line officially closed completely on and from Monday 29th April, 1935.

In the coming days, the locomotive would return to Galway with any remaining wagons from each station, and the now empty passenger carriages from the last train into Clifden. It is possible that a few local people 'in the know' might have hitched a last nostalgic ride en route.

The GSR had already made arrangements to remove old furniture, supplies and stationery from all stations and offices. They would proceed to offer all of the railway track bed and all the stations for sale.

Not everybody lamented the passing of the railway; on 6th April a Miss H.C. O'Dowd of Oughterard had written to the GSR saying that she was 'absolutely delighted' that the railway was closing, as she 'wasted time' while waiting for the train at the station. One hopes that she was suitably impressed with the replacement bus service!

On 16th July, 1934, 'Woolwich' (officially 'K1' class) No. 385 is being prepared on shed in Galway for a Dublin train. This locomotive entered traffic with the GSR in 1928 and lasted in service until 1962. The locomotive shed was narrowed in width in 1961 when the present bay platform was being put into place. It is now out of use. *H.C. Casserley*

Chapter Six

Train Services

Before considering the services provided by the new railway, it is interesting to consider what forms of public transport existed previously. In 1815, an Italian businessman who had made his home in Ireland established regular horse-drawn mail coach services along several main national routes throughout Ireland. His name was Carlo Bianconi, and he had arrived in Ireland from Italy aged 16 in 1802. He eventually married into a wealthy Dublin family, and they moved to Co. Tipperary, by which time he had not only established Ireland's first regular public transport system, but also opened several coaching inns along routes which he served. Bianconi died in 1875, but his 'long car' and mail car services were to continue in operation in some areas long after the railways had come. These horse-drawn vehicles became known as 'Bianconis' or 'Bians'.

In 1837, Bianconi established a passenger and mail service between Galway and Clifden. The road then was little better than a 49 mile stony track or glorified footpath, so a journey out through Connemara was very remote, and took all day. A four-wheeled car left Clifden, and another left Eyre Square, Galway, each day at 9.30 am. These cars carried passengers and any light goods they had with them. Arrival at the other end of the journey was between 5 pm and 6.30 pm, depending on weather, load, and road conditions. Another two-wheeled car left each end with the mails. Many of these mail cars carried the legend 'Royal Mail' on them. The larger Bianconi cars could carry up to 10 people plus a quantity of luggage or mail. No protection from the elements was available at all, apart from a rough blanket or tarpaulin for passengers to put over their knees. In Connemara's wild stormy winters, this would have been a journey for the very brave only. The fare was seven shillings and sixpence, plus a tip for the driver. This would equate, at the time of writing, to roughly €0.47c.

In 1865, therefore, public transport in the region was provided by these means as follows:

Route	Service	Dep.	Approx. arr.	Notes
Galway-Clifden	Post car (mail)	1.30 am	7.30-8.30 am	a
Galway-Clifden	'Large' (Long car)	9.30 am	5.00-6.00 pm	b
Galway-Clifden	Long car	2.00 pm	9.00-10.00 pm	c
Clifden-Galway				d
Clifden-Westport	2 'horse cars'	9.00 am	3.00 pm	e
Westport-Clifden	2 'horse cars'	9.30 am	3.30 pm	e

a   Carrying mail which had arrived in Galway by train (the railway had reached Galway in 1851).

b   Passenger carrying.

c   Connection from 8.00 am train from Dublin. A 14 hour journey from Dublin to Clifden with little in the way of comfort or refreshment stops, over half of which was in the open air on stony roads, must have been a serious ordeal.

d   Similar services to the above in reverse; exact details not recorded.

e   Passengers and mails.

Selection of tickets used on the line.
From the collections of Col Eugene Field and the author

MIDLAND GREAT WESTERN RAILWAY.

THROUGH BOOKED PARCEL.

From_____ to _____

Via _____

CARRIAGE PAID

CONDITION.— All Consignments are received subject to the rights of the Company, under 1 Wm. IV., chap. 68, and other statutes, and in addition to name the Company will not be liable for loss of, or injury to any Goods described in the first section of said statute which shall exceed *Ten and not exceed Two* pounds in value unless at the time of delivery thereof for the purpose of being carried or of accompanying the person of a Passenger, the value and nature of such Goods shall have been declared to the Company by the person sending or delivering same, and such reasonable charge as a compensation for the increased risk in the carriage thereof, as the Company shall in such case require, or an engagement to pay the same shall have been accepted by the Company.

Following Bianconi's death, many of his routes ceased or were taken over by others. The Galway-Clifden cars were operated by a Mr K. O'Brien who took over in 1867. A year later, a Mrs Carrigan was recorded as 'managing' them.

Following the opening of the railway from Dublin to Galway in 1851, tourist traffic began to increase dramatically, and the cars were used to provide the growing stream of intrepid tourists with the means to travel on a round Connemara trip, over several days. The route taken was from Galway to Clifden, then onwards to Leenane, and northwards to Westport, Co. Mayo, where connections were made with MGWR trains from there back to Dublin. The whole trip took several days.

After the railway opened to Clifden, the use of these cars over the route was discontinued straight away, but for many years afterwards they remained in use beyond Clifden, principally for the use of tourists making the round trip from Clifden via Leenane to Westport. By this stage, the railway at Westport had been extended to Achill Sound, with a hotel owned and operated by the MGWR at Mallaranny. Tourists were therefore able to stay overnight in Westport and proceed by train to Mallaranny the following day. Horse-drawn cars continued to connect the new terminus at Achill with the interior of Achill Island, reached by bridge, for some years afterwards.

Once the Clifden line had opened to traffic, two trains were initially provided in each direction. Both carried passengers and goods ('mixed trains'). No Sunday service was provided. A third service was soon added, but this carried goods only. Over the life of the railway, the public service varied between two and three trains per day over the whole route, but at various times extra workings took place, notably on market or fair days.

The initial service provided only went as far as Oughterard. On and from 1st January, 1895 this was as follows:

Up trains	Passenger	Mixed*	**Down trains**	Mixed*	Passenger
	am	pm		am	pm
Oughterard	9.25	2.00	Galway	10.45	3.45
Moycullen	9.54	2.39	Moycullen	11.20	4.11
Galway	10.18	3.04	Oughterard	11.49	4.38

* Mixed trains carried passengers and goods. Passenger coaches were situated at the front immediately behind the locomotive, as the goods wagons and cattle trucks were all loose coupled and unbraked with a brake van at the rear of the train.

It will be noted that Ross station was not yet open. The train took 11 minutes extra when operating as mixed, suggesting that the time spent at Moycullen was of the order of up to 15 minutes to attach or detach wagons of goods.

By 1896, an extra train was operated between Clifden and Recess on Fair Days as a trial. It left Clifden at 5.30 pm and returned in the early evening. It must have attracted some custom as it became a permanent feature on Saturdays as well as Fair Days.

The summer timetable for 1897 showed three departures from Clifden daily at 7.40 am and 2.10 pm for passenger trains and 1.05 pm for a goods train. Times were shown in the format then used, with 'am' and 'pm' universally used instead of the 24 hour clock system. Thus, times quoted in this book follow that pattern. Journey time over the whole route was generally 1 hour and 55 minutes for a passenger train, but a mixed train was a lot slower due to the necessity to load or unload wagons in stations, usually by detaching or adding them from the train. Thus, a typical mixed train was timed to allow eight to 15 minutes in each station, which meant that it took around 2 hours 55 minutes. In the case of the 7.40 am from Galway, three hours and two minutes were allowed for the 49 miles.

In the opposite direction, trains left at similar times, though the 7.20 am departure appears to have been the goods train in the down direction. For example, the afternoon down train left Galway at 2.30 pm and crossed the 2.10 pm up train at Oughterard. It is not known what became of the locomotive and rolling stock used for the Saturdays-only local as far as Recess, but a footnote in the Working Timetable mentions that on Saturdays a train of empty carriages left Oughterard at 5.43 pm for Galway. One wonders why, with a little more imagination, the Recess local could not have been extended onwards to Galway instead. Instead, having left those attending the fair at Recess, it appears to have continued empty to Oughterard before returning. This is likely to have been related to crew rosters.

It is worth looking in detail at the 1.05 pm goods departure. Having stopped for 10 minutes at Ballynahinch, it had to wait at Recess from 2.04 to 2.57 pm. This very lengthy wait was to enable the 2.10 pm passenger train to Galway to pass it. Once it left there, it had another 10 minute wait at Maam Cross. As well as the usual shunting, it was here that this train crossed the 2.30 pm down passenger train. The stop at Oughterard was 15 minutes, from 4.15 to 4.30 pm, and while it omitted a stop at Ross, another 15 minute stop at Moycullen led to its eventual arrival in Galway at 5.46 pm.

By March 1898, greater attention was being paid to the developing tourist traffic, particularly in connection with the new Railway Hotel at Recess. At this time the company made some alterations to the timetables to ensure that trains which could be expected to carry the greatest number of tourists had good connections in Galway station with services from there to Dublin and other points elsewhere. In June, new lower fares were introduced between Dublin and Clifden. These would include hotel accommodation at Recess, and would run for the tourist season until the end of September. An identical scheme for combined rail and hotel tickets was available for the Dublin-Westport-Achill route, with accommodation at the railway's hotel at Mallaranny. For a passenger who had to travel between Galway and Dublin (Broadstone), the connecting trains generally took about 4½ hours. By the 1920s this had been reduced to around four hours. Integration of railway services, the hotels, and cheap fares was to become a frequently visited theme. The following year, the committees of management of the two hotels requested that the offers referred to above would apply for extended periods, in this case from 1st May to 1st November.

The 1904 timetable shows departures at 8.45 , 11.05 am and 6.50 pm from Galway, the 8.45 running on Wednesdays and Saturdays only. The 11.05 took three hours, the others two, therefore this would have been the mixed train conveying goods to all intermediate stations. In the opposite direction, trains left Clifden at 9 am (Wednesdays and Saturdays only), and daily at 12.50 and 3.30 pm. In this direction, the 3.30 was the slow train, arriving in Galway at 6.35 pm in time to connect into the evening train to Dublin. Dublin connections were provided for both daily trains in each direction, but not the early Wednesday/Saturday ones. The 'Tourist Express' service, which would have been the morning train, carried the line's first and only dining car from June 1904. Dining cars were not a common feature on any MGWR route, and were entirely absent from most; for example, the dining car never ran on the Achill line, still less neighbouring branch lines to Loughrea, Ballinrobe or Killala.

Ross station had been an unwitting latecomer to the line, as many details at the station were not complete when it opened. One gets the impression that the provision of a station here may have been something of an afterthought, as from the outset it did not have all the facilities that other stations had. But traffic did develop to a greater extent than expected, something that could not be said for most rural railway stations in Ireland. By February 1908 the goods loading bank at Ross was extended and a weighbridge was added. From then on, timetabling had to take into account the likelihood of a slightly longer station time needed in order to load or unload goods wagons. By 1915, it was necessary to extend the station's facilities further by the addition of a cattle bank. Prior to that, cattle from this village for loading onto the train had to be walked to Moycullen station! In addition to providing convenience for local farmers, the railway now had the ability to generate extra revenue, as a journey from Ross to Dublin incurred slightly greater railway mileage than one from Moycullen.

An example of the passenger service from September 1908 may be considered typical for the early years of the line's operation, as follows:

Down trains		*Mondays to Saturdays*				*Sundays*
		a		*b*	*c*	*d*
		am	*am*	*pm*	*pm*	*am*
Kingstown Pier	*e*	5.37				
Dublin (North Wall)	*e*	8.05f				
Dublin (Broadstone)		7.00	9.15		4.15	
Galway *arr.*		10.35	1.42 *pm*		8.50	
Galway *dep.*	4.25	10.50	2.30	5.00	*g*	6.00
Moycullen	5.02	11.12	3.01	5.22		6.22
Ross	5.21	11.23	3.12	5.33		6.33
Oughterard	5.55	11.35	3.25	5.43		6.45
Maam Cross	6.37	11.56	3.46	*h*		7.06
Recess Hotel Platform	7.01	12.11i	4.01i			7.22
Recess Station	7.20	12.15	4.05			7.26
Ballynahinch	7.49	12.27	4.17			7.38
Clifden	8.10	12.42	4.32			7.53

a – Down day mail train. On the 'Limited Mail' train, higher fares were charged. A breakfast car for first and second class passengers was provided between Broadstone and Galway, where this train connected with the local train, formed by the locomotive and coaches which had formed the 7.30 departure from Clifden to Galway that morning.
b – Saturdays-only local train from Galway; no connection from Dublin.
c – Night mail.
d – No connections from Dublin on Sundays. Crosses up train at Ballynahinch.
e – No connection from Dublin.
f – This connection from the London & North Western Railway station at North Wall, Dublin, was only provided Tuesday to Friday inclusive.
g – No onward connection, though mails for Clifden could be loaded onto the 4.25 am train the following morning.
h – This train only came as far as Oughterard, and returned at 6.00 pm to Galway.
i – This was a request stop. Passengers alighting at the hotel had to advise the guard or station master at the preceding station (Maam Cross).

TABLE No. 12. **Clifden Branch—DOWN TRAINS.**

Distance from Br'dstone. M. C.	STATIONS			WEEK DAYS						
			1	2 Pass W.& S.O.	3	4 Pass	5	6 Pass	7
				a.m.		a.m.		p.m.	
—	Dun Laoghaire Pier dep.		..	..	..	6 10		..	..
—	N. Wall, L. M. & S. "		..	..	..	..	..	..	
—	Broadstone "		..	..	..	7 10	..	2 30	..
1 33	Liffey Junction "		..	..	..	..	..	..	
126 35	Galway arr.		..	..	..	10 50	..	6 35	..
						Mixed			
—	Galway† dep.		..	8 45	..	11 5	..	6 50	..
134 28	Moycullen† {arr. {dep.		.. ..	9 7 9 8	.. ..	11 32 11 42	.. ..	7 11 7 12	.. ..
138 61	Ross {arr. {dep.		.. ..	9 18 9 19	.. ..	11 53 11 58	.. ..	7 22 7 23	.. ..
143 20	Oughterard† {arr. {dep.		.. ..	9 29 9 30	.. ..	12 12 12 22	.. ..	7 33 7 35	.. ..
153 36	Maam Cross† {arr. {dep.		.. ..	9 49 9 53	.. ..	12 46 12 56	.. ..	7 54 7 56	.. ..
162 67	Recess† {arr. {dep.		.. ..	10 13 10 14	.. ..	1 19 1 29	.. ..	8 16 8 17	.. ..
168 16	Ballynahinch† {arr. {dep.		.. ..	10 25 10 27	.. ..	1 44 1 50	.. ..	8 28 8 29	.. ..
175 46	Clifden† arr.		..	10 45	..	2 10	..	8 46	..

No. 2.—*Cross 9.0 a.m. Up at Maam Cross.*
No. 4.—*Cross 12.50 p.m. Up Passenger at Recess.*
† Electric Train Staff Stations.

TABLE No. 13 **Clifden Branch—UP TRAINS.**

Distance from Clifden. M. C.	STATIONS		8	9	10 Pass W. & S.O.	11 Pass.	12	13 Mixed	14
					a.m.	p.m.		p.m.	
—	Clifden dep.		..	..	9 0	12 50	..	3 30	..
7 30	Ballynahinch {arr. {dep.		.. ..	.. ..	9 15 9 16	1 5 1 6	.. ..	3 50 4 0	.. ..
12 59	Recess {arr. {dep.		.. ..	.. ..	9 27 9 28	1 17 1 20	.. ..	4 15 4 25	.. ..
22 10	Maam Cross {arr. {dep.		.. ..	.. ..	9 48 9 50	1 40 1 41	.. ..	4 48 5 0	.. ..
32 26	Oughterard {arr. {dep.		.. ..	.. ..	10 9 10 12	2 0 2 2	.. ..	5 14 5 34	.. ..
36 67	Ross {arr. {dep.		.. ..	.. ..	10 22 10 23	2 12 2 13	.. ..	5 48 5 53	.. ..
41 18	Moycullen {arr. {dep.		.. ..	.. ..	10 33 10 36	2 23 2 26	.. ..	6 6 6 10	.. ..
49 11	Galway (Platform) arr.		..	..	11 0	2 50	..	6 35	..
—	Galway dep.			..	..	3 35	..	7 30	..
—	Broadstone arr.		..	..	..	7 20	..	11 30	
175 46	N W'll, L.M.& S. "		..	...	..	..	..	..	..
—	Dun Laoghaire Pier		..	..	..	8 25	..	..	..

No. 10.—*Cross 8.45 a.m. Down at Maam Cross.*
No. 11.—*Cross 11.5 a.m. Down Mixed at Recess.*

Full train service in 1920.

Goods trains are not shown in the above as these did not appear in public timetables (from which this extract is taken). As already mentioned, most of the goods on the line travelled by mixed train. As an aside, it was on another ex-MGWR branch line that Ireland's last mixed trains ran as late as November 1975; this was the Attymon Junction to Loughrea line in eastern Co. Galway.

Up trains			Mondays to Saturdays				Sundays
			a		*b*	*c*	*d*
		am	pm	pm	pm	pm	am
Clifden		7.30	1.30	*e*		7.20	7.30
Ballynahinch		7.46	1.46			7.46	7.46
Recess Station		7.58	1.58			8.11	7.58
Recess Hotel Platform		8.00*f*	2.00*f*			8.16	8.02
Maam Cross		8.17	2.17			8.54	8.19
Oughterard		8.30	2.39		6.00	9.35	8.41
Ross		8.50	2.50		6.11	9.54	8.52
Moycullen		9.01	3.01		6.23	10.18	9.03
Galway	arr.	9.22	3.22		6.45	10.45	9.24
Galway	dep.	9.40	3.40*g*	4.25			
Dublin (Broadstone)		2.15	7.12	9.05			
Dublin (North Wall)		2.45	7.45				
Kingstown Pier			8.00				

a – Connects at Galway with 3.40 pm up mail train to Dublin.
b – Saturdays-only local train to Galway; no connection onwards to Dublin.
c – No connection onwards to Dublin.
d – No connections to Dublin on Sundays. Crosses down train at Ballynahinch.
e – Passengers from the 1.30 train from Clifden not wishing to pay the higher fares on the 3.40 train to Dublin could travel on this one at normal fares.
f – This was a request stop. Passengers alighting at the hotel had to advise the guard or station master at the preceding station (Ballynahinch).
g – On the 'Limited Mail' train, higher fares were charged. A dining car for first and second class passengers was provided between Galway and Dublin.

The short working on Saturdays-only between Galway and Oughterard was not always a feature of the service. Having disappeared from the timetable by the time the GSR took over, it strangely reappeared in 1931, lasting until closure at the end of 1934. It is difficult to be certain of a reason for this service, as somebody availing of the return trip would barely have an hour in Oughterard. Looking at the Sunday service, two trains were required, as the up train left Clifden before the down train arrived. Had the departure of the 7.30 train been put forward to 8.00, or the 6.00 from Galway retimed to leave at 5.30, a single train would have sufficed. However, this could have had implications for crewing arrangements, as the same driver, fireman and guard would have had to do the entire return trip with little opportunity to have a break.

The very early departure from Galway of the first train of the day, at 4.25, was to facilitate the carriage of mails, but it will be noted that both this train and the evening 7.20 from Clifden were the only trains to make an obligatory stop at the Recess Hotel Platform. Whilst all other trains stopped there on request only, the early departure and obligatory stop may have been connected with deliveries of supplies to the hotel, or the convenience of hotel staff travelling to and from Galway.

TABLE No. 12.   **Clifden Branch**—DOWN TRAINS   17

Distance from Br'dstone.	STATIONS		WEEK DAYS						SUN-DAYS
			1 Weds. and Sats. only Pass	2 Pass	3 Goods	4	5 Pass.	6 Pass.	7
M. C.			a.m.	a.m.	p.m.		a.m.		
—	Kingstown Pier	dep.	..	6 5	..	..	..	..	..
—	N. Wall, L. & N. W.	ʋ	..	..	..	..	11 30	..	..
—	Broadstone	,,	..	7 25	..	..	1 30p'm	..	..
1 33	Liffey Junction	,,	..	..	..	..	..	..	..
126 35	Galway	arr.	..	11 23	..	..	5 56	..	..
—	Galway	dep.	7 30	11 40	12 5	..	6 15	..	..
134 28	Moycullen	{arr.	7 51	12 1	12 33	..	6 36	..	..
		{dep.	7 52	12 2	12 43	..	6 38	..	..
138 61 ˙	Ross	{arr.	8 2	12 12	12 54	..	6 48	..	..
		{dep.	8 3	12 13	12 59	..	6 49	..	..
143 20	Oughterard	{arr.	8 13	12 23	1 1)	..	6 59	..	..
		{dep.		12 25	1 35	...	7 1	..	..
153 36	Maam Cross	{arr.		12 45	1 57	..	7 21	..	..
		{dep.		12 50	2 12	..	7 24	..	..
	Recess (Hotel Platform)	{arr.		1 4	2 30	..	7 48	..	..
		{dep.		1 6	2 35 .	..	7 50	..	..
162 67	Recess	·arr.		1 8	2 38	..	7 52	..	..
		ˎ dep.		1 9	2 55	..	7 53	..	..
168 16	Ballynahinch	ˎarr.		1 20	3 8	..	8 4	..	..
		{dep.		1 21	3 25	..	8 5	..	..
175 46	Clifden	arr.		1 36	3 45	..	8 20	..	..

. No. 2—*Cross 12 Noon Up at Maam Cross.*
No. 3.—*Cross 12 noon Up at Oughterard and 3.0 p.m. Up at Ballynahinch.*
No. 5.—*Cross 3.0 p.m. Up Goods and 5.5 p.m. Up Passenger at Moycullen.*

TABLE No. 13.   **Clifden Branch**—UP TRAINS.

Distance from Clifden.	STATIONS		WEEK DAYS					SUNDAYS	
			8 Pass. Weds. and Sats.	9 Pass.	10	11 Goods	12 Pass	13	14
M. C.			a.m.	p.m.	..	p.m.	p.m.		
—	Clifden	dep.	..	12 0	..	3 0	5 5	..	..
7 30	Ballynahinch	{arr.	..	12 15	..	3 21	5 20	..	..
		{dep.	..	12 16	..	3 35	5 21	..	..
12 59	Recess	{arr.	..	12 27	..	3 50	5 32	..	..
		{dep.	..	12 28	..	4 5	5 33	..	..
	Recess (Hotel Platform)	f arr.	..	12 30	..	4 9	5 35	..	..
		{ dep.	..	12 31	..	4 14	5 36	..	..
22 10	Maam Cross	{arr.	..	12 46	..	4 37	5 51	..	..
		{dep.	..	12 49	..	4 52	5 52	..	..
32 26	Oughterard	{arr.	..	1 11	..	5 19	6 14	..	..
		{dep.	8 45	1 15	..	5 39	6 17	..	..
36 67	Ross	{arr.	8 55	1 25	..	5 53	6 26	..	..
		{dep.	8 56	1 26	..	6 3	6 27	..	..
41 18	Moycullen	{arr.	9 6	1 36	..	6 17	6 36	..	..
		{dep.	9 9	1 39	..	7 5	6 40	..	..
49 11	Galway (Platform)	arr.	9 31	2 3	..	7 32	7 5	..	..
—	Galway	dep.	..	2 25	..	..	7 45	..	..
175 46	Broadstone	arr.	..	6 20	..	..	12 15	..	..
	N W'll, L & N W	,,	..	7 0	..	..	..	..	..
—	Kingstown Pier	,,	..	7 20	..	..	..	..	..

No. 9.—*Cross 11.40 a.m. Down at Maam Cross and 12.5 p.m. Down Goods at Oughterard.*
No. 11.—*Cross 12.5 p.m. Down Goods at Ballynahinch and cross 6.15 p.m. Down and shunt for 5.5 p.m. Up at Moycullen.*
No. 12.—*Pass 3.0 p.m. Up Goods and cross 6.15 p.m. Down Passenger at Moycullen.*

Electric Train Staff Stations—**Galway, Moycullen, Oughterard, Maam Cross, Recess, Ballynahinch, Clifden.**

From the MGWR's working timetable for 1st October, 1924. By the time the next one would be produced, the line would be part of the Great Southern Railways, encompassing almost every single railway line in Ireland, south of Sligo, Cavan, Kingscourt and Dublin.

By 1915, pressures were to begin to appear on timetabling. The MGWR's senior engineer, Purcell O'Neill, wrote to the Chairman, M.F. Keogh, to inform him that the track on the Clifden line was all original, and it needed to be relaid - in common with track over a large proportion of the entire MGWR system. As far as the Clifden line was concerned, this would mean relaying significant stretches of the original 65 lb. rails with heavier (85 lb.) material salvaged from the main Galway-Dublin line. The main line would then be upgraded with new and heavier rails as it was carrying increasing traffic. In the meantime, some speed restrictions would be imposed at the worst parts of the Clifden line to which the track relaying budget did not stretch. The resultant slowing of services would in a short time contribute - along with improving local roads and mechanised road transport - to the railway's demise. By 1928, only small repairs would be carried out at the worst spots, and some temporary speed limits over short sections were as low as 10 mph (15 km/h). By this stage, wear and tear of rails was one issue - but life expired sleepers (some quite rotten) was another cause.

The 1924 timetable shows the usual three departures each day, two for passengers and one for goods. The passenger trains left Galway at 11.40 am and 6.15 pm, both with connections from Dublin. During the day, a goods train left at 12.05 pm. In the opposite direction, the passenger trains left Clifden at 12 noon and at 5.05 pm; the goods at 3 pm. In addition, there was a short passenger working on Wednesday and Saturday mornings which left Galway at 7.30 am for Oughterard, arriving there at 8.13. It returned at 8.45 am, bringing passengers into Galway for 9.31 am. Interestingly, in later years there would be a Saturday-only passenger train just as far as Oughterard, but it operated in the late afternoon instead!

Early services with one goods and two passenger trains per day were not to last. Goods traffic was never heavy, so it made sense to combine one of the passenger train with the goods. Thus, the goods train became a mixed train sometime after 1920. Certainly, by 1926, and now under the control of the GSR, the now familiar pattern of one passenger and one mixed train per day remained, though fair days required extra trains. In 1930, an extra service was added for a time, consisting of a passenger train on Wednesdays-only between Galway and Oughterard. This left Galway at 7.30 am, taking 40 minutes to get to Oughterard, and returning at 8.35 am, allowing a connection into the 9.20 am train for Dublin.

By 1931 an extra passenger train operated in each direction on Saturday mornings only, leaving Galway and Clifden at 8.40 and 7.20 respectively. A year later, possibly in an effort to try to regain some of the traffic lost to road transport, another extra Saturday service operated in the late afternoon between Oughterard and Galway only. This would remain the basis of the service until closure.

Towards the end, passenger traffic figures on the overall route had been falling off for some years, but special occasions could still result in heavy traffic. On 18th August, 1934, 120 people boarded a special train at Clifden alone, with the same number again wanting to join at Recess. The occasion was a train chartered for a Gaelic Athletic Association (GAA)* match, to which several extra carriages had to be added in Galway. Based on numbers, the train probably loaded to six or seven passenger carriages in all. Goods traffic was also decreasing rapidly, with annual figures of tonnages carried over the line equating to a mere 13 tons per day. In all but a few exceptional circumstances,

---

* The GAA is the governing and administrative body for Gaelic sports in Ireland.

Table No. 11.   Galway to Clifden.

Distance from Broadstone.	STATIONS			1.	2. Mixed	3.	4. PAS.	5.	6. PAS.	7.
M. C.					a.m.		a.m.		p.m.	
—	BROADSTONE	...	dep.			...	7 20	...	2 30	...
126 35	GALWAY ...	...	arr.			...	11 0	...	6 40	...
—	GALWAY † ...	...	dep.	...	7 30	...	11 10	...	7 0	...
134 28	MOYCULLEN †	... {	arr.	...	7 55	...	11 27	...	7 17	...
			dep.	...	8 3	...	11 28	...	7 18	...
138 61	ROSS ...	... {	arr.	...	8 14	...	11 38	...	7 28	...
			dep.	...	8 19	...	11 39	...	7 29	...
143 20	OUGHTERARD †	... {	arr.	...	8 33	...	11 50	...	7 40	...
			dep.	...	8 45	...	11 51	...	7 42	...
153 36	MAAM CROSS †	... {	arr.	...	9 9	...	12 14	...	8 5	...
			dep.	...	9 19	...	12 15	...	8 6	...
162 67	RECESS † ...	... {	arr.	...	9 43	...	12 35	...	8 26	...
			dep.	...	9 53	...	12 36	...	8 27	...
168 16	BALLYNAHINCH †	... {	arr.	...	10 8	...	12 48	...	8 39	...
			dep.	...	10 14	...	12 50	...	8 40	...
175 46	CLIFDEN †	...	arr.	...	10 35	...	1 7	...	8 57	...

No. 2 to Cross No. 9 at Oughterard. No. 4.—Cross 11 at Ballynahinch.
† Electric Train Staff Stations. No. 6 to cross 13 at Moycullen.

Table No. 12.   Clifden to Galway.

Distance from Clifden.	STATIONS.			8.	9. PAS.	10.	11. Mixed.	12.	13. PAS.	14.
M. C.							p.m.		p.m.	
—	CLIFDEN ...	...	dep.	...	7 20	...	12 20	...	5 40	...
7 30	BALLYNAHINCH	... {	arr.	...	7 37	...	12 41	...	5 57	...
			dep.	...	7 38	...	12 51	...	5 58	...
12 59	RECESS ...	... {	arr.	...	7 50	...	1 6	...	6 10	...
			dep.	...	7 51	...	1 15	...	6 11	...
22 10	MAAM CROSS	... {	arr.	...	8 11	...	1 39	...	6 31	...
			dep.	...	8 12	...	1 45	...	6 32	...
32 26	OUGHTERARD	... {	arr.	...	8 34	...	2 9	...	6 54	...
			dep.	...	8 35	...	2 16	...	6 55	...
36 65	ROSS ...	... {	arr.	...	8 46	...	2 29	...	7 6	...
			dep.	...	8 47	...	2 32	...	7 7	...
41 18	MOYCULLEN	... {	arr.	...	8 57	...	2 45	...	7 17	...
			dep.	...	8 59	...	2 50	...	7 19	...
49 11	GALWAY	...	arr.	...	9 15	...	3 15	...	7 36	...
—	GALWAY ...	...	dep.	...	9 20	...	3 30	...	7 55	...
175 46	BROADSTONE	...	arr.	...	1 20	...	7 15	...	11 55	...

Great Southern Railways working timetable 1st July, 1931.

Table No. 11.   Galway to Clifden.

Distance from Broadstone.	STATIONS		1.	2. PAS.	3. PAS.	4. PAS.	5.	6. PAS.	7.
M. C.				a.m. Sats. only		a.m. 7 20		p.m. 2 30	
—	BROADSTONE ...	dep.			...		...		...
126 35	GALWAY	arr.		only	...	11 0 Mixed (a)	...	6 40	...
—	GALWAY †	dep.	...	8 40	...	11 15	...	7 0	...
134 28	MOYCULLEN † ...	arr.	...	8 57	...	11 40	...	7 17	...
		dep.	...	9 0	...	11 50	...	7 18	...
138 61	ROSS	arr.	...	9 10	...	12 1	...	7 28	...
		dep.	...	9 11	...	12 6	...	7 29	...
143 20	OUGHTERARD † ...	arr.	...	9 22	...	12 20	...	7 40	...
		dep.	...	9 23	...	12 32	...	7 42	...
153 36	MAAM CROSS †	arr.	...	9 46	...	12 56	...	8 5	...
		dep.	...	9 47	...	1 6	...	8 6	...
162 67	RECESS † ...	arr.	...	10 7	...	1 30	...	8 26	...
		dep.	...	10 8	...	1 46	...	8 27	...
168 16	BALLYNAHINCH †	arr.	...	10 20	...	2 0	...	8 39	...
		dep.	...	10 22	...	2 6	...	8 40	...
175 46	CLIFDEN †	arr.	...	10 40	...	2 29	...	8 57	...

† Electric Train Staff Stations.
(a) Commencing with 21st September.

Table No. 12.   Clifden to Galway.

Distance from Clifden.	STATIONS.		8.	9. PAS. Sats. (a) only	10.	11. PAS. (a)	12.	13. Mixed. (a)	14.
M. C.				p.m.		p.m.		p.m.	
—	CLIFDEN	dep.	...	7 20	...	1 15	...	3 30	...
7 30	BALLYNAHINCH ...	arr.	...	7 37	...	1 32	...	3 51	...
		dep.	...	7 38	...	1 33	...	4 1	...
12 59	RECESS ...	arr.	...	7 50	...	1 45	...	4 16	...
		dep.	...	7 51	...	1 46	...	4 25	...
22 10	MAAM CROSS ...	arr.	...	8 11	...	2 6	...	4 49	...
		dep.	...	8 12	...	2 7	...	5 5	...
32 26	OUGHTERARD ...	arr.	...	8 34	...	2 29	...	5 29	...
		dep.	...	8 35	...	2 30	...	5 36	...
36 65	ROSS ...	arr.	...	8 46	...	2 41	...	5 49	...
		dep.	...	8 47	...	2 42	...	5 52	...
41 18	MOYCULLEN ...	arr.	...	8 57	...	2 52	...	6 5	...
		dep.	...	8 59	...	2 54	...	6 10	...
49 11	GALWAY (PLATFORM)	arr.	...	9 15	...	3 10	...	6 35	...
—	GALWAY	dep.	...	9 20	...	3 30	...	7 55	...
175 46	BROADSTONE ...	arr.	...	1 20	...	7 15	...	11 55	...

(a) Commencing with 21st September.

Great Southern Railways working timetable 14th September, 1931. The underline indicates crossing place with another train (although the cross at Recess in train 4 is missing).

there was no doubt that a few small lorries could adequately deal with this traffic. For passenger and goods traffic, the newly tarmacadamed road was proving more flexible, with door to door deliveries much easier than transhipment from the nearest station, often a considerable distance away.

Timetables for every single year of the line's existence have not survived, although few changes occurred. Most rural Irish lines had a service of two or three trains per day, and Clifden was no exception. All trains served all stations – there no express or limited stop services. Throughout the life of the Clifden line (and for many decades later) train services tended to have summer and winter versions, with extra services in the high season. It is therefore possible that the service shown was augmented in the summer months with another passenger service. Sometimes this was achieved by simply adding a passenger coach onto the goods train. It will be seen that journey times for passenger trains varied from 1 hour 56 mins to 2 hours 5 mins.

The goods train had to stop and shunt at each station, so the 49 mile route took an exhausting 4 hr 32 mins for the 3pm up goods train. Approximately 15 minutes were allowed at all stations except Moycullen, where the train remained for 48 minutes. This extended delay allowed the 5.05 pm passenger train to overtake it. The timetables are reproduced to show some variations in the service.

Once the GSR took over in 1925, little changed and the service settled down to a standard pattern for some years during the mid and late 1920s and until the early 1930s. The extracts are from 1931, where the overall service is the same as before although (from September) instead of the first train of the day from Galway and the midday return service carrying goods, the goods now travels later. This meant that any cargoes consigned from Dublin would only arrive at 2.29 pm, rather than 10.35 am. In the return direction, goods consigned to Dublin would not arrive in the capital until five minutes before midnight. The passenger trains still completed the journey in just under two hours, but the mixed trains took around three. By now the stop at the Recess Hotel Platform had long disappeared from the timetable, the hotel having been destroyed in 1922.

By 1934 the service had been reduced to cut costs, and the following timetable (*page 88*) came into effect on and from 10th September, 1934. The track was by now in a poor condition and resultant speed restrictions were now making the service less competitive than ever. On Mondays to Fridays there were only two trains in each direction. In the up direction there was no morning train at all on the same day. The first departure from Clifden, at 1 pm, took 2 hours 20 mins to get to Galway, while the 4.35 pm mixed train took over three hours to make the journey, stopping at all stations to shunt goods wagons. In the down direction things were no better. The only train until the evening service was the 11.15 am departure from Galway which took a massive 3 hrs 17 mins for the journey, an average of some 15 miles per hour. The 6.50 pm from Galway took over 2½ hours. When one bears in mind that in order to get from Dublin to Clifden, a 2.40 pm departure from Dublin would not bring you to your destination until 9.24 pm, it is easy to see why the line was losing passengers. The situation was alleviated somewhat by the retention of a third service on Saturdays only over the whole line, plus a short working on Saturday afternoon as far as Oughterard and back. This would be the last timetable issued for the Clifden line.

CO-ORDINATION OF RAIL AND ROAD SERVICES.

CLIFDEN BRANCH.

PROPOSED REDUCTION OF TRAIN MILEAGE

PROPOSED TRAIN SERVICE.

Work as passenger and goods line with assistance of buses during the Summer months, as under. The question of complete conversion to a Goods line (at least as between Clifden and Oughterard) to be re-considered when Winter train service is being arranged.

SUMMER SERVICE.

	Saturdays Only. Passr.	Mixed.	Passr.	Saturdays Only. Passr.
	a. m.	p. m.	p. m.	p. m.
Clifden.	-	12.20	5.40	-
Oughterard.	8.45			7.45
Galway.	9.25	3.15	7.30	8.30

	Mixed.	Saturdays Only. Passr.	Passr.	Saturdays Only.
	a. m.	a. m.	a. m.	p. m.
Galway.	7.40	7.15	11. 5	6.50
Oughterard.		7.59		7.33
Clifden.	10.42	-	1. 0	-

PROPOSED BUS SERVICE.

	a. m.	p. m.
Clifden.	8. 0	-
Oughterard.		5.30
Galway.	11.10	6.30

	p. m.	p. m.
Galway.	4.30	6.30
Oughterard.	5.30	
Clifden.	-	10. 0

I.O.C. to be prepared to run extra services on Wednesdays and Saturdays, Galway to Oughterard and back from 3.30 p.m. to 5.0 p.m., if required, to compete with pirate buses.

The Galway Co. Council recently obtained a decree against the Connemara Bus Company for damage to a road between Maam and Clifden, via Leenane. Our proposed route will not traverse that particular section of road, but it is possible that in course of time our buses will inflict damage on the direct road which we purpose to use, and the I.O.C. must be prepared to expect similar legal action from The Galway County Council, should such damage occur.

It is not yet clear if the road which passes our Ballinahinch station will be suitable for a bus, but if it proves unsuitable, it will be necessary to take the direct road which passes about 1½ miles distant from our station.

Saving in train mileage for three months as compared with usual Summer mileage ... 6,760 miles.

Loco. saving ... £470 for three months.

Initial proposals for closure of the Clifden line were circulated amongst nine members of the GSR's senior management on 15th June, 1934. Closure was proposed for the end of August; this would have given little time for preparations, had the decision not been postponed until the following year.

The extracts from the GSR timetables illustrate differing schedules in the high season and winter seasons. It was customary for many years for railway companies to have different timetables for each season, to take into account changing passenger usage and the needs of cattle fairs and other seasonal agricultural traffic. Timetable amendments on the Clifden line would also have to take into account the equivalent changes to main line connections at Galway. Occasionally, outside entities like the Post Office would have their own proposals taken into account which could result in rescheduling of trains to suit mail traffic.

The last full timetable for the line was issued on 10th September 1934. Services had never changed hugely; the last was fairly typical. All that was missing was any quantity of passenger traffic on the actual trains!

Table No. 11. Galway to Clifden.

Distance from Broadstone.	STATIONS		1. PAS.	2. PAS.	3. PAS.	4. PAS.	5. PAS.	6. PAS.	7.
M. C.				a.m.		a.m.	p.m.	p.m.	
—	**BROADSTONE** ... dep.			Sats. only	...	7 20	Sats. only	2 40	...
126 35	**GALWAY** ... arr.				...	11 0 Mixed		6 30 Mixed for Clifden only	...
—	**GALWAY †** ... dep.		...	8 15	...	11 15	4 15	6 50	...
134 28	MOYCULLEN HALT † ...	{ arr.	...	8 32	...	11 40	4 32	7 15	...
		dep.	...	8 33	...	11 48	4 33	7 16	...
138 61	ROSS ...	{ arr.	...	8 44	...	11 59	4 43	7 27	...
		dep.	...	8 45	...	12 3	4 44	7 28	...
143 20	OUGHTERARD † ...	{ arr.	...	8 55	...	12 17	4 55	7 41	...
		dep.	...	8 59	...	12 27	...	7 42	...
153 36	MAAM CROSS † ...	{ arr.	...	9 32	...	1 0	...	8 15	...
		dep.	...	9 33	...	1 10	...	8 16	...
162 67	RECESS † ...	{ arr.	...	9 53	...	1 34	...	8 40	...
		dep.	...	9 54	...	1 45	...	8 41	...
168 16	BALLYNAHINCH HALT †...	{ arr.	...	10 0	...	2 3	...	8 59	...
		dep.	...	10 10	...	2 8	...	9 0	...
175 46	**CLIFDEN †** ... arr.		...	10 34	...	2 32	...	9 24	...

† Electric Train Staff Stations.

Table No. 12. Clifden to Galway.

Distance from Clifden.	STATIONS.		8.	9. PAS. Sats. only	10.	11. PAS.	12. PAS. Sats. only	13. Mixed.	14.
M. C.						p.m.	p.m.	p.m.	
—	**CLIFDEN** ... dep.		...	7 20	...	1 0	...	4 35	...
7 30	BALLYNAHINCH HALT ...	{ arr.	...	7 44	...	1 24	...	4 59	...
		dep.	...	7 45	...	1 25	...	5 5	...
12 59	RECESS ...	{ arr.	...	8 3	...	1 43	...	5 25	...
		dep.	...	8 4	...	1 44	...	5 30	...
22 10	MAAM CROSS ...	{ arr.	...	8 24	...	2 5	...	5 54	...
		dep.	...	8 25	...	2 6	...	6 5	...
32 26	OUGHTERARD ...	{ arr.	...	8 58	...	2 39	...	6 38	...
		dep.	...	8 59	...	2 40	5 15	6 45	...
36 65	ROSS ...	{ arr.	...	9 9	...	2 50	5 26	6 58	...
		dep.	...	9 10	...	2 51	5 27	7 1	...
41 18	MOYCULLEN HALT ...	{ arr.	...	9 20	...	3 1	5 37	7 14	...
		dep.	...	9 21	...	3 3	5 38	7 17	...
49 11	**GALWAY (PLATFORM)** arr.		...	9 38	...	3 20	5 55	7 42	...
—	**GALWAY** ... dep.		...	...	...	3 30	...	7 55	...
175 46	**BROADSTONE** ... arr.		...	...	...	7 15	...	12 0	...

—— Indicates where trains cross or pass each other.

Great Southern Railways working timetable 14th September, 1934.
The last before the line closed.

Chapter Seven

Mishaps and Incidents

As one might expect, various incidents took place over the life of the railway with unintended consequences, but luckily no major accident or multiple loss of life ever took place. It is, however, worth looking at what did happen, to give an idea of the challenges faced on a daily basis by those who worked and managed the railway.

As in other areas, it is unfortunate that there were some who saw the new railway as a suitable source for insurance claims. Naturally, when circumstances arose in which claims might be made, the railway might or might not be at fault, but they were anxious to send out signals that they would not just pay out without questioning the circumstances in detail.

No sooner had the line opened than a dispute took place between the station master at Oughterard, W. O'Gara, and his foreman. The foreman denied that the signature on the receipt for his £1 13s. 4d. wages was his. He accused O'Gara of signing it, but O'Gara denied this. Officialdom took the view that O'Gara was the culprit, reprimanded him, and told him that if he did it again he would be sacked immediately. As early as April 1896, the level crossing gates at Maam Cross were smashed when they were struck by the 1.20 pm train from Clifden. The gatekeeper was disciplined for not having them secured properly, and the driver for not stopping in time. A week later, the signalman at Moycullen and driver Robert Coppenwhite had to forfeit their Christmas gratuity, as the former had handed the wrong staff to the driver, who had taken it without checking. Since they were different colours and had different shaped ends, this does seem careless; however unlikely in the circumstances, the presence of a train coming the other way was a possibility. Coppenwhite could have put his whole train in grave danger, and the mixing up of staffs was always treated by railway companies as an extremely serious breach of procedure.

The same driver was summoned again to the presence of the management only a month later, having run through level crossing gates at Rineen crossing, Moycullen. This time it was not his fault, as the gatekeeper (Burke) had not only left them shut across the track, he had no lights on them, so the driver could have been forgiven for not seeing that they were across the track until far too late. This time, Burke forfeited his Christmas bonus. In June 1897 the gates near Clifden station were smashed when the train ran through them. The gatekeeper, Mrs Hussey, was held responsible and forfeited half of her Christmas bonus; the damage had cost £2 10s. to repair.

The first record of a derailment occurred at Oughterard on 8th May, 1896, when the leading wheels of locomotive No. 91 came off the track there while shunting. It is possible that lighter track used in some sidings (which had originated on the Achill line) might have played a part in this.

Perhaps concerned by the possibility of losing his own Christmas bonus, the gatekeeper at Recess station noticed that pedestrians were leaving a gate across the railway open after passing through. He shut it and locked it, and refused to let anyone else cross the line. The MGWR were duty bound to take him to task for this, but they sympathised with his concern for the safety of trains and footpath users alike, and simply cautioned him. Elsewhere on the line, a similar incident had occurred, which led to the company being rebuked by the Board of Trade in June 1896 for obstructing road traffic, especially when a local doctor said that he had been delayed. A dispute arose in the summer of 1895 when none other than Richard Berridge complained to the company that he had not been given back a key for a locked gate across the track where it crossed his lands. The MGWR's Engineer answered by saying that the situation of the gates was dangerous enough in the first place, but this was exacerbated by his claim that Berridge's staff 'always left them open' with the result that cattle strayed on the line and risked causing an accident. It is not recorded how the dispute was settled!

On 27th May, 1896, the 10.15 am down train hit some sheep on a remote part of the line. The impact was such that it caused damage to the drain cocks on the locomotive. This can't have had a happy outcome for the sheep!

An incident in Moycullen station around the same time resulted in the locomotive and leading coach of a passenger train derailing. Apparently, the driver had driven over the points too quickly. Some severe jolting was experienced by some of those on board, to the extent that two passengers required treatment from a doctor and made insurance claims against the MGWR. On 1st May, 1897, the down morning goods train suddenly encountered a track repair crew at milepost 173. They had a small trolley on the track, and must have heard the train coming. However, they had neither a lookout man nor any flag signals, so the locomotive hit the trolley, causing £3 damage to the locomotive and 10 shillings' worth of damage to the trolley! Given the light and simple nature of permanent way trolleys, and the fact that any damage was recorded in financial terms, and that it was hit by a steam locomotive, it was probably destroyed completely! The acting man in charge, O'Flaherty, was dismissed for having no warnings in place for the driver. Such an oversight could well have resulted in death or injury to one of the track gang. A month later, speed was said to be the cause of a locomotive having become derailed in Moycullen station.

Staff often carried out tasks in these times which would not be allowed in modern times. It was common practice, for example, for railway staff to push goods wagons which had been uncoupled from trains, if they were light enough, to avoid time spent shunting. The practice was frowned upon except in a few carefully controlled circumstances as it could lead to runaways if not handled delicately, or damage or injury to whatever (or whoever) got in their way. A milesman, Michael Lynch, claimed that he received an injury while doing this at Maam Cross on 25th August, 1898 and wanted £100 compensation. The MGWR investigated, and their minute books record that the incident was 'alleged'; whatever the truth, Lynch received nothing.

Errors in operation could result in dismissal. If the mistake or carelessness was serious enough, this could be instantaneous. Allowing a signal to be changed to allow a train to move before it was safe to do so was very much in this category (as it would be today). On 4th May, 1899, the porter at Recess,

Thomas Tobin, was lucky to keep his job after doing this. He appears to have allowed the 3 pm train to leave before opening the gates, resulting in the train hitting them. 'Next time', he was told, 'you will be dismissed'.

Generally, trains ran on time, which was not always a reliable assumption to make on some isolated rural railway lines. But here, main line trains between Galway and Dublin had to be connected with. Timings allowed were generous, and the track and locomotives were well maintained. Occasionally, severe delays could occur, however, such as on 2nd August, 1899. On this day, the electric train staff system failed completely between Recess and Clifden, leading to delays of 1¾ hours to trains.

Not all mishaps were man-made. On 6th August, 1899, following a prolonged period of very rainy weather the line was washed away in two places, at milepost 149¾ and at milepost 157½. The former was the more serious, resulting in 100 yards of track becoming impassable. Repairs to such things in those days would be effected as quickly as possible, with staff working night and day to remedy the damage.

Vandalism is not something that might be associated with rural Connemara in the late 19th century, but on 23rd July, 1899 a stone was thrown at the train near Moycullen. The carriage window was broken. The local Royal Irish Constabulary (RIC) were informed but no culprit was found, still less any reason. On other occasions, stones were placed on the track here and there; while the potential for harm was there, no incident of this nature ever caused mischief on the Clifden line. In late 1899 two youths were taken to court and prosecuted for damaging the crossing gates at Moycullen when the gateman had been absent.

A broken window was one thing in a carriage, but a bizarre incident took place on 26th January, 1900 when the 2.30 pm down train arrived in Clifden missing a door! This had apparently fallen off - possibly it had not been properly secured after repair, and vibration of the carriage while in motion had opened it. That could have caused it to flap about, but while damage might have occurred, it is unlikely that this alone would have resulted in the whole door coming off. The door was found a mile west of Recess, which raised another issue – why had station staff at Ballynahinch not spotted it when the train paused there? Why had no passenger noticed it? Had somebody tampered with it en route? The carriage concerned was a standard six-wheeled third class coach, No. 78.

Another issue was that the train crews and station staff apparently were not doing enough to stop people smoking in the non-smoking compartments. In February 1900 this issue was brought to the attention of the Board of Trade, who appropriately reprimanded the company. Staff were instructed to apply the rules more firmly.

In October 1902 stormy weather took its toll when a wagon was blown along the track in Clifden station overnight. It smashed against the goods shed doors, damaging them. No mention is made in notes taken at the time as to why the wagon handbrake was not on, or why it was not adequately secured. Windy weather is common in this area, and there are reports of the gates at the adjacent level crossing blowing open on several occasions, resulting in the 2 pm train colliding with them on 4th December, 1905, and a similar occurrence happening a month later between Moycullen and Oughterard. The gatekeeper had not secured them properly.

On 31st January, 1903, the driver of the 4.30 pm up train from Clifden was to cause chaos en route to Galway. The train was mixed, thus it had to stop to shunt at most stations. The locomotive was No. 5 *Mars*, and for all the world the driver, a William Blackmore, might well have been on that planet as he was blind drunk. At Maam Cross, during the course of shunting a few wagons, he managed to rough shunt a wagon, damage some electrical apparatus, and cause damage to passenger coach No. 20 (which presumably had passengers in it!). At Moycullen, he ran hard against the buffer stops in the siding while shunting, causing damage. When officialdom found out, his trail of destruction was rewarded with forfeiting his Christmas bonus, and a transfer - still as a driver - to another district. This raises an interesting matter; the taboo of drink. While today, such an action would be very quickly reported by anyone witnessing it - staff or public - this was not always the case. Today, the individual would certainly be dismissed and taken to court and convicted as well; he could well end up in jail. So why did nobody report him - how was he allowed to continue to Galway with his train? In the past, there was a simple answer - there was a greater degree of toleration at unofficial level, or local level, for such things. Officially, the rules were of course as strict as they would be today; a railwayman was expected to be completely sober while on duty. But it was not always applied to the letter. Shortly before the Clifden line had opened, another driver in Galway had been reported for 'behaving in a peculiar manner' while in the company of the signalman there, who was 'found in his cabin stupid from drink and unfit for duty'. This time, the signalman was indeed sacked.

The Maam Cross signalman was taken to task in October 1903 after the driver of the 5.10 pm Clifden to Galway train, on approaching the station, found a train pulling out from the platform towards him! The signalman had not set the line correctly, and was cautioned. This could have had very nasty repercussions had the 5.10 been late, as the down train would have met it at speed somewhere out west and a collision might have taken place. Thankfully nothing like this happened, but the first fatality was to happen on 10th November, 1904. A passenger named Thomas Keane was boarding the 2 pm down train at Oughterard when he fell down between the carriage steps and the platform edge. The train moved, and he was badly crushed, dying later in hospital. After an inquiry had taken place, it transpired that he had crossed the tracks to board the train, rather than the footbridge. Consequently, the station staff had not seen him; perhaps he was running a little late and taking a short cut. The Oughterard Board of Guardians criticised the MGWR for not having a notice about using the footbridge, despite this being obvious - this, we must remember, was in the days long before every single possible move by a member of the public had to be explained by prominent signage as today. They also questioned the staffing arrangements, saying that there were not enough staff in the station. The MGWR had the same arrangements of staffing, and the same arrangements for safely crossing the track as virtually every other railway station in Ireland or Britain, and denied any responsibility. The Board of Trade then asked them to explain the staffing arrangements. It appears that misadventure on the part of the passenger was the cause; certainly, no action was taken against the railway.

In dry weather, locomotive exhausts could set fires due to sparks from the chimney. On several occasions in the dry spring of 1905 fires took place alongside the track at Oughterard and on Richard Berridge's land at milepost 144. The standard position of railway companies tended to be that if the fire spread, as it did in these cases to adjoining property, they would deny liability unless the neighbouring landowner could prove that the fire was actually caused by the locomotive, and not (for example) a spark from a pile of burning rubbish. In these cases, the MGWR played the normal line, denying liability.

An unusual incident was recorded in May 1905, when a policeman noticed a station master, no less, removing wooden planking from the sides of a wagon. It is not recorded at which station this occurred, but the man concerned, Mr Stewart, was demoted as a result. His reasons for removing timbers from the wagon are not recorded either.

Boardroom minute books recorded a number of other incidents along the lines of those above in the early years of the 20th century, with broken crossing gates a recurring feature due to a number of reasons, most of which had simple carelessness as the common denominator. Runaway wagons were another feature - sometimes high winds and a lack of handbrake power was to blame, other times sloppy adherence to correct shunting procedures.

A bizarre incident took place in May 1907 when the station master at Ross, William Nolan, was called upon to pay £8 11s., which was described as proceeds from 'the late station master, Maam Cross'. If he did not do so within one week, he would be dismissed. One wonders how he came by this money, or what it was meant to be for. Evidently, he had inappropriately received or taken it. It is not known who the 'late' station master at Maam Cross was, or what had happened to him.

Clues abound, as has already been seen, of casual operation leading to minor accidents and damage, as well as financial irregularities. Frequent occurrences of level crossing gates being smashed were sometimes due to their incorrect use by adjacent landowners, but more often than not the errors were made by those employed by the company. Gatekeepers and shunters seemed to be the prime culprits, but vigilance by locomotive crews was also found to be lacking at times. Was life more casual away from the watchful eye of management in Galway and Dublin? A runaway fish van at Oughterard smashed the gates on 10th August, 1908, and the failure of the station porter to light the lamps on those at Recess led to another gate smash on an October evening in 1910.

In August 1910, the goods clerk at Clifden had been discovered stealing money from the goods office, a sacking offence with possible consequences of prosecution. The man must have been well regarded as he was given a chance to resign quietly if he made good the difference. A few years later, in April 1923, a 'Major financial irregularity' was uncovered in Galway station. This involved the senior goods clerk (a man named Casserly), and quite a few other staff being sacked, demoted, transferred or disciplined for a range of irregularities, in which they were all involved. Falsification of account books and records, leading to the theft of £826 was uncovered. It transpired that fraudulent procedures on a sophisticated scale were providing a very lucrative income to some of the staff, as this represented a considerable sum of money at the time -

more than 10 years' wages for many of the staff involved. Galway station would end up with a significant number of personnel changes as a result. Without explanation, staff records indicate that Casserly was reinstated - possibly in a similar position - later in the year!

Political events in Ireland were entering a fraught period in the late 1910s and early 1920s, as Ireland's struggle for independence began to dominate rural life. However, it was not only at home that matters were unsettled. The outbreak of World War I in 1914 also began to make itself felt due to wartime restrictions on coal and other goods. Fires in station waiting rooms were to be lit from locally obtained wood and turf, or not at all; coal was only to be used in the very coldest of weather at major stations, and even then only with the express permission of the MGWR's traffic manager in Dublin. In order to be as economical as possible with locomotive fuel, the full goods train service was curtailed, including the closure of the recently opened Shantalla siding. Restrictions were also imposed on the carriage of livestock and various categories of general goods. It would be October 1919 before a full and unrestricted goods service was restored to the line. Passenger services had also been reduced on various lines, including that to Clifden, and full service was eventually resumed on 2nd August, 1920.

Another wartime fuel economy measure was the suspension of the tourist coaches operated by the MGWR. This service was discontinued on 1st September, 1914 as that year's season drew to a close. It would be 1921 before it was restored, using new vehicles ordered that year, as the originals had been adapted to carry turf and other materials during the recent turbulent times. The new tourist cars were not to last for long, as the clouds were now gathering in relation to domestic political upheaval.

On and from 1st January, 1917, all of Ireland's railways had come under Government control. Canvassing for traffic and all forms of competitive traffic were to cease. This measure was intended to provide maximum capacity to the railways to move troops about, or military supplies. By the early 1920s, disruptions to train services began to be felt in various areas, as Nationalist groups attempted to curtail the ability of the British army to move about the country. In those days, mass movement of troops could only be done by rail. When British personnel would join a train, the crew would often refuse to move the train. On 3rd July, 1920, services were disrupted on the Clifden line when a large number of 'Black and Tans' entered the early morning train in Galway. This resulted in a complete suspension of the service for two days.

On St Patrick's Day, 1921 a train of 'Black and Tans' arrived in Clifden, where they burned down 14 homes and murdered an innocent bystander. Ireland was in the throes of its struggle for independence, and over the next 12 months disruptions to the train service occurred, with some bridges being blown up in the winter of 1921/22, even as arrangements regarding the separation of the country into two separate political entities were in progress. Further disruption was imminent. At the end of September, the railway had to discontinue the carriage of mail by train as the Irish Civil War had broken out. The issue at stake was the acceptance, or non-acceptance, of the Anglo-Irish Treaty of December 1921, which had paved the way for the division of the newly named Northern Ireland and the Irish Free State. Anti-treaty forces battled with Free State troops in many areas, and on the Clifden line it was seen to be safer to have mails escorted by military personnel instead of on the train. Similar measures applied to the Westport-Achill line.

The Government control of the railways, initially intended to last until 1919, ended up being extended for another two years until 15th August, 1921.

Following the Anglo-Irish Treaty in December 1921, the Galway to Clifden railway found itself within the newly created Irish Free State*. A short but bitter civil war followed, between the pro-treaty (Government) forces, and those opposing it. This lasted until early 1923 and was to cause considerable disruption to the railway and society in general. The principle was the same, as Free State troops depended on railway travel just as much as their British predecessors had – the idea among the anti-treaty forces was to attack the railways to prevent Government troops moving around.

During the Irish Civil War period, 1922/23, a number of incidents were recorded on the line:

8th July, 1922: Laghtgannon bridge blown up and the track cut, resulting in train services being suspended. No train, post or newspapers reached Clifden until 15th but even then train services had yet to be fully restored.

29th July, 1922: The Marconi Wireless Station at Derrygimlagh (outside Clifden) was burned down.

5th August, 1922: Laghtgannon bridge repairs were completed. By now, the anti-treaty ('Irregular') forces in Clifden had been defeated, and the town was under control of the Irish Government forces, headed by Col Brennan and Dick Joyce of Leenane.

21st September, 1922: Two miles of track were lifted between Oughterard and Clifden and as a result a goods train which came upon the scene was derailed. The locomotive was damaged, as well as two oil tank wagons and several wagons carrying pigs. Further damage was done to several bridges.

30th September, 1922: As a result of the events of 21st, train services were fully withdrawn in order to carry out various repairs to damage which had been carried out.

8th October, 1922: The MGWR's Recess Hotel burned to the ground in the early hours of the morning, when armed men arrived and gave the staff half an hour to evacuate the place. No casualties resulted but the hotel was completely destroyed, never to be rebuilt. The MGWR claimed £50,000 compensation from the new Irish government as a result. Around the same time, the town of Oughterard was occupied by Nationalist (anti-treaty) forces to prevent Government forces making a base in the town.

17th October, 1922: After a three month closure of the line, a limited service - including the carriage of mail - was reinstated, initially as far as Maam Cross only. Since the suspension of services, several railway carriages had been marooned at Oughterard, and these were brought back to Galway. They were lucky to be left unscathed; vehicles left parked up in other parts of Ireland would often attract the attention of the 'Irregulars' and be burned.

22nd October, 1922: Maam Cross signal cabin was burned and train services restricted to Galway-Oughterard. Now Clifden had been retaken by the 'Irregulars' and it would be December until Government troops recaptured it.

28th October, 1922: Services from Galway to Oughterard were in operation, but between there and Clifden had been abandoned due to occupation by 'Irregular' forces.

In early December: A locomotive travelling from Maam Cross to Galway was fired upon just east of Oughterard. Luckily, no injuries were recorded.

9th December, 1922: Clifden was retaken by Government forces and by 30th, both the full Clifden line and the equally disrupted Achill line were operating normally.

* The 'Free State' was renamed as 'Ireland' following constitutional changes in 1937.

Altogether, closures and disruptions had affected the train service for over seven months. But all was not yet well, as the 'Troubles' dragged on into 1923.

February 1923: Armed men arrived at Clifden station, disconnected and removed all telephone apparatus. This would also have damaged the signalling equipment.

24th May, 1923: A train travelling to Maam Cross was taken over by armed men at Ross station and derailed after the solitary passenger, a solicitor named Ward, was ordered off it.

A total of 15 locomotives were damaged to varying extents during the political upheavals of 1922/23, one of them (No. 93 *Butterfly*) being destroyed entirely in Sligo on 10th January, 1923. Apart from the above, no serious damage of this nature occurred on the Clifden line.

In other parts of Ireland, particularly the south-east, similar actions took place. In Donegal, there were several instances of trains being fired on, and in Co. Wexford signal cabins and station buildings were burned down, track damaged, and locomotives derailed. The Clifden line got away fairly lightly in comparison.

From 1928 speed limits were introduced in several locations due to the deteriorating standard of the track. The railway was now 33 years old, and much of the original track materials were still in use and becoming worn. The GSR maintained that they did not have the £20,000 required to upgrade the track. The beginning of what would become a gradual period of economy, culminating eventually in closure, had begun.

The MGWR recorded in detail every letter written by their Secretary, or received from outside, as well as each and every instance of irregularity in the operation of the railway. After 1925, as just one part of the much bigger Great Southern Railways, records of such things are very much more sparse. Daily operation of the Clifden line had settled into a regular pattern, so it is probable that fewer incidents were recorded in the 1925-35 period. Certainly, within the last 10 years of the railway's life, no major upheavals took place.

ITINERANT VENDORS OF FRUIT AND CHOCOLATES.

Itinerant Vendors must not be permitted to sell fruit and chocolates, etc. in the Company's trains.

Fruit conveyed in Guards' vans of trains must be charged for in accordance with the scale applicable to the traffic.

ITINERANT MUSICIANS IN TRAINS.

Itinerant Musicians plying their vocations in the Company's Trains or on the premises must be warned to desist. If they continue playing or singing after having been so warned their names and addresses should be obtained and circumstances reported to Traffic Manager.

SMOKING IN NON-SMOKING COMPARTMENTS—(Rule 159).

The names and addresses of Passengers **persisting** in Smoking in other than Smoking Compartments must be obtained, and the case reported to the Traffic Manager.

Railway (and other) bye-laws were rigidly enforced in an era where order and discipline was expected of all members of the public, whatever their circumstances. To have names taken, or to be reported to a manager, might not seem unduly intimidating in these times, but in the 1920s, when this notice dates from, those reported could be sure that it would be followed up, and that a court appearance and very stiff fine was a certainty. This notice applied to the entire MGWR railway system, including the Clifden branch.

Chapter Eight

Working the Line

Trains had to be made up in a certain way, due to the fact that the passenger vehicles, and a few non-passenger types like horse boxes, were vacuum braked, while general goods wagons were loose-coupled and were controlled by the handbrake in the guard's van. This operating instruction makes it clearer:

MIXED PASSENGER AND GOODS TRAINS.

The particular Trains by which unbraked (i.e., not fitted with Vacuum Automatic Brake) Goods and Cattle Wagons may be run with Passenger Vehicles will be described in the Working Time Tables as "Mixed Trains." The running of these Mixed Trains will, under the Regulation of Railways Act, be subject to the following conditions, namely :—

(a) That the Engine, Tender, and Passenger Vehicles of such Mixed Trains shall be provided with Continuous Brakes worked from the Engine.

(b) That the Goods Wagons shall be conveyed behind the Passenger Vehicles with Brake Van or Brake Vans in the proportion of one Brake Van, with a Guard in it, for every ten Wagons or fractional part of ten Wagons.

(c) That the total number of Vehicles of all descriptions on any such Mixed Train shall not exceed 25.

(d) That the maximum speed of any such Train throughout the journey between Stations shall not exceed 25 miles an hour ; and

(e) That all such Trains shall stop at all Stations, or at intervals not exceeding ten miles, or in the case of stations more than ten miles apart, at each of such Stations.

Trains for the conveyance of Horses, Cattle, or other stock, when Vehicles are added for the conveyance of Passengers, shall be subject to the same regulations and conditions as apply to Mixed Trains ; provided, however, that for the purposes of this Order, Drovers, Grooms, or other persons travelling in charge of such stock shall not be deemed to be Passengers.

Guards working Mixed Trains must, in all cases, describe them as such on their journals, and also on the statement handed to the Drivers.

BANK ENGINES IN REAR OF PASSENGER OR MIXED TRAINS.

1. Referring to Rule 179 of Book of Rules and Regulations, under no circumstances must an Engine be attached to the rear of or allowed to push a Passenger or Mixed Train over an incline unless specially authorised. In every case where it is necessary to provide assistance for Passenger or Mixed Trains, the Assistant Engine must be attached in front and run to the next Station, where there is a cross-over road.

2. This order will not apply in cases of an accident to Passenger or Mixed Trains between Stations.

PASSENGER AND MIXED TRAINS SHUNTING INTO SIDINGS WHERE THERE ARE GOODS SHEDS.

Whenever it is necessary to shunt a Passenger Train or a Mixed Train into a Siding where there is a Goods Shed, on no account must any Carriage, in which there are passengers, be allowed to be shunted into or through the Goods Shed.

The operating sections of the line, controlled by electric train staff, were:

M.	ch*.	From	To	Colour of staff	Form of head of staff
7	73	Galway	Moycullen	Red	Round
8	72	Moycullen	Oughterard	Blue	Triangular
10	16	Oughterard	Maam Cross	Red	Round
9	31	Maam Cross	Recess	Blue	Triangular
5	29	Recess	Ballynahinch	Red	Round
7	30	Ballynahinch	Clifden	†	

* A now long-discontinued system of measurement in Ireland; there were 80 chains in one mile, or roughly 53 to the kilometre.

† In the March 1904 instructions, the details shown were of a single staff from Recess to Clifden. By 1920, there were two sections; Recess-Ballynahinch and Ballynahinch-Clifden.

WORKING OF CLIFDEN BRANCH TRAINS INTO GALWAY STATION.

The Passenger Trains from the Clifden Branch into Galway Station are to be propelled from the Junction points into the arrival Platform at Galway. The number of Vehicles on each Train must be limited to eight (including Brake Vans). A Brake Van must be placed at each end of the Train.

The Guard of each Train must ride in the Brake Van at the front end of the Train as it is being so propelled and he must keep a sharp look-out. He must not, under any circumstances, be engaged in any work which would in any way interfere with his keeping a proper look-out.

The speed of these Trains when entering Galway Station is limited to five miles per hour.

The buffer stops at the Arrival Platform at Galway must, after sunset, or in foggy weather, or during falling snow, have a Red Lamp (lighted) placed on same in accordance with Rule 114 of the Book of Rules and Regulations.

If the number of Vehicles on a Train exceeds eight the Train must stop clear of the Junction when the Engine is to be uncoupled and run round the Train so that it may be hauled into the Station.

As has been seen, direct access from the passenger platforms in Galway station to the Clifden line was not possible, as trains had to reverse in and out of the station. This operating instruction (MGWR, 1920) refers.

Ross station was not a block post. Sidings controlled by a key on the train staff were those at Shantalla siding in Galway, Ross station, and Recess Hotel Platform.

Details have survived of operational procedures when cattle trains were operated over the line in connection with local fairs. Cattle trains required extra time and were loose-coupled. It was necessary to ensure that animals would not fall while in transit. The maximum load permitted for a loaded cattle special over the line was 34 wagons, though a footnote adds, '…when necessary load may be increased to 37 loaded wagons'. One wonders why such guidelines were issued at all, as a further footnote mentions that all such limits, for all lines, 'may be increased when necessary in order to clear off all stock and save running an additional Train; but in such a case this must only be done after consultation between traffic and Loco. Staff'. Pencilled notes on a 1914 gradient profile document refer to loads of 35 wagons being permissible between Galway and Oughterard, and 30 between there and Clifden.

Whether the apparent absolute maximum of 37 wagons were hauled, the load remained within the capabilities of the 0-6-0 locomotives generally used on the line. Double-heading of locomotives was therefore unnecessary; just as well, as weight restrictions on bridges were such that double-heading was prohibited on the Clifden line.

Locomotives were crewed by men based at Clifden and Galway. While occasionally crews would work into Clifden from further afield, Athlone in particular, the recollections of a retired Galway driver as told to the author were that Clifden men never worked beyond Galway in the eastern direction. This probably applied to train guards as well as drivers and firemen.

Trains had to be made up with wagons for the various destinations in the right order, so they could be dropped off en route with a minimum of shunting. This would reduce any potential stress to the animals on board. Times allowed were as follows:

Section	Load not exceeding 30 wagons* (minutes)	Load exceeding 30 wagons* (minutes)
Galway-Moycullen	19	24
Moycullen-Oughterard	22	26
Oughterard-Maam Cross	25	30
Maam Cross-Recess	23	28
Recess-Ballynahinch	13	16
Ballynahinch-Clifden	18	22

* This figure was included in the 1920 and 1924 instructions; in 1904, it is given as 31).

This represented an average speed of about 20 mph (32 km/h) for loads over 30 wagons. Such occurrences would not have been common on the Clifden line, with most loads somewhat lighter. The maximum speed reached by such trains was probably of the order of about 25 mph (40 km/h).

G. S. R. (22).
10,000—L7—2/35.A.T.&Co..Ltd.°

BRITTLE GOODS
SHUNT
WITH GREAT CARE.

Labels such as this were affixed to wagons carrying delicate cargoes. Despite being wrapped in straw or old newspaper in crates, care had to be exercised, as broken goods on delivery would result in a compensation claim against the railway company.

On the night before a fair, the station master or equivalent was instructed to liaise with local cattle dealers to advise them when the special trains had to be loaded, as adherence to the timetable was obviously of critical importance. In return, dealers would be advised about time scales for loading of livestock.

Cattle drovers and grooms, when travelling with their cattle or horses in special livestock trains had their own accommodation in vans with extremely basic seating accommodation. It was noted that when a mixed train conveyed livestock, and drovers or groom accompanied them, they were 'not to be deemed to be passengers' – in other words, they were not allowed into the normal passenger coaches, instead travelling with their animals in horse boxes or drover's vans.

There were strict rules about how not only cattle or horses, but also poultry could be carried. A note in the various appendices to working time tables refers thus to the carriage of geese, hens and turkeys. Station staff were to check on the welfare of animals and if necessary they might have to be unloaded to refresh them, or allow the rescue of an animal which had fallen. This, if it happened, would be a very time consuming matter involving a possibly unscheduled shunting operation so that beasts could be unloaded at a cattle bank. It was noted that if railway staff discovered a turkey or goose in distress, to the extent that it was unlikely to survive, they were empowered to kill it! If a larger animal died in transit, a vet had to be called at the next station where the train would stop, in order to remove the animal and examine it. Trains conveying livestock were to be given priority over all other trains except passenger trains.

As the land yielded traffic in the form of cattle, so did the sea. In the years between 1897 and 1900, despite Clifden not having a siding direct to the quayside, fish traffic from the station rose from a respectable 343 tons, up to 1,437 tons. Most of this was mackerel from Cleggan Fisheries which had been able to greatly expand its production now that a fast service to Dublin was available. It was not only Clifden which produced traffic of this nature. In 1900, Ballynahinch alone loaded 397 tons of fish, most of which would have come in from Roundstone by road.

Virtually all goods wagons and all cattle trucks were loose-coupled, but passenger coaches were all vacuum braked or piped. Mixed trains had to be assembled with all the vehicles with continuous vacuum brakes at the front. Thus, the locomotive was always immediately followed by the passenger carriages, with goods or livestock wagons at the back. Brake power for these was, of course, provided by the guard's vans, and to provide adequate braking power, one van was required for each 10 wagons. Speed was not to exceed 25 mph on mixed trains.

To avoid passengers disembarking by mistake on a goods platform, an instruction was issued to the effect that when a mixed train was shunting in a station, vehicles containing passengers were not to be shunted through goods sheds. Instead, they would be left, passengers included, at the platform, while the locomotive detached the wagons and moved them about the station as needed. Each station had a fixed crane for loading and unloading goods from wagons. Most could lift one ton, though Galway had a 5 ton crane. At all stations, these cranes were deemed suitable for lifting passenger's property, general goods and livestock. At Clifden, Recess, Oughterard and Moycullen they could also lift furniture and (horse-drawn) carriages. Ross eventually had a mobile (rail mounted) crane.

Most of the passenger carriages used throughout the life of the line were of the non-corridor variety. Apart from this resulting in few passengers having access to lavatories - few carriages had them anyway - it meant that a ticket checker was unable to walk through the train. This, of course, was the case on most rural lines, and prior to around 1890 virtually all trains anywhere in Ireland. Thus, ticket inspection stops were included. On the Clifden line, passenger tickets were inspected at Recess, Moycullen and Galway.

In 1920 an extra siding was laid at the Recess Hotel Platform, a small halt just east of Recess station, built to serve the MGWR's nearby hotel. Access to the siding was controlled by an Annett's Lock, the key for which was part of the Maam Cross-Recess station train staff. The siding faced Clifden, so only down trains were able to access it. Therefore, wagons for this siding were to be placed at the rear of the train next to the brake van, so they could be dropped off conveniently. When collected from there, the same procedure applied.

SIDING AT RECESS HOTEL PLATFORM.

The above Siding will be used exclusively for traffic to and from the Company's Hotel when sent in such quantities as to necessitate the use of separate wagons.

The following instructions in regard to the working must be strictly observed :—

(1) The Points leading into this Siding are locked by means of an Annett's Lock, the key of which is attached to the Train Staff for the Maam Cross-Recess Section.

(2) The Siding will be worked when required by the Down Trains.

(3) The wagons must be placed next Rear Brake Van so as to ensure that the operation of running them into the Siding will be performed as expeditiously as possible.

As well as handling supplies for the hotel, passenger's luggage was dealt with at the Hotel Platform Halt, and staff picked up and dropped off for the hotel. The hotel manageress was empowered to issue free travel tickets for hotel staff. A footnote in the operating regulations urged staff to ensure that passenger's luggage was conveyed in parcel vans or the guard's van on relevant trains, and not in fish vans! Guests staying at the MGWR's hotels at both Recess and Mallaranny on the Achill line could have their luggage sent ahead and delivered by railway company staff for a charge of 9d. per item. Modern budget airlines were not the first to charge for such things! This amount was actually a significant enough charge for the early 20th century.

To allow sufficient time for shunting procedures at each station, signal cabins were manned as follows:

Galway	7.30 am-11.30 pm
Moycullen	8.45 am-7.45 pm
Oughterard	8.30 am-8.30 pm
Maam Cross	9.30 am-8.30 pm
Recess station	9.00 am-8.45 pm
Ballynahinch	9.00 am-9.00 pm
Clifden	9.00 am-9.15 pm

(The hotel platform halt had no signal box.)

Recess Hotel Platform Request Halt was opened in 1902 to allow easier access to the hotel which was a short distance away from the station. Recess station is a short distance ahead, this view looking towards Clifden. A short siding would later be installed here for unloading hotel supplies. After the hotel was destroyed by fire the halt fell into disuse.

Before the train entered Recess station, a special platform was provided for hotel traffic. After the hotel had been burned down the halt fell into disuse. However, as this view from around 1929/30 shows, it remained *in situ* for many years more. Here, we look towards Galway; the main road lies to the left, and the hotel opened off this. Behind the photographer a short siding opened off the main line for the use of wagons being unloaded by hotel staff.   *Stations UK*

Signals were lit by oil lamps. In order to avoid unnecessary waste of oil, all signal lamps were to be extinguished at night after passage of the last train, and lit again in the morning before the first one. Lamps and signals were regularly inspected to ensure that the light was bright enough for drivers to see at an appropriate distance. Initially, it was the custom on many Irish railways to have level crossing gates placed across the road normally, defaulting to a position where the right of way was set for the train. These were opened and closed as necessary to allow road traffic through, except when a train was coming. By 1920, operating regulations instructed gatekeepers to have the gates shut across the railway at night, and special notice would have to be given should there be a necessity to operate a special train during these hours. By day, they were to be shut across the road 30 minutes before the first train was due. As road traffic developed and increased, the reverse position was adopted, as today, with gates only being shut to road traffic to allow a train past.

Staff working hours were longer in the past than nowadays, but the MGWR still issued instructions covering occasions when extra hours were required, such as on days when special trains were operating. Staff were required to have nine hours rest (or eight in emergencies) in between ending their shift the previous day, and a possible early start the following day. For busy periods, arrangements were made to bring extra staff in to assist with such tasks as shunting wagons. Locomotive drivers and firemen were to be advised of any potential lengthy waits, or any instances where locomotives would be idle for longer periods than normal, so that they would be better able to regulate their locomotive fireboxes. A grim warning was carried in an operating instruction issued in October 1924:

Both guards and drivers are to clearly understand that they will be held responsible for getting their trains to destination as quickly as possible, and any lax working or waste of time will be specially dealt with.

In reality, this could mean suspension without pay, or heavy deductions from their week's wages.

For shunting operations, the standard hand signals used on most railway systems in Britain and Ireland applied. When visibility was restricted, or after dark, horns and whistles were used. One blast meant 'go ahead'; two = set back; three = stop; and four = ease couplings.

Breakdowns were rare, but a breakdown van with basic tools was stabled in Galway in case of need. Major failures were dealt with by the MGWR at Broadstone Works up to 1924, and for a few years after the takeover by the GSR the following year. By degrees, these responsibilities were transferred to the former Great Southern & Western Railway's Inchicore Works. A carriage & wagon examiner was employed in Galway station. In the 1920s, this person had a dual role - he was also the locomotive foreman. A pedal-powered inspection trolley was kept at Mullingar for use, if required, on both the Clifden line and several other remoter stretches of line in the west.

In Galway, just west of the River Corrib viaduct, the Shantalla Quarry siding diverged from the main running line. This line, like the siding at Recess Hotel platform, was controlled by an Annett's Lock which was incorporated into the Galway-Moycullen train staff. As noted elsewhere, little use was made of this siding as the quarry was nearing the end of its life even as the railway was being built. Sidings at Ross station were also thus controlled.

Quarrying was carried out at various locations in the area, generally on a small scale. One such operation, however, which was to provide traffic for the railway was the marble quarry near Recess. This was where the famous Connemara Marble with its beautiful green tints comes from. In June 1896 a refurbished mobile crane was brought to Recess station, where it was placed in a siding in order to deal with the loading of this material onto trains. One wonders how quantities of marble had been loaded prior to its arrival - such manoeuvres would have been quite awkward.

The railway company had correctly predicted that tourism would be a major source of traffic, though no railway can depend entirely on a purely seasonal traffic, and Ireland's tourist season was then quite short. Fishing provided some traffic, but the bread and butter was local people going about their daily business. The line's promoters had hoped that the railway would encourage commerce and thus slow the catastrophic trail of emigrants from the area, but in reality it simply made it easier to emigrate - an experience replicated on other rural lines all over Ireland. Many people congregated with their families for fond farewells at the stations, knowing that they might never see home again as they set off for Pennsylvania, New York, or elsewhere. The famine's legacy in emptying the countryside remained recent memory. Many a strained face looked out of the carriage window, thinking over their families left behind moments ago, the long journey ahead, and imagining their new life. How the open wild scenes of Connemara must have contrasted with the bustling streets of New York or London when they got there!

In 1902, the MGWR agreed to let an unused office in Clifden station to the Congested Districts Board (CDB), a Government body, providing that they suitably indemnified the company. The CDB used it as a telegraph office. The station at Ballynahinch was quite remote, and had no need of a telegraph office. However, the CDB asked the company if they would provide one. They were happy to do, provided spare space could be found for it, and provided that the railway would not be burdened with the operator's wage bill. It is not known whether the CDB took up the offer, though the point illustrated is the spare capacity in many station buildings on lines such as this; often, they were built to cope with a much busier life than they ended up having in reality.

Details have survived of the contracts to carry mails between Galway and Clifden. In 1902, the MGWR told the Post Office that the current fee of £620 per year was not enough to cover a night mail train service. Such an operation meant paying night shifts to signalmen and station staff along the route, as well as the cost of coal for a locomotive to haul a train containing little more than half a dozen mail bags. The Post Office responded by asking the company if they could not use a small petrol-powered vehicle, to which they replied that they did not have one. The Post Office then agreed to discuss the MGWR's asking price of £1,200-£1,400 for the time being, but after three months of communication, no agreement was reached, the MGWR apparently having to make do with a lesser amount. Research into the contracts made between other railway companies across Ireland show that the Post Office was very cost conscious, and tended to drive a hard bargain wherever they went. An interesting postscript to this exchange was that a few years later, a similar issue would arise on the Achill branch, but this time the MGWR would respond by acquiring a small petrol-driven vehicle. On the Clifden line until 1918, at the request of the Post Office, a train left Galway at 4.30 am, taking the mails which had arrived on the previous afternoon's 'night mail' train from Dublin. This train would have the mail in Clifden by about 7.00 am, ready to be locally delivered before business hours commenced. This train left Clifden on its return journey at 7.20 am. However, a train at this hour attracted virtually no other business on its outward journey, so it was discontinued after 1918 to save coal.

In February 1905 the Post Office asked for permission to place a letter box in the station premises at Clifden; this was agreed to. They were not the only outside agency to request permission to use the station for other purposes. Apart from local car drivers being allowed to shelter their horses at various stations, the Consolidated Petroleum Oil Company was granted permission to install oil tanks at Oughterard and Clifden stations. This allowed them to bring oil to these locations by train, and store it for local resale. By 1909, the sale of 'motor spirit' - petrol - was authorized at Recess station on the Clifden line, and at Mallaranny on the Achill line. The MGWR had cars and tourist coaches stationed at these places, and filling stations as we now know them did not exist. Effectively, the necessity to maintain supplies at these locations was put to advantage by allowing them to function as local filling stations.

In 1908 the first passenger special train to run right through from Clifden to Dublin (Broadstone) was operated. Unfortunately, details of this have not survived. Among notes which appear from time to time in old railway papers on unrelated matters, we also learn that in the early 1930s, sugar beet was being loaded in Moycullen for onwards transport. On occasions, instructions were given for a couple of empty wagons to be left there by a preceding good train to facilitate loading of this.

In December 1909, Richard Berridge sought permission to build a shed for his horse at Ballynahinch station. The company agreed, and allowed him £10 to build it provided he paid an annual rent of £2. Berridge also constructed a shelter at the station for the postman to use when awaiting the mails off the train. This time he acted without telling the company, but they agreed to let it stay. One wonders why the postman could not use the station facilities.

By 1911 the railway had been operating for 16 years, but no station master's house had been provided at Moycullen, where the incumbent had to live in a gatekeeper's house. These were very substantially smaller than the type of accommodation normally afforded to a station master who held a considerable position of respect in the local community. After deferring any decision on what to do, after a few months and some complaints by the station master, the company agreed to enlarge his house. While no record exists to confirm it, the possibility is that his wife was a gatekeeper. Generally the railway was a firm but fair employer. Slight deviations from strict disciplinary or operational standards were swiftly and uncompromisingly dealt with - often harshly, in some cases with instant dismissal. However, for those staff who were diligent or as the railway companies put it, 'good servants of the company', they were often looked after above and beyond the actual statutory duties of the railway company as they were then. In 1916, the widow of a deceased railway inspector named Joyce was given free use of a gate house at the level crossing at Oughterard, and a job as gatekeeper there, as she would have fallen upon hard times otherwise. The house required some repairs, so the railway was happy to expend £58. A nearby level crossing there was found to be in poor order a few years later, and had to be renewed entirely, and the gate house rebuilt.

Periodic inspections of the whole railway system were undertaken by senior management, at least on an annual basis. Usually, this would be conducted with a special train organised for the purpose. Maintenance trains also had to be arranged from time to time; these would need a slot within the day's normal timetable. A note from 12th February, 1915 shows how one such operation was included. A permanent way special train left Dublin (Broadstone) at 5.00 am, to arrive at Clifden at 5.05 pm, having shunted on its outward journey at Killucan to allow the Limited Mail to pass, and at Recess it had to be detained to allow the 2.30 pm Galway to Clifden train to overtake it. The goods train coming the other way, on the other hand, had to give way to this train, otherwise its journey to Clifden would have taken even more than the twelve hours and five minutes allocated!

At Ballynahinch, an inspection in 1920 found that the level crossing gates at Ballynahinch were not properly interlocked with the signals; this was a requirement for safe operation and had evidently been overlooked since the line had opened 25 years earlier! The company remedied this deficiency without delay.

On 1st September, 1927, the GSR signed an agreement with the Post Office which provided for timings for mail trains to be observed as shown below. The number of mail bags was specified also, and it will be seen that Ballynahinch and Recess generated more mail than Clifden. The reason is that these places were central, and mail deliveries would have reached larger areas from those stations. Up to nine mail bags were to be carried in each direction, with further to be carried by the night mail trains. These ran as follows:

Down Night Mail (from the night before)*
Galway (depart) 11.15 am (five minutes earlier June-September) - to Clifden

Up Day Mail
Clifden (depart) 3.30 pm (5.40 pm June – September) – to Galway

* Railways always referred to journeys towards the headquarters of the line as 'up', and away from it as 'down'. Therefore, all trains from Galway to Clifden were 'down' trains, while all leaving Clifden were 'up' trains.

The agreement was to run from 1927 until 31st August, 1937, though by then the railway had been closed and the agreement superseded.

Throughout the life of the Clifden line, the arrangements for working trains in and out of Galway station involved reversing the train within the station. Trains had to be hauled out across the Lough Atalia bridge, where they would stop, and the locomotive would change ends before continuing to Clifden. A brake van was to be provided at each end of the train. On their return, they would come in from the branch, stop on the bridge and reverse into the platform. If the load exceeded eight vehicles, the locomotive had to run-round and haul the train in. For shorter trains it was deemed sufficient for trains to propel (reverse) in and out of the station, providing that the train guard was watching from his balcony and leading the reversing train in by flag. Special attention had to be paid by station staff to have the red light at the buffer stops lit after dark or in dull weather.

Following the closure of the Clifden branch, the GSR reorganised the signalling in Galway station, as no need existed any longer for an arrival/departure platform for Clifden trains. This extract from a current weekly circular informs train crews of amended signals on approaching the station.

Chapter Nine

Locomotives and Rolling Stock

Locomotives

Since the railway to Clifden operated for just 40 years, and the average lifespan of a steam locomotive or passenger coach could be up to double that, it will come as no surprise to learn that the stock used upon commencement of services was largely still in use not only when the line closed, but for many years afterwards. Railway companies in these times generally saw 40 years as a reasonable lifespan for a steam locomotive, though examples of many types were to be found in use well beyond this. Some locomotives in use on the line were still hauling trains even as steam traction ended on the Coras Iompair Eireann (CIE) system in 1963.

As the MGWR's stock of rural branch lines was expanding considerably following the passage of the 1889 'Balfour Act', by the time the Clifden line was open, more and more new passenger carriages were being built to standard designs for use across the MGWR system. The same was true of locomotives. Thus, no stock was built specifically for the Clifden line itself; it merely shared a common stock with other lines.

As far as locomotives were concerned, 'K' class 2-4-0s, or 'L' or 'Lm' class 0-6-0s were most commonly associated with the line. Twenty 'K' class were built by Broadstone Works between 1893 and 1898. These had the classic Atock-designed 'flyaway' cab roof; a trade mark feature of MGWR locomotives which looked attractive, but was as abysmal a design as possible in practical terms as they offered the crew little protection from the elements. Three hours or so on the footplate of a goods train out to Clifden, virtually in open air, often with biting winds and driving rain lashing around the unfortunate driver and fireman was not for the faint hearted. After the MGWR became part of the GSR in 1925, these cabs gradually disappeared, being replaced with more conventional and practical ones. These engines were otherwise a very successful design with all but two of them outliving the Clifden line by over 20 years. By 1960, six were still in use, mostly on the Sligo line, and two of these managed to remain in traffic until the end of steam traction on CIE in early 1963. They were the last 2-4-0 tender locomotives in use in Ireland and Britain combined. In GSR days they were renumbered and reclassified as 'G2' class.

While these locomotives were frequently employed on the line, especially on passenger trains and in the earlier years, the locomotives which came to be most associated with it were the ubiquitous 'L' or 'Lm' class. Ten, designated as 'L' class, were built for the MGWR by Sharp, Stewart & Co., Atlas Works, Manchester in 1876, though they were subsequently rebuilt at Broadstone as 'Lm'. The rebuild involved the provision of steel frames instead of iron, new boilers and larger tenders, and other minor differences. Another 20 'L' class appeared from Broadstone between 1885 and 1889, with another 10 'Lm' class following between 1891 and 1895. A further six, designated 'Ln' had been built in 1879/80. As Broadstone Works was building these, it was operating at full capacity, so another

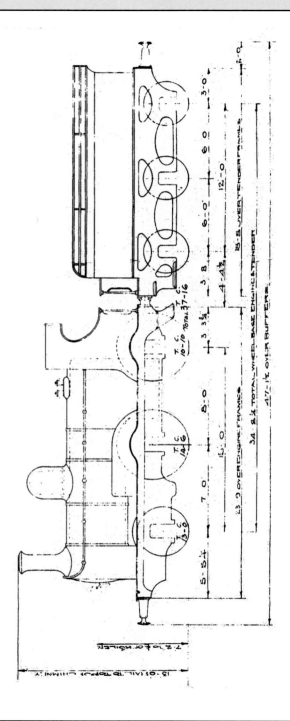

The MGWR employed their attractive and long-lived 'K' class 2-4-0s on the Clifden line principally in the early years; the 'L' class would be more common later. Pictures of the 'Tourist Train' generally feature the 'K' class, which were speedy and economical. The illustration is of how they appeared following post-1925 receipt of GSR pattern chimney and cab. Initially, they had the Atock-designed 'flyaway' cab which was attractive looking but utterly impractical in terms of providing any shelter for the crew! Twenty were built between 1893 and 1898, of which no less than six survived in front line passenger traffic into the 1960s, by which time they were mostly to be found on the Sligo line; the last 2-4-0 tender locomotives in service in Ireland. Two survived until the end of steam traction on CIE in 1963.

The following two pictures illustrate the varying appearance of the Broadstone-built 'K' class 2-4-0s over the years. The GSR re-designated then as 'G2' class and renumbered them in the 650-668 series. *Above:* No. 33 *Arrow* (later GSR No. 657) is seen at Clifden about 1903. The locomotive is in original condition, with lined green livery, Atock-designed 'flyaway' cab, and MGWR pattern smokebox door and chimney. It was built in 1898 and withdrawn from traffic in 1961. Compare with the following picture. *Real Photographs*

As 'G2' class No. 654, the former MGWR No. 28 *Clara* is seen in Dublin in the late 1930s. In contrast to the picture above, the attractive lined green livery has given way to the all-over grey of the GSR, and the name removed. The locomotive now sports a conventional Inchicore cab, chimney and smokebox door. This example of the class was built in 1897 and withdrawn in 1963. *Irish Railway Record Society*

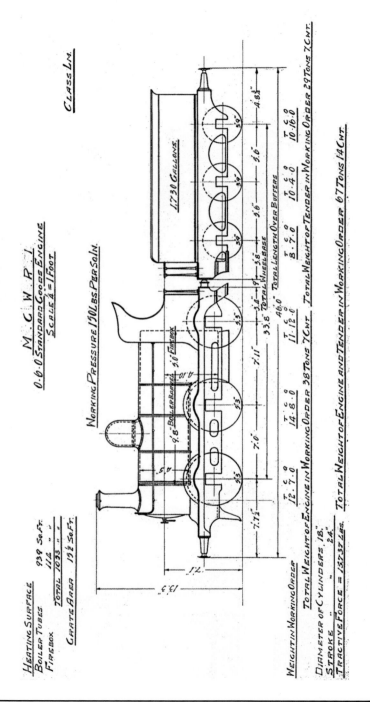

M.G.W.R.¹

0-6-0 STANDARD GOODS ENGINE

SCALE ⅛ = 1 FOOT

CLASS LM.

WORKING PRESSURE 150 LBS. PER SQ.IN.

1730 GALLONS.

HEATING SURFACE
BOILER TUBES   939 SQ.FT.
FIREBOX   114 "   "
                 ————————
     TOTAL 1053 "   "
GRATE AREA   15½ SQ.FT.

WEIGHT IN WORKING ORDER

TOTAL WEIGHT OF ENGINE IN WORKING ORDER 38 TONS 7 CWT.   TOTAL WEIGHT OF TENDER IN WORKING ORDER 29 TONS 7 CWT.

TOTAL WEIGHT OF ENGINE AND TENDER IN WORKING ORDER 67 TONS 14 CWT.

DIAMETER OF CYLINDERS, 18."
STROKE   "   24."
TRACTIVE FORCE = 15,737 LBS.

Throughout the life of the line, most trains were hauled by the MGWR's 'L' class 0-6-0s, and their derivatives, the 'Lm' and 'Ln' class. Fifty-eight were built in total between 1876 and 1895, all but nine of which survived into Great Southern ownership in 1925. Many outlived the Clifden line, despite some half of the class having been built before it ever opened. Nineteen were still on CIE's books into the 1960s and No. 593 (MGWR No. 139, originally named *Tara*) was the last one to be withdrawn as late as 1965. It had survived in use until the end of steam traction in the Republic of Ireland in 1963, along with eight others of the class which were withdrawn in that year. No. 603 (ex-MGWR No. 65) also officially lasted until 1965, though it had been out of use for some years. No CIE steam locomotives hauled trains after early 1963.

12 were ordered to MGWR design from manufacturers elsewhere. Six each were built by Sharp, Stewart & Co. who had now moved to Glasgow, and Kitsons of Leeds. These locomotives were designed, built and intended as goods locomotives, very much the equivalent of Inchicore's output of '101' ('J15') class 0-6-0s for the Great Southern & Western Railway (GSWR). However, they were eminently suitable for the sometimes lengthy mixed trains on the Clifden line, and became the standard class used. When the well-known English enthusiast, Henry C. Casserley, visited the line in 1934, he noted three locomotives in use on the line, all of this class: Nos. 582, 583 and 589. All three of these had been built at Broadstone in 1892. Two were to survive until the end of steam on CIE in 1963, almost 30 years after their last journeys through Connemara. The GSR renumbered and re-designated these locomotives as the 'J18' and 'J19' classes. Technically they were similar to each other, and to the 'Ln' class; six locomotives built between 1879 and 1880. If we look at the 'L', 'Lm' and 'Ln', or 'J16', 'J18' and J19' classes as a single group, there were 58 of them, the largest number of the same class of locomotive in Ireland excepting the GSWR's '101' ('J15') class.

Little first-hand information has survived to give us an idea of how these engines performed in day-to-day service, and what they were like to work on. However, the late R.N. Clements is reputed to have timed a 'J18' at 68 miles per hour on a main line run near Dublin. Former Waterford engine driver, writer and railway historian, the late Jack O'Neill, recounted his experiences on No. 602 which arrived in Waterford (deep in GSWR territory!) in the early 1930s, still in MGWR condition with 'flyaway' cab. He observed that it was strong, steady running and comfortable to work on. However, the GSWR equivalent, the 'J15', was stronger.

Locomotives which operated on the Clifden line

MGWR 'K' (GSR '650'/'G2') class 2-4-0 (built by MGWR, Broadstone, Dublin)

MGWR No.	Name	Post-1925 GSR No.	Built	Withdrawn	Notes
13	Rapid	659	1893	1961	
14	Racer	650	1893	1959	
15	Rover	660	1895	1959	
16	Rob Roy	651	1895	1959	
17	Reindeer	661	1894	1959	
18	Ranger	652	1893	1954	
19	Spencer	653	1894	1963	Lasted until end of steam traction on CIE.
20	Speedy		1896	1923	Destroyed in Civil War, Killala, 1923.
21	Swift	662	1896	1955	
22	Samson	663	1896	1959	
23	Sylph	664	1896	1961	
24	Sprite	665	1897	1959	
27	Clifden	666	1897	1957	
28	Clara	654	1897	1963	Lasted until end of steam traction on CIE.
29	Clonsilla	655	1897	1961	
30	Active	656	1898	1957	
31	Alert	667	1897	1957	
32	Ariel	668	1898	1959	
33	Arrow	657	1898	1961	
34	Aurora	658	1898	1954	

'G2' class 2-4-0 No. 653 in GSR condition, with Inchicore cab and chimney. This picture was taken at Athlone, but these locomotives were regulars on the Clifden line in its earlier days.

Irish Railway Record Society

MGWR No. 95 *Bulldog* outside the goods shed at Clifden. The picture is described as having been taken in 1895, just after the railway opened. If this is so, it is probably the earliest surviving photograph from the line. The presence of weeds, however, in the immediate foreground, may indicate that it was a short time later.

P. O'Cuimín

Between 1879 and 1895, the 0-6-0 locomotives of the 'L', 'Ln' and 'Lm' classes were built, all of which would eventually have so many minor variations that some became 'one-offs'. The GSR variously classed them as 'J16', 'J18' and 'J19' classes. To all intents and purposes, they were effectively the same class despite the variations, as the basics were much the same. Thus, in practice, they were operated as a common fleet. They are listed below according to MGWR classification.

MGWR 'L' (GSR 'J18'/'J19') class 0-6-0
(86-55 built by Robert Stephenson & Co., others by MGWR, Broadstone, Dublin)

MGWR No.	Name	Post-1925 GSR No.	Built	Withdrawn	GSR classification and notes
86	Bullfinch	577	1876	1928	J18
87	Buzzard		1876	1925	
88	Buffalo		1876	1925	
89	Bison		1876	1925	
90	Beaver		1876	1925	
91	Bear	579	1876	1928	J18
92	Bittern	575	1876	1957	J18
93	Butterfly		1876	1923	Destroyed in Civil War at Sligo, 1923.
94	Badger		1876	1923	
95	Bulldog	573*	1876	1927	J18

The following 'L' class were designated as class '594' or 'J19' by the GSR:

55	Inny	594	1885	1961	J19
56	Liffey	595	1885	1957	J19
57	Lough Corrib	596	1885	1959	J19
58	Lough Gill	597	1885	1959	J19
59	Shannon	598	1885	1963	J19
60	Lough Owel	599	1885	1963	J19
61	Lynx	600	1888	1957	J19
62	Tiger	601	1888	1959	J19
63	Lion	602	1888	1959	J19
64	Leopard		1888	1923	Destroyed in Civil War at Streamstown, 1923.
65	Wolf	603	1888	1965	J19. Not used after 1963.
66	Elephant	604	1889	1961	J19
67	Dublin	605	1888	1957	J19
68	Mullingar	606	1887	1962	J19
69	Athlone	607	1889	1961	J19
70	Ballinasloe	608	1888	1959	J19
71	Galway	609	1887	1954	J19
72	Sligo	610	1888	1963	J19
85	Meath		1886	1924	
140	Wren	611*	1886	1925	J19

* GSR No. allocated but never carried.

The 'J18' class No. 594 is seen at Clara. In GSR days this was the staple motive power on the line. The locomotives used on the line each day were based in Clifden and Galway, but would return to Dublin when major overhauls were necessary.   *Irish Railway Record Society*

The last locomotive to wear the old MGWR green livery was 'Lm' ('J18') class No. 74 *Luna* built in 1891 and scrapped in 1957. This picture was taken in Broadstone station, Dublin in GSR days.
                    Irish Railway Record Society

MGWR 'Lm' (GSR '573'/'J18'/'J19') class 0-6-0
(Nos. 74-84 built by MGWR, Broadstone, Dublin, others as shown)

MGWR No.	Name	Post-1925 GSR No.	Built	Withdrawn	GSR classification and notes
73	Comet	582	1892	1959	J18
74	Luna	576	1891	1957	J18
75	Hector	612	1891	1961	J19
76	Lightning	569*	1892	1925	J18
77	Star	589	1892	1963	J18
78	Planet	570*	1893	1925	J18
79	Mayo	578*	1892	1927	J18
80	Dunsandle	574	1891	1963	J18
81	Clancarty	613	1893	1963	J19
82	Clonbrock	583	1892	1963	J18
83	Lucan	571*	1892	1925	J18
84	Dunkellen	572*	1891	1925	J18
130	Ajax	584	1895	1955	J18. Built by Sharp, Stewart.
131	Atlas	585	1895	1960	J18. Built by Sharp, Stewart.
132	Pluto	586	1895	1957	J18. Built by Sharp, Stewart.
133	Titan	587	1895	1961	J18. Built by Sharp, Stewart.
134	Vulcan	588	1895	1963	J18. Built by Sharp, Stewart.
135	Arran Isles		1895	1923	Built by Kitson & Co., Leeds. Damaged beyond repair in Civil War at Streamstown, 1923.
136	Cavan	590	1895	1961	J18. Built by Kitson & Co., Leeds.
137	Maynooth	591	1895	1959	J18. Built by Kitson & Co., Leeds.
138	Nephin	592	1895	1962	J18. Built by Kitson & Co., Leeds.
139	Tara	593	1895	1965	J18. Built by Kitson & Co., Leeds. Not used after 1963

MGWR 'Ln' (GSR '563'/'J16'/'J19') class 0-6-0
(Built by MGWR, Broadstone, Dublin)

MGWR No.	Name	Post-1925 GSR No.	Built	Withdrawn	Notes
49	Marquis	563*	1879	1928	
50	Viscount	564*	1879	1925	
51	Regent	565*	1880	1926	
52	Baron	566*	1880	1927	
53	Duke	567	1880	1950	The only example to carry its GSR No.
54	Earl	568*	1880	1925	

* GSR number allocatd but never carried.
All locomotive names were removed by degrees after 1st January, 1925.
'L' class Nos. 86-95 were all rebuilt during their careers and classd as 'Lm'.

The locomotives were originally painted a mid-emerald green, believed to be similar to that used by the Great Central Railway in England. They were adorned with black and white lining, with red buffer beams and black smokeboxes and chimneys. Locomotive frames and cab roofs were green also,

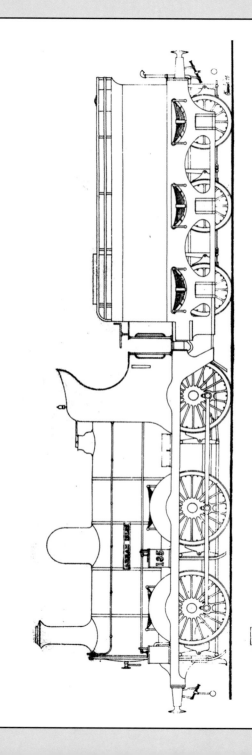

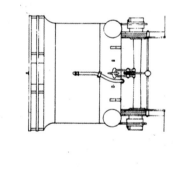

'Lm' class locomotive in original style (Kitson, 1895).
Designed by Martin Atock.

Coupled wheels	5 ft 3 in.
Tender wheels	3 ft 9 in.
Cylinders	18 in. x 24 in.
Weight in working order	66 tons
Livery	Emerald green, lined black and white

Outline drawing of 'J18' class locomotive.

Author's Collection

'Lm' ('J18') class No. 75 *Hector* in GSR condition as No. 612 in the early 1930s. It appears that the engine has been recently painted in the all-enveloping dark grey livery current at the time. The GSR removed the attractive lining and the picturesque nameplates from all MGWR engines. The utilitarian appearance of the grey livery is accentuated by the fact that even the number on the cabside is not picked out in a lighter colour, as was usually the case. This engine was built by the MGWR in Broadstone in 1891, and worked for 70 years on all kinds of traffic, including Clifden branch trains. It was withdrawn in 1961. *Irish Railway Record Society*

Afternoon train getting ready to leave Clifden for Galway in the last full year of operation. The locomotive is No. 589, a standard 'Lm' ('J18') class 0-6-0. *H.C. Casserley*

but smokeboxes and chimneys, as common on almost all railways, were black. Copper pipework was polished. The MGWR named virtually all of its engines and their cast nameplates had deep red (vermilion) backgrounds, with polished letters and numbers. Locomotive numbers were individual brass polished figures rather than numberplates.

When the 'Tourist Express' was introduced, the company unveiled a new livery. While the initial intention appears to have been to apply it to this train only, further locomotives and carriages were thus painted between 1903 and 1906. However, it never became popular as it did not wear well, as a result of which most stock remained the way it had been. The 'Tourist Express' was hauled by locomotives painted in this livery of 'royal blue', with black and yellow lining. Cab roofs were black instead of green, but smokeboxes and chimneys remained black. Locomotives thus attired soon reverted to the green, though for locomotives painted after 1906 the green tended to be of a somewhat lighter shade. Some carriages were painted to match, but they too soon reverted to their previous brown livery.

Weather was not as warm outside the tourist season. A wild winter day in Connemara is not for the faint hearted, therefore trains were provided with footwarmers, which were heavy metal containers with hot water in them. Galway and Clifden stations kept a supply of these for placing in trains between 1st October each year and 31st March the following year. These were to be placed in first class, second class, and ladies-only compartments.

After 1913, the MGWR painted its locomotives in black. Initially, all thus treated were plain black, but after 1916 mixed traffic engines and superheated passenger engines had red lining too, with the insides of frames also red. Goods locomotives – including those of the type to power most trains on the Clifden line - remained plain unlined black all over. The letters 'M G W R' were carried on the tender sides, picked out in gold and red.

From 1925, all stock on the line was gradually repainted into the GSR's standard livery, used everywhere from Sligo to West Cork, and Belturbet to Rosslare. For locomotives, this livery was quite singular in its lack of any sort of variety. All locomotives of all types (bar three on the Cork line), on all lines which came under the GSR banner, whether standard or narrow gauge, were painted in what the GSWR had introduced as an economy measure seven years earlier – plain grey all over. The shade was described as a 'dark battleship grey' which when newly applied had a slight bluish tint in sunlight. Unusually, the smokebox and chimney, inside frames, wheels and cab interiors were also coloured thus, the only relief being the red buffer beams, which sometimes had a thin black line around them. Locomotive numbers were now carried on standard Inchicore cast plates, also painted over plain grey, but with the numerals and raised rim either polished metal, or more usually painted light yellow. Over the years, the only variation came with cab interiors painted a mid-brown on some locomotives, but not all. Externally, no lettering, lining, emblems, coats of arms or numerals of any kind were added. It was as if the locomotives had been through a grey paint sheep dip. Dull as this livery was, it was to endure right through GSR days, long after the Clifden line was dismantled, and into CIE history; in fact, most of the locomotives still running

'Lm' ('J18') class No. 133 *Titan* seen here resplendent in its lined green livery in Dublin (Broadstone) about 1900. One of just five of the class which was built by Sharp, Stewart & Co. of Manchester. It entered service in 1895 and was withdrawn in 1961, having been renumbered 587 by the GSR in 1925, when it also lost its name.   *Irish Railway Record Society*

'Lm' ('J18') class No. 591, formerly No. 137 *Maynooth* at Dublin (Broadstone) in the 1950s. This picture shows this class of locomotive in the form that they were in in the later days of service on the Clifden line and elsewhere.   *Irish Railway Record Society*

at the end of the steam era in 1963 were still painted thus. The attractive green MGWR livery didn't disappear overnight; not every locomotive in Ireland would be repainted grey in one day. Thus, it was 1931 before the very last green locomotive was repainted. This was 'Lm' class No. 74 (GSR No. 576), very much one of those engines likely to go to Clifden as well as other places on the former MGWR system. While the author has no record of it, No. 74 may therefore have been to Clifden in original guise until shortly before the line closed. When the famous railway traveller, T.R. Perkins, visited the line in June 1932, he noted both the carriage he travelled in on the Clifden line, and also the one he one he occupied on the Achill line, as still bearing the worn remains of MGWR livery.

To add to their austere (but practical) new image, all MGWR locomotives lost their often picturesque and imaginative names on repainting into GSR livery.

It will be seen that the MGWR had a very individual policy of naming all of its engines. Most railway companies only allocated names to express passenger engines, or the like, but even lowly shunting engines received names on the MGWR. The variety of names was very colourful: birds, insects and figures from Greek and Roman mythology mingled with geographical names, or names of British titles, like *Marquis*, *Duke* or *Earl*. When a locomotive was scrapped, its number and name was often transferred to a newly built one. Thus, for example, the numbers 73-84 were originally allocated to an old class of locomotive which were all broken up in 1891/92, but later transferred to newly commissioned locomotives.

In the aftermath of the opening of the Clifden line the 'K' (GSR 'G2') class 2-4-0s were to be found on most passenger services. These extraordinarily long-lived locomotives were a great success design-wise, and several were still in front line passenger service as late as the early 1960s, when they were some 80 years-old. The details of the 'K' class were as illustrated on page 108.

No. 27 *Clifden* was allocated the number 666 by the GSR. Consequently the engine was nicknamed 'The Beast' by drivers - a reference to the Biblical connotations of its new number. Some drivers were reported to be cautious or superstitious about driving it.

Goods trains appear to have been handled from the outset by the 'J18' class of 0-6-0s, referred to earlier. By the 1920s these had taken over all traffic and were to provide the staple motive power over the line until closure. Thus, the 'J18' may be considered the typical Clifden locomotive. No photographic evidence known to the author exists of any other type of locomotive whatsoever on the line.

No internal combustion vehicles ever ran on the Clifden line. It was steam powered in its entirety from start to finish. The only other vehicles ever to operate on the line would have been rail bicycles used by maintenance workers.

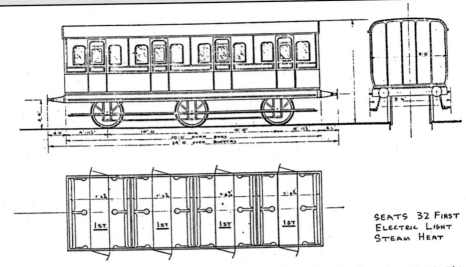

SEATS 32 FIRST
ELECTRIC LIGHT
STEAM HEAT

A standard MGWR first class coach, of the type used on the Clifden line throughout its life. This particular example was one of several built in 1905 with a new, higher roof profile. Earlier examples had a flatter roof in common with most carriages of the day. It will be seen that neither through corridor nor toilet facilities were available. Passengers would use station breaks - if they were quick enough - to use facilities there. Lighting in this case was electric, most carriages were gas lit at the time.

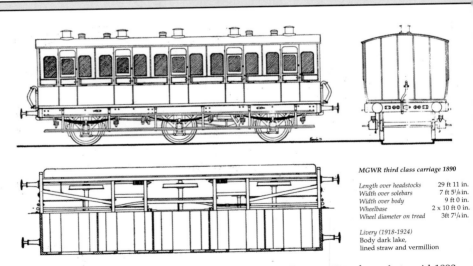

MGWR third class carriage 1890

Length over headstocks	29 ft 11 in.
Width over solebars	7 ft 5⅛ in.
Width over body	9 ft 0 in.
Wheelbase	2 x 10 ft 0 in.
Wheel diameter on tread	3ft 7¼ in.

Livery (1918-1924)
Body dark lake,
lined straw and vermillion

A standard third class coach, as built in large numbers by the MGWR in the early to mid-1890s. They seated 50 people each, ten in each compartment on bench seats. Comfort levels were basic. Three examples have survived, though none in operable condition. These are located at Whitehead, Co. Antrim (in the care of the railway Preservation Society of Ireland); Downpatrick, Co. Down (in the care of the Downpatrick & Co Down Railway, where it shares accommodation with a similar second class example); and at time of writing one is stored in the car park at the Station House Hotel, Clifden.

Rolling stock

From the outset, passenger accommodation on the Clifden line was in the MGWR's standard designs of six-wheeled non-corridor coaches. As the MGWR had expanded in the 1880s/1890s, around 300 new carriages were built to the company's existing standard designs. Over a quarter of these were the long-lived five-compartment third class coaches, which though spartan in comfort would become the standard passenger vehicle on the line during its entire life. They were 30ft in length, seating 60 people (6 per side), and weighing 12½ tons. MGWR coaching stock had many distinctive features, such as their window frames - square corners at the bottom, curved at the top, and their elegantly angled door grab handles. Communication cords were carried outside initially, with the small rings attached along the side just under roof level being another of the MGWR's design trademarks.

The extensions to the MGWR system created a need for more passenger vehicles, and while these vehicles were initially built with the following new lines in mind, they would end up in use all over the system:

Galway-Clifden
Westport-Achill
Ballina-Killala
Clonsilla-Kingscourt and Athboy

First class carriages had four or five compartments, second class five, and third class six. Since these vehicles had no side corridor or central aisle, each compartment had no means of communication with the next, and nobody could walk up and down the train. Therefore, the bench seats in each stretched from one side of the carriage to another. Tickets were checked in stations rather than by an on-board railway official. With four people per seat in a first class coach and six people per seat in a second or third class coach, seating capacity of typical coaches ranged from 32 to 60. Through corridors and toilets were a luxury yet to be introduced, and those equipped with lighting were gas lit. The guard travelled in a separate coach, sometimes with two or three extra passenger compartments in it, sometimes none.

The MGWR abolished second class in 1914, considerably in advance of most other neighbouring railway companies. From then on, second class coaches were altered to first or third, and these two classes remained for the future.

Passenger carriages, like locomotives, saw little variety over the life of the line. From the introduction of the 'Tourist Express', some main line bogie carriages began to appear, but the standard MGWR 30 ft six-wheeled vehicles remained the standard.

At least one old photograph shows an elderly four-wheel coach, probably dating from the early to mid-1870s, in a train consist at Clifden. Few carriages like this saw service into the 20th century.

Once the 'Tourist Express' started operating, dining car services came to the line - at least as far as an early photograph suggests. This may have been a publicity shot, as other information suggests that the dining car only went as far as Galway, with passengers changing trains to continue to Clifden. It is possible

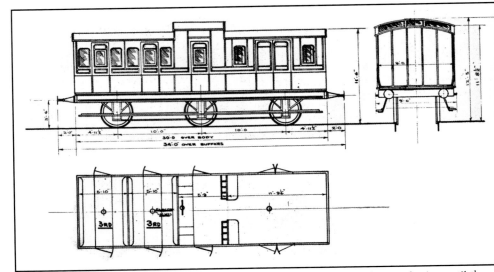

A standard MGWR brake third class coach built in the 1885-95 period, many lasting until the early 1960s. In later years, the central raised roof observation section had been removed in most survivors and replaced by a side ducket. *Author's Collection*

Six-wheeled brake third No. 18M, built by the MGWR and seen at Broadstone. Vehicles of this type generally took up the rear on Clifden trains. There are two compartments for third class passengers, each seating ten people, plus a substantial area for parcels, small goods traffic, and of course the train guard. *Irish Railway Record Society*

that the dining car travelled the whole way initially, but in subsequent seasons it appears to have been used only on the main line between Dublin and Galway. In any event, passengers needed to have the means to access it, but the few existing photographs of this train tend to show at least one, and maybe more non-corridor six-wheeled vehicles among the train. Thus, it was probable that the corridor bogie vehicles included were reserved for first and second class passengers, with third class travelling separately. It is unlikely that many third class passengers would have been able to afford the delicacies on offer in the dining car, but if they did they could possibly enter it while the train was situated at a station platform during a scheduled stop en route.

Carriage livery on the MGWR was a mid-chestnut brown until 1918. In the early years it is likely that coaches had a varnished finish, but if so it had certainly been superseded by painted brown when the Clifden line opened. For most of the life of the line, this was the norm. Originally, lining was in gold with the MGWR coat of arms and ornate numerals and lettering displayed on the sides. From 1902 some vehicles began to appear in the 'Tourist Express' livery, which for passenger coaches was the same royal blue used on locomotives decorated for this purpose. These carriages were lined in gold, with white upper panels. Like the locomotive version, the blue did not wear well and was soon discontinued. Following the resumption of the brown livery after February 1905, the gold lining began to be replaced by yellow. Dining cars, the Royal Saloon and some bogie coaches were to remain blue and white for a time, but gradually reverted to brown. Roofs were initially white but later grey. Chassis and drawgear were black. After approximately 1918, the MGWR changed its carriage livery to a very deep maroon, but with similar lining and numerals. The GSR continued with a similar shade after 1925, though now with GSR crest, lettering and numerals. Lining was yellow. In 1930 the GSR started painting main line bogie carriages only in a new livery of chocolate brown with cream upper panels and black lining. Another variation had cream upper panels, but brown mouldings, and yellow lining instead of black. Vehicles thus painted began to appear alongside the maroon ones. Six-wheeled coaches and those only used on local trains or branch lines remained in the dark crimson shade, though in some cases, six-wheeled passenger brake vans began to be painted all in the new brown shade. Further livery changes to a lighter mid-maroon colour were just being introduced by the GSR as the Clifden line was closing, but at that stage were confined to brand new Dublin suburban and Cork main line stock, the so-called 'Bredin' coaches. This would become the standard GSR carriage livery for the remainder of its existence, but the Clifden line was now consigned to history.

After the amalgamation in 1925, ex-MGWR coaches spread further afield onto the lines of other constituent companies. These 'Midland Six-Wheelers' were even to be found in West Cork and the former Dublin & South Eastern Railway system, including the much lamented Harcourt Street line in Dublin. Long after many newer coaches had been scrapped, some found their way into a reserve of old carriages held in Cork for occasional overload excursion traffic, largely in the Cork area. This reserve included the last remaining six-wheeled coaches in passenger traffic in Ireland with a few lasting until early 1964. A few survived with seats removed as maintenance tool vans and crew vans in breakdown

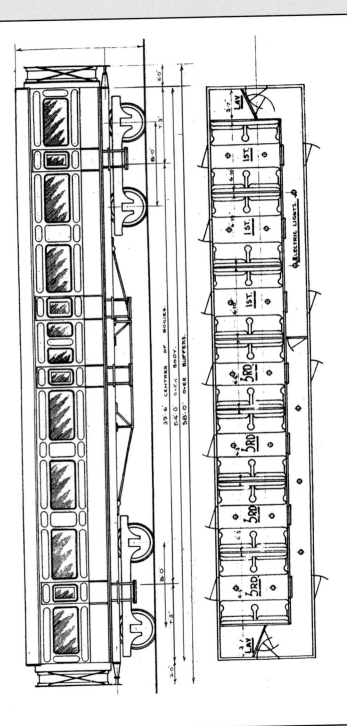

Bogie coaches were rare visitors to the Clifden line. However, vehicles such as these made occasional appearances on excursion trains from time to time. This example carried 24 first class and 32 third class passengers; note the door in the corridor to separate one from the other. Carriages were brown until *circa* 1918, with the exception of a few years from 1902 when some vehicles of this type, but by no means all, wore the elegant blue and white 'Tourist Train' livery for a while. After 1918 all carriages began to be painted a very deep maroon colour, which was continued into GSR days.

MGWR first/third composite coach No. 163M, just after being repainted in the GSR's late 1920s carriage livery of chocolate brown and cream. The coach had a chequered history, having been built in 1903 as composite coach No. 44. It would have appeared on the 'Tourist Express' in this form in the MGWR's blue and white livery for that service. In 1914 it was upgraded as fully first class, and renumbered 30. By this stage, it probably received the company's standard plain brown livery. In 1930 it was altered again to accommodate stretchers and wheelchairs, as an ambulance coach and again renumbered at 163M, the 'M' suffix being applied by the GSR to all carriages of former MGWR parentage. It is probable that this is when the picture was taken. This carriage lasted in use until 1961.

Irish Railway Record Society

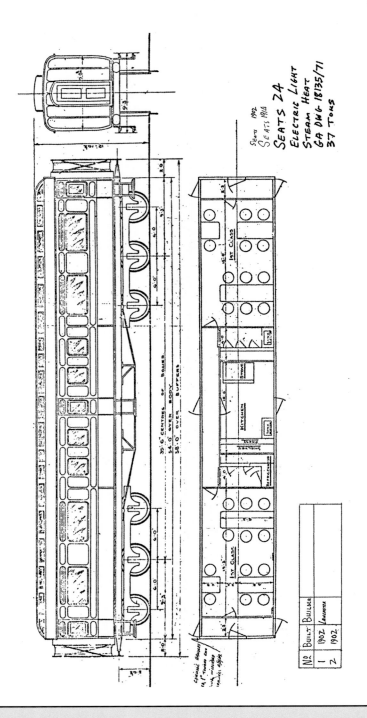

For the introduction of the 'Tourist Express', two first class dining cars were built in 1902. These were very well appointed vehicles, with construction outsourced to the Lancaster Railway Carriage & Wagon Co. in England. Unusually for Irish railway carriages, they were 12-wheeled. One survived in much modified form, having long been converted into an ordinary carriage, then a departmental vehicle, into the 1970s.

trains. Several have survived to this day, No. 84, built in 1897, is stored outside the Station House Hotel (formerly the railway station) at Clifden. Former No. 62 (built 1892) is in the care of the Railway Preservation Society of Ireland at Whitehead, Co Antrim, and Nos. 53 (1892) and 39 (1896) at the Downpatrick & Co. Down Railway. A heavily rebuilt one is stored in the open outside Cork. None, at the time of writing, are restored to traffic; it may be hoped that in the future it may be possible to travel in one again at Downpatrick, where No. 39 displays traces of 'Tourist Train' dark blue on one end, and thus would almost certainly have been used on the Clifden line at some stage. At the time of writing, it must be conceded that all four of these vehicles would by now require a total rebuild by specialists, which would be extremely costly and time consuming.

One photograph of a train on the line in its twilight years in the early 1930s shows two six-wheeled vehicles plus a bogie non-corridor third; a typical train make up for those times. However, towards the very end, this had declined to two six-wheeled passenger coaches (one first class and one third), and a six-wheeled passenger brake van. The same type of coaches would have been on the line at the start of services. Among specific vehicles which were regulars was six-wheeled first class coach No. 15 which was built in 1892 as a second class vehicle, but converted to first in 1914. In this guise it remained in traffic for another half-century, not finally being broken up until 1964.

Unlike locomotives, passenger and goods stock was not renumbered by the GSR. Instead, the letter 'M' to denote 'Midland' was added. Thus carriage No. 62 became 62M, and wagon 208 would be 208M. This system was applied to other constituent parts of the GSR also, except for those of the erstwhile GSWR, which retained their original numbers. For example, former Dublin & South Eastern Railway stock occasionally seen in Clifden would be suffixed 'D'.

Goods stock was of standard MGWR and Railway Clearing House designs. Most stock used on the Clifden line would have been standard four-wheeled goods vans, ventilated vans, horse boxes, cattle trucks and open wagons.

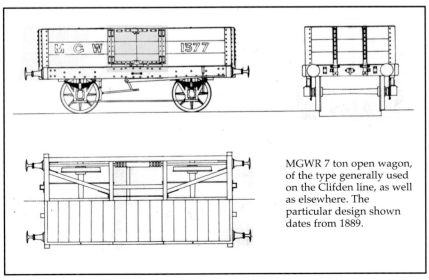

MGWR 7 ton open wagon, of the type generally used on the Clifden line, as well as elsewhere. The particular design shown dates from 1889.

A standard MGWR 7 ton goods van with removable central roof section, from a design dated 1893. The central roof section was covered by specially made tarpaulins which could be removed to provide ventilation if the vans were used to carry cattle, but covered up for general use. It may be assumed that after use as temporary cattle trucks, they were thoroughly washed out before re-use to carry conventional goods! These vans were thus known to railwaymen as 'soft-tops' or 'convertibles'. Variations of the type were commonplace on virtually all Irish railways, the last examples remaining in use until the late 1950s. The photograph inset shows a similar 'soft-top' in the 1950s built to a different design.

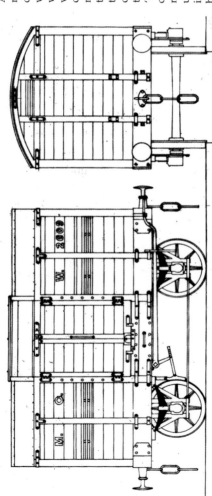

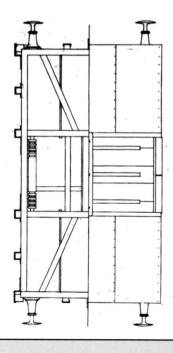

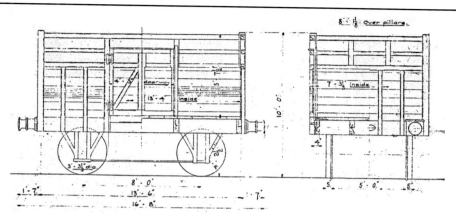

A standard design of cattle wagon, shown as roofless in this diagram. Board of Trade regulations required these wagons to be roofed from 1904. Cattle traffic was a most important source of income on almost all Irish railways, and until its final demise in 1975 would result in huge traffic on fair days. Special arrangements had to be made to ensure a sufficient supply of wagons at the relevant locations, as well as special timetable arrangements to cope with the traffic offered. It was customary in these times for livestock to be exported live, thus heavy traffic to Dublin would emanate from cattle fairs all over the country.

A butter wagon, often found in passenger train consists, as dairy products needed to reach their destination as quickly as possible in the days before refrigerators were invented. This vehicle, No. 91, is in MGWR livery. Like carriages, wagons of MGWR origin had 'M' added to their numbers by the GSR after the 1925 amalgamation. *Irish Railway Record Society*

Despite their presence in huge numbers all over the MGWR system, not a single one has survived. The last MGWR wagon seen by the author, and almost certainly the last in traffic, was bogie flat wagon No. 1M, which was still lying in the North Wall goods yard in Dublin as late as 1980.

The MGWR painted goods wagons, vans and cattle wagons an overall very dark grey with white lettering and numerals. Goods brake vans were mid-green, possibly the same shade as on locomotives, but with black chassis. Chassis and ironwork were the same grey colour. Initially horse boxes were probably brown, as the general convention was that railway companies painted such vehicles in passenger liveries, rather than as goods vehicles. This was on account of the fact that horses tended to be transported with passenger trains to avoid the rough shunting which would have been the norm with loose-coupled goods trains. There has been a suggestion, however, that at one stage these may have been green, though it is not possible to be sure of this. Certainly, once the MGWR changed its carriage livery to deep maroon in 1918, these vehicles followed suit. There is no record of any having acquired the short-lived blue livery, and it is highly unlikely that any did.

After 1925 the GSR continued to paint goods stock in plain grey, much the same shade as that of the MGWR but somewhat lighter than their dark locomotive grey. All that changed otherwise was that the smaller 'M G W R' lettering was replaced by the large 'G S' which that company used on all goods stock, and the addition of an 'M' to the vehicle number.

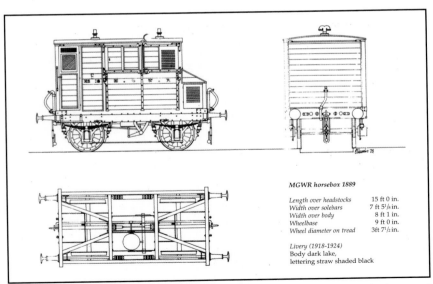

MGWR horsebox 1889

Length over headstocks	15 ft 0 in.
Width over solebars	7 ft 5¹/₈ in.
Width over body	8 ft 1 in.
Wheelbase	9 ft 0 in.
Wheel diameter on tread	3ft 7¹/₂ in.

Livery (1918-1924)
Body dark lake,
lettering straw shaded black

All Irish railway companies had horse boxes, generally used to transport the horses of gentry, or on race days to transport horses to the nearest stations to race meetings. The designs varied, the one shown being that of the MGWR, dated 1889. Notes attached to the original suggest that these were painted dark maroon between 1918 and 1924. This would correspond to the period when the MGWR passenger vehicles were also that colour, so it is likely that they were mid-brown before that.

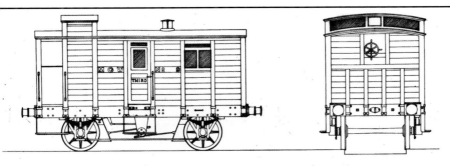

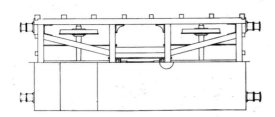

A goods brake van of 1874 design. Vans of this type were well established in use when the Clifden line was opened and many remained in traffic for many years afterwards. Generally, goods vehicles were painted grey or black by almost all railway companies, the MGWR included, but these vans were a very dark green, with white lettering and black ironwork. By 1924 they were a mid-green, and after 1925 all grey.

MGWR brake van No. 19, apparently still in MGWR livery when photographed at Broadstone, Dublin, in the late 1930s. By this stage, in GSR times, it was officially 19M. Vans like this were used often on the Clifden line.   *H.C.A. Beaumont*

Standard pattern of wagon number plate used by the MGWR.   *Author*

   After the 1925 amalgamation, goods wagons tended to become more widely travelled across the whole GSR system. While locomotives and carriages were to be seen on lines other than those for which they were built, it was the norm for these to remain more or less within original territory. The author has seen photographs of wagons built in Dundalk in service in West Cork in the 1950s, and wagons more accustomed to the quays of Waterford or the banks of the River Lee in Cork, in places like Sligo, Enniskillen and Galway. By degrees, the GSR built its own standard goods wagons, and towards the end of the life of the line these were to be seen in Clifden.

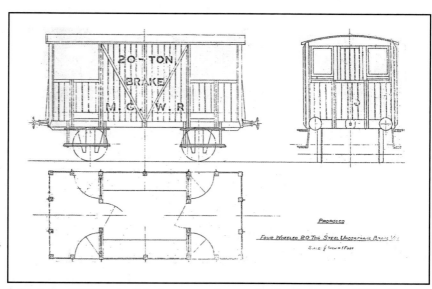

Later design of 20 ton goods brake van, used as standard by the time the Clifden line was closed. Some examples of these would see another 20 years use afterwards, all over the former MGWR system.   *Author's Collection*

Chapter Ten

After the Railway closed: Roads and Greenways

Following closure the GSR lost no time in removing the railway lines and fittings and disposing of the land. Removal of the railway track commenced at the Galway end in the summer of 1935, reaching Oughterard during summer 1936, with most removed by the end of that year. A few remnants of track were still visible in Clifden station for several years later.

Almost immediately the Galway county surveyor wrote to the GSR to enquire whether the 'site of the ruins of Recess Hotel and Grounds' was for sale. The GSR was happy to divest itself of this property and on 2nd September, 1938 they agreed to sell this for five shillings per acre, plus fishing rights in Glendollagh Lough for £100 - if such rights, despite being enjoyed by hotel guests throughout the hotel's existence - could be proved! The buyer was a Colonel Kilkelly, who also offered to buy the station and goods store. The store and station house changed hands for £250 and £400 respectively, the latter sale to include any peripheral station outbuildings.

An early priority was to dispose of the Corrib viaduct. Initially this was offered to the City authorities for £10, by some accounts reduced to £5. It could have made a useful road crossing, but Galway's city fathers did not want to be burdened with it. They were probably discouraged by the likely long term maintenance costs, including the necessity to have staff on hand to open or shut it for shipping. The opening span would itself require long term care and maintenance. Thus, it was sold for scrap to the Hammond Lane Foundry in Dublin in May 1937. Removal was complete by early 1938. Local rumours persisted for some years later that the scrap was used to make bombs to drop on Germany during the war, or that it was disposed of in several other unusual ways, but there was no foundation in these. For one thing, the war did not start until two years later. Another false story suggested that the entire railway line was sold to the railway administration in Nigeria. Often, when railway lines were dismantled in these times, various colourful 'urban legends' would arise as to how materials were disposed of! Rarely did such accounts have any substance.

Following closure, dismantling of the track by the scrap company took place using small trolleys and a tractor, rather than the conventional means of using a dismantling train with heavier lifting equipment. This rare scene is of this work in place near Moycullen. The demolition of the track was carried out by degrees over the several years after closure, with some isolated short bits of track still extant in the late 1930s.

Shane Joyce

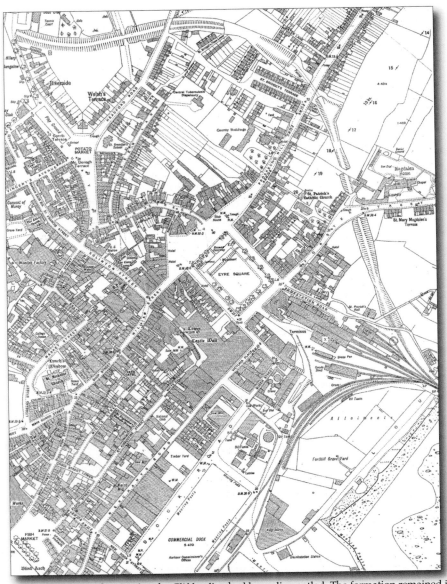

Galway station as it was shortly after the Clifden line had been dismantled. The formation remained intact for some years before significant expansion of the city in the 1950s and 1960s. Compare with the map on page 30, as this illustrates the differences in Galway city over the 40 years during which the railway was in operation. At bottom right, the main line enters from Dublin, and once across the Lough Atalia bridge, the lines fan out with the passenger station straight ahead, goods and cattle yards to the left, and the former Clifden line curving away to the north. It will be seen that the former branch line now ends as a siding adjacent to the locomotive turntable. This siding is still extant, hidden by ornamental grasses, as is the turntable, though both are now disconnected from the other tracks. The passenger station remains the same. The area where the sheep loading pens, goods shed and goods sidings are is all now cleared as a car park. Trains arriving from Clifden would set out across the Lough Atalia bridge, then proceed backwards into the branch platform into the 'mechanical garage' (marked 'X' on the map). A train leaving for Clifden would reverse out from there over the bridge, before pulling forward past the turntable and heading north.

Following closure, dismantling of the line was carried out over the ensuing years by small gangs based at various locations and working for the overall demolition contractor. This view was taken at least a year after closure, as weeds may be seen all over the railway track. While in operation, these would have been kept under control by the annual visit of the weed spraying train.

Jim Deegan

On 12th July 1937, as the viaduct structure was being dismantled, one large beam fell and two demolition workers were thrown down with it. Luckily, they landed in the water, clear of the beam.

At one time there had been another rumour regarding the bridge; that a young lady used to cross the Corrib by walking across the top of the beams … if true, the removal of the bridge would have prevented any injury to anyone attempting such a risky feat!

With the Clifden branch now closed, the old arrival platform in Galway station was no longer needed, and this was taken out of commission on 10th November 1935, during a period of general economies being made along the Dublin-Galway and other routes. Subsequent alterations to Galway station building saw this platform disappear, but to this day the end of an adjacent platform on the down side can be glimpsed opposite the existing passenger platform, just outside the overall platform canopy.

On 6th May 1935, the GSR advertised for tenders to purchase dismantled track and other scrap materials. A few weeks later the Chief Engineer and signals & telegraphs engineer were therefore given instructions to remove all the track, signalling and telegraph instruments, the latter now being available for spare stock for use elsewhere. The firm of Joyce, Mackie & Lockheed was appointed as auctioneers to sell all rental property, stations and the route of the track bed to adjacent landowners. By June 1935 it had been decided by the GSR that only a few small sites were to be retained, as follows:

Moycullen	Old cattle loading banks for loading livestock into cattle lorries.
Ross	Old cattle loading banks (as above).
Oughterard	Old cattle loading banks (as above), plus possible acquisition of a separate premises, or retention of part of the railway premises as a road services depot.
Maam Cross	Station Master's Residence for depot keeper, and three sheep pens.

Above: Clifden station about two years after closure,
with remnants of track still extant.
Irish Railway Record Society

Right: The station remained largely unaltered in 1970.
Author

Twenty years after the line closed, this is all that remains of the road bridge adjacent to the
Corrib viaduct. The stone abutment on the right has been cleared away in this view from April
1955.
H.C. Casserley

Recess	Crossing cottage for depot keeper, and three sheep pens (crossing cottage later extended and used as goods store). Goods store for road traffic built across trackbed adjacent to cottage.
Ballynahinch	All to be sold.
Clifden	Locomotive crew dormitory for conversion into a house for depot keeper, goods store for road goods depot. Locomotive shed to be altered as garage for bus (in addition to which, extra bus garage accommodation was to be obtained in Galway).

The tender mentioned 43¼ miles out of the 49. This was because the GSR planned to retain some six miles of track themselves. This was normal practice, as it is possible that this represented several short stretches deemed suitable for reuse elsewhere, rather than scrap. In this case, the GSR's Chief Engineer, A.W. Bretland, wanted this amount of rail to replace worn out tracks on the Cork & Bandon line. We cannot be certain whether these track materials ever did make their journey south, as Bretland was told to wait until the company evaluated how the new road services were shaping up. Could it be that even at this late stage, options were being kept open in case re-opening of a part of the line might be called for?

One short stretch of the track to remain was the section of line from Galway Station to the end of the Corrib bridge, which was to be retained as a siding. This short siding remained in place for some years, and although shortened now to a hundred metres or so inside the station limit, remains as a short remnant to this day. The passenger footbridge from Oughterard was removed in its entirety for re-use at Ballyglunin, Co. Galway. Following the cessation of use of the second platform there in the 1960s, it was removed again to Ballinasloe, Co. Galway where it remains to this day.

Maam Cross station, June 1961. Despite 26 years having passed since closure, the entire station remains, bar the signal cabin and the water tank from above the stone base on the left. The photograph is taken looking towards Clifden, with the goods and cattle platform on the extreme left, and the passenger platforms on the right. Just out of the picture on the left was the goods shed, which still stands. The attractive red brick station building is, however, no more. However, revival through the Connemara Railway project at Maam Cross includes plans to rebuild the structure as it was.   *David Soggee*

The tunnel under Prospect Hill, Galway *circa* 1960. Contrast this photograph with the image of the tunnel under construction on page 18. *J.P O'Dea*

Ballynahinch signal box pictured in the early 1960s. A replica stands in the same position today. *J.P O'Dea*

The stations themselves had already been cleared out, with GSR lorries removing furniture, stationery and other equipment on 29th April, 1935. Now, unfortunately, it was time to pay off or re-deploy the staff. The result was that some 58 jobs were lost as follows:

	Traffic Dept	Locomotive Dept	Permanent Way Dept
Retired	2	3	4
Track inspector*	–	–	1
Paid off women gatekeepers†	2	–	–
Temporary staff paid off	1	–	30
Staff transferred to other locations	4	3	–
Staff transferred to road services	5	–	–
Staff temporarily transferred pending decision on fate#	3	–	–
Totals	17	6	35

* Fate to be decided later.
† Generally 'women gatekeepers' were the wives of men who worked elsewhere on the railway. The closure of the railway would therefore often result in the loss of two incomes to the household, albeit the gatekeeper's allowance being small. Gatehouses were provided free of rent in compensation, and a small patch of land was often provided adjacent to the house, on which the occupant could grow vegetables.
# One of these staff was transferred to Athlone.

The loss in wages to the area was some £7,000 per annum. Station masters, of whom there were seven, were paid £220 each per year. Clifden also had two porters and a head porter, and signal porters at Recess, Maam Cross and Oughterard. Track maintenance staff consisted of 10 gangs of four men each, each paid £3 per week. Two engine drivers and two firemen were also employed on the line. Signalmen and junior staff made up the rest of the payroll.

A typical gatekeeper's house on the line, this one shown in 2002.   *Author*

The very attractive Ross station, at the village of Rosscahill, 2002. While some evidence of alteration is to be seen, the building remains largely in original condition.   *Author*

The former goods shed at Ross was typical of many in small MGWR stations, was accompanied by a small goods platform. Pictured here in 2002, all was silent; but when the line was operating this was the least busy station anyway.   *Author*

The high quality stonework of the culverts and minor bridges on the line is evident to this day. This picture was taken just west of Oughterard station in 2002, 67 years after the line closed.

Author

As the railway was dismantled by a number of local contractors with comparatively light equipment (see pages 135 and 137), many steel bridges were left intact and remain so today. This bridge spanned the river just west of Recess station, also still extant and seen in the background, looking towards Galway in 2002.

Author

Ballynahinch in 2002: (*above*) the river bridge, (*lower*) the station building from the approach road. The attractive coursed brickwork is evident. This was a feature of a number of stations on the line. *(Both) Author*

Clifden station, 2002, now the bar and restaurant of the Station House Hotel. The former water tower survives intact. The signal is a modern prop, but fits in well. Compare these views to the one on top page 172. *(All) Author*

Oughterard station from the approach road,
2002. *Author*

Water tower at Oughterard, still extant in
2002. The station was by this stage a
business premises. *Author*

Preparations for a section of cycleway on the old line near Ballinafad, 2019.

(Both) Jim Deegan

At Maam Cross, a heritage railway project commenced in time to mark the 125th anniversary of the opening of the line in 2020. Temporary track was laid again for the first time in 85 years. The setting in the spectacular Connemara scenery is evident, and the original water tower and goods shed are still standing (*right*). A replica level crossing has been installed. The view is looking towards Galway and the station building was originally on the left, knocked down in the 1960s and replaced by the farm sheds seen here.

Jim Deegan

In many locations, the railway bed so carefully laid down in the 1890s is still in use. Parts of the modern road were widened or diverted over the old railway bed from the 1960s onwards, and plans are in hand to convert other large stretches of the line into a cycleway, as was done with the entire Westport-Achill line. There is a successor to the old tourist cars between Clifden and Westport - during summer months there is one Bus Eireann service in each direction over the route.

Speculation is often rife after a railway has closed as to how it would have fared if it had survived. If traffic on the Clifden line had been very considerably more substantial, and this had been maintained throughout the 1950s, and the line survived today, it is still hard to imagine that any stations other than Moycullen and perhaps Oughterard would have survived. As in most of Ireland, goods services and facilities would be a thing of the past. Modern passenger trains of the type operating into Galway would simply proceed onwards to Clifden, at the rate of perhaps three or four per day. Certainly, a revival of the line as far as Moycullen would be a very beneficial move to ease the commuter bottlenecks on the road from there into Galway each working day, with an extra stop in the vicinity of the University, probably close to where the Shantalla siding once diverged.

Today, the remains of the railway repose, mute witness to the hopes of the original promoters. As the decades advance sections of the trackbed sink back into nature or have modern roads or laneway built over them, leaving no trace. Stations mostly remain, although the fortunes of each vary. For example, Maam Cross station building has vanished, though the goods shed and platform remain. The site of these has been acquired, at time of writing, by Jim Deegan, a railway enthusiast with strong connections to, and interests within the area. The proposal is that the site will be developed into a railway heritage centre providing a snapshot of the Irish country railway and will explore themes of early to mid-20th century social history including emigration, revolution and Connemara tourism. Oughterard station building is incorporated into an industrial premises, while that at Recess is a private house and Clifden station itself is part of a hotel complex.

Galway station in early 2019. The remnants of the end of one of the older platforms, once used for goods and mail is shown on the left. This would be removed in connection with track alterations a short time later to make way for a new storage siding. Compare this with the view on page 56.   *Author*

Work in progress on the Maam Cross Connemara Railway Project in 2021.   *(All) Jim Deegan*

Chapter Eleven

Road Services

Once all train services had ceased the GSR was faced (as in other areas now bereft of railways) with establishing replacement road services - buses for passengers and lorries or vans for goods services. Rural road transport had been provided by the Irish Omnibus Company (IOC), with a nationwide fleet of some 70 buses until July 1929 when the GSR absorbed the IOC.

Mails were now carried either on the roof rack of the bus, where the mail bags were open to the elements - or in lorries. Almost immediately the Post Office complained that the lorry used by the GSR to carry mail bags had a leaky tarpaulin, and this was replaced. By June 1935, the GSR was reporting that the new method of mail transport was a great success, and was to be extended to Roundstone and Cashel.

At first, the new bus services were similar to the displaced rail services, as seen overleaf. It will be seen that the bus appears to have travelled via the main road, not via Ballynahinch, thus leaving that place off the public transport route. Lorry deliveries to there would have continued, though. No Sunday services were provided.

Other teething troubles with the new road services were to occur. By July, cattle markets were in full flow. The GSR had made no provision for extra cattle lorries as the line closed, instead opting to utilise their existing stock. Cattle drovers complained that they had nowhere near the capacity needed, but the GSR pointed out that they had brought seven cattle lorries into the area, a figure justified by recent returns of cattle carried by rail in the equivalent period in the previous few years. However, the cattle men retorted that it was all very well providing seven lorries, but enough cattle to fill 15 had turned up! The lorries ended up making two return trips, packed full. They ran to the times of the old goods trains, thus making connection with the afternoon goods train from Galway to Dublin. But this was not enough - some cattle had to be left behind, at great inconvenience to the cattle dealers, before making their journey the following day. Whether related or not, officials from Galway County Council were to complain of instances of lorries 'blocking up the roads' and 'driving dangerously'! Ironically, this echoed criticisms raised in Clifden in the early years of the railway in terms of the congestion of horse-drawn vehicles at the station when trains arrived.

Immediately after closure of the railway, the road freight department of the GSR continued to use railway goods sheds at each station for storing goods delivered by lorry, but this changed by degrees and was eventually discontinued. For example, Recess station building was sold off for use as a private dwelling but as a result of the sale, the GSR had to make plans to build a new goods store for their road traffic services. This work was carried out in 1940, with the new store placed across the old trackbed beside the crossing keeper's cottage. The construction was by a Mr T. McWilliams and cost £218. By 1936, the GSR had built 100 new lorries for general use across the country.

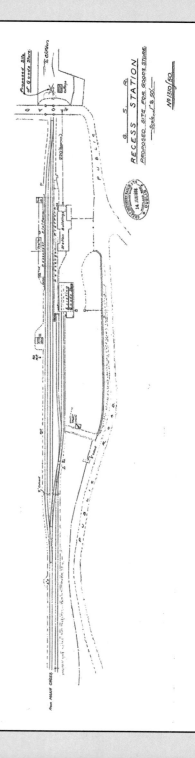

Plan of Recess station and proposed alterations dated 14th June, 1938. By this stage the railway was closed, but the replacement road freight services still used the goods store. In order to facilitate the disposal of the entire station site, it was proposed to build a new store across the road, on the Clifden side of the former station. This new building would straddle the old track bed beside the former gatekeeper's cottage, which the company had retained for use by the goods agent. The store was not in fact built, but the plan is of interest as it shows the layout of the station when it was open and operating.

Author's Collection

GREAT SOUTHERN RAILWAYS
(OMNIBUS DEPARTMENT.)

GALWAY *and* CLIFDEN SERVICE

PATRONS PLEASE NOTE ON AND AFTER MONDAY, 29th APRIL, 1935, THE FOLLOWING SERVICES WILL OPERATE BETWEEN GALWAY AND CLIFDEN ON WEEK-DAYS ONLY.

		a.m.	a.m.	p.m.	p.m.
GALWAY	dep.	* 8.15	11.15	* 4.15	6.45
MOYCULLEN	„	8.35	11.35	4.35	7. 5
ROSS	„	8.47	11.47	4.47	7.17
OUGHTERARD	„	9. 0	12. 0 P.M.	5. 0 STOP	7.30
MAAM CROSS	„	9.30	12.30	—	8. 0
RECESS STATION	„	10. 0	1. 0	—	8.30
CLIFDEN	arr.	10.45	1.45	—	9.15

		a.m.	p.m.	p.m.	p.m.
CLIFDEN	dep.	* 7. 0	12.45	*—	5. 0
RECESS STATION	„	7.45	1.30	—	5.45
MAAM CROSS	„	8.15	2. 0	—	6.15
OUGHTERARD	„	8.45	2.30	5.10	6.45
ROSS	„	8.57	2.42	5.22	6.57
MOYCULLEN	„	9.10	2.55	5.35	7.10
GALWAY	arr.	9.30	3.15	5.55	7.30

* Saturdays only.

BUSES START FROM GALWAY RAILWAY STATION AND CONNECT WITH ALL TRAINS.

HEAD OFFICE :—
   TRANSPORT HOUSE,
      BACHELOR'S WALK,
         DUBLIN.
Phone 52351 (Ten Lines).
10/4/35.

W. H. MORTON,
General Manager.

[P. 6/1.]   BROWNE AND NOLAN, LTD., DUBLIN.

Replacement bus service, to be introduced after the railway closed; 10th April, 1935.

Author's Collection

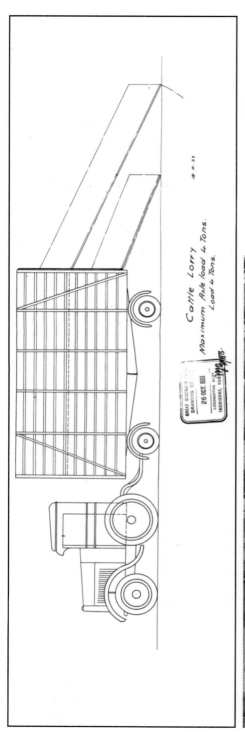

Cattle Lorry

Maximum Axle load 4 Tons.

Load 4 Tons.

GREAT SOUTHERN
DRAWING OF
26 OCT. 1933
LOCOMOTIVE DEPT
INCHICORE, DUBLIN

Above: Cattle lorry design, October 1933. Vehicles of this nature were proposed for cattle traffic after this and other lines closed. The design originated in the GSR's Inchicore Works, and was drawn by H.J.A. Beaumont, the chief mechanical engineer's chief draughtsman.   *Author's Collection*

Newly-built lorry suitable for carrying cattle and general goods, 1935. Vehicles such as this replaced the goods service.   *Author's Collection*

GSR bus, pictured at Leenane in July 1934. These buses continued the traditional Irish rural bus livery of red and white, started by the Irish Omnibus Co. when buses first operated, and only interrupted by the all-enveloping CIE green of 1945-63. Vehicles such as this replaced the passenger railway services. *H.C. Casserley*

Over the years, the public bus service transferred from the GSR to CIE, which was formed in 1945 as an amalgamation of the GSR and road transport interests, the Grand Canal Co., and the Dublin United Tramways Company. In 1950 CIE was nationalised, and the bus and road freight services between Galway and Clifden fell into state ownership. In 1987, CIE was split into three subsidiaries which at the time of writing remain state owned. Iarnród Eireann/Irish Rail was one, and it assumed responsibility for the railways, while Bus Eireann/Irish Bus now operates the public bus service over the route. At the time of writing, three services per day cover the whole route for all of the year except July and August. Two additional short daily services operate only between Galway and Oughterard. The summer service has five return trips plus the two short ones. Nowadays, some services travel via the main road, but others serve Roundstone. Road freight services operated by CIE were gradually de-regulated and the state now plays no part in road haulage in the area.

GALWAY/CLIFDEN SERVICE

WEEKDAYS ONLY

		a.m.	*p.m.	p.m.			a.m.	p.m.	p.m
Galway ...	dep.	11.30	5.00	6.45	Clifden	dep. 8.30	12.45	5.0
Newcastle	...	11.42	5.12	6.57	Ballinahinch Cross	8.50	1. 5	5.2
Moycullen	...	11.53	5.23	7. 8	Recess ...	9.10	1.20	5.3
		p.m.			Maam Cross ...	9.35	1.45	6.0
Ross Station	...	12. 6	5.36	7.21	Oughterard ...	10.10	2.10	6.2
Oughterard	...	12.20	5.50	7.35	Ross Station ...	10.13	2.24	6.3
Maam Cross	...	12.45	6.15	8.00	Moycullen ...	10.25	2.37	6.5
Recess ...	...	1.10	6.40	8.25	Newcastle ...	10.35	2.48	7.
Ballinahinch Cross		1.27	6.57	8.42	Galway arr.	10.45	3.00	7.1
Clifden ...	arr.	1.45	7.15	9.00				

*Saturdays only.

Replacement bus services, from GSR (Omnibus Services) leaflet, 1941. Compare this with that of 1935 on page 153, which seemed more logical.

Appendix One

The Midland Great Western Railway

The MGWR, eventually Ireland's third largest railway company, was incorporated in 1845 to build a railway to Mullingar and Longford, and eventually Galway, from its terminus at Broadstone, just north of Dublin's city centre. Its authorised capital was £1,000,000 to cover the first stages of construction to Mullingar and Longford, as well as the outright purchase of the Royal Canal, along the banks of which its line was laid for some distance out of Dublin. This allowed this stretch of railway to be constructed without the purchase of further land, and also eliminated canal competition for goods traffic.

Construction commenced in January 1846, at the height of the Great Famine, thus providing very valuable employment opportunities in the districts through which it passed. By May 1847 the first section to Enfield, Co. Meath, was opened to traffic, and Mullingar received its first train in October 1848. From here the line struck out due west, crossing remote areas of bog, this presenting a number of constructional difficulties in itself. By August 1851, Galway was connected to the rail network, with a fine cut stone station situated at the edge of Eyre Square, right in the city centre. It was from here that trains were to commence their journey westwards to Clifden some 44 years later.

By the start of the 20th century, the total mileage of the MGWR main line and branch lines was 538 miles (866 km), serving an area roughly triangular in shape. The main line was Dublin-Galway, and a secondary main line (officially referred to as the 'Principal Line') connected Dublin with Sligo. Various branch lines operated within this geographical area. In addition, two lines struck north - one to Navan and Kingscourt, Co. Cavan, with a branch off it to Athboy, and another from Inny Junction (near Mullingar) to Cavan town, with a branch to Killeshandra.

Mainly in the 1880s and 1890s, branch lines had been built from the main Galway line to Edenderry, Clara and Loughrea; from the Sligo line to Ballaghaderreen, and the 'Mayo Branch' acquired. This was the Athlone to Westport line, which would become the MGWR's third trunk route, and which had started life as the Great Northern & Western Railway. Having reached Westport, branches were built at the western end of this route under the Balfour Act: Claremorris to Ballinrobe, Manulla Junction to Ballina and onwards to Killala, and Westport to Achill Sound. The Killala and Achill lines were constructed at the same time, and under the same legislation, as the Clifden line, and would also succumb in the 1930s.

The Waterford, Limerick & Western Railway Company (WLWR) operated a route which ran north to south through MGWR territory, this connecting Sligo with Limerick via Claremorris and Athenry. At times, the MGWR had permission to operate into Limerick over this route, just as the WLWR had permission for its trains to use the MGWR's Collooney to Sligo line. However, use of the MGWR's powers were short-lived as the working arrangement required the MGWR to pay an unsustainable portion of receipts from such services to the WLWR.

From January 1925, all major railway companies whose lines lay entirely within the Irish Free State were amalgamated into the Great Southern Railways. Little changed under GSR operation, though in 1937 Broadstone terminus in Dublin was closed, with trains from the MGWR lines diverted into the former Dublin & South Eastern Railway (DSER) station at Westland Row, Dublin, which was somewhat nearer to the city centre. At the start of 1945 the GSR itself amalgamated with the Dublin United Tramways Company and the Grand Canal Company to form Coras Iompair Eireann (The Irish Transport Company). CIE thus took over the operation of the former MGWR system, though by that stage the Ballina-Killala, Achill and Clifden lines had closed. In 1950, CIE was facing mounting losses owing to road competition, and it was nationalised.

Subsequent consolidation of the railway system in the 1950s saw further withdrawals of services. The Cavan and Meath lines lost their passenger services at first, but were later to close entirely. The Ballaghaderreen, Edenderry and Streamstown-Clara lines closed in the 1960s, leaving the Attymon Junction-Loughrea line as the last traditional rural branch line railway not only in MGWR territory, but throughout Ireland. Services on this line ended in November 1975, mixed trains and cattle traffic to Loughrea Cattle Mart remaining to the end, long after it had ended elsewhere.

Between 1973 and 1985, trains using the main line from Galway, and those approaching Athlone from the Mayo branch were diverted away from their traditional route through Mullingar. Again, the Dublin terminus changed; now, such services would travel along the erstwhile Great Southern & Western Railway's Athlone-Portarlington line to join the Cork-Dublin main line there, ending up (as they still do) at Dublin (Heuston) Station, formerly Kingsbridge Station.

At the time of writing, all three of the MGWR's main routes operate, with Sligo trains now operating from Dublin (Connolly) - formerly the Great Northern Railway's Amiens Street terminus. Westport and Galway trains operate as described above into Dublin (Heuston). The Mullingar-Athlone middle stretch of the MGWR's main line has been closed to passenger traffic since 1985 and is now part of a cycle network, though at the time of writing still in railway ownership. The track remains *in situ* at the time of writing.

Thus, trains from the MGWR system have the strange distinction of having used not only their original Broadstone Terminus, but also the DSER one at Westland Row, the GNR one at Amiens Street, and the GSWR one at Kingsbridge!

After the GSR amalgamation in 1925, maintenance of locomotives and carriages was gradually transferred to the GSWR's Inchicore Works, but Broadstone remained as a locomotive depot until the early 1960s, just as steam traction was being finally abolished from regular services in the Dublin area. It retained its connection with public transport after that, as the large areas of the station no longer needed for railway use were turned over to CIE's buses. Today, Broadstone is the major national garage and repair facility for Dublin city and provincial buses.

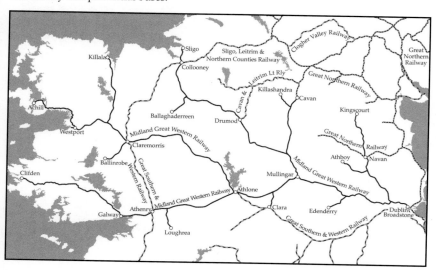

GALWAY & CLIFDEN RY.

Corrib River Bridge.

(Amended Design)

— Scale 20 feet to 1 inch —

Ryan & Townsend

The final plans for the Corrib viaduct, dated 28th March, 1891, and signed by Ryan & Townsend (Engineers). The entire structure was 488 ft long.

	Description	Unit	Quantity	Rate £ s. d.	Amount £ s. d.
1.	Wrought iron in permanent caissons	Tons	50	36 0 0	1,800 0 0
2.	Cast-iron in beltplates, fixed and lifting spans, &c., and in checkplates of lifting spans	"	9	13 10 0	121 10 0
		"	18½	8 10 0	157 5 0
3.	Cast-iron in balance weight				
4.	Steel in main girders, wind bracings and cross girders of fixed spans, and cross girders and rail bearers on piers	"	250	22 0 0	5,500 0 0
		"	86	22 0 0	1,892
5.	Steel in Hobson's patent arch plate flooring of fixed spans				
6.	Steel in main girders, cross girders, rail bearers, floor bars, wind bracing, and hand-rail standards of lifting span	"	9	24 0 0	216 0 0
7.	Steel in rollers, and pins of rollers, and fixed bearings of large spans	"	2½	32 0 0	80 0 0
8.	Machinery in lifting span, including steel axles, cast-iron pedestals, cast-iron section, and pinions, and chains, shafts and bearings, winch gear and brake, also apparatus as specified for locking and wedging tail end	Lump sum			550 0 0
9.	Bolts, nuts, and washers, including lewis bolts and lead filling	Cwt.	12	24 0	14 8 0
10.	Excavation in cylinders, including air pressure or otherwise, clearing of water, pumping and staging	Cub. yds.	275	3 0 0	825 0 0
11.	Excavation in foundations of No. 2 Pier, including coffer dam, or otherwise clearing of water, pumping and staging				
12.	Excavation in abutments				
13.	Concrete in cement in cylinders and elsewhere—strength {4 to 1 {5 to 1 {6 to 1	"	116 400 68	2 0 0 0 8 0 1 5 0	232 0 0 160 0 8 85 0 0
14.	Brickwork in cement, in cylinders	"	68	1 3 0	78 0 0
15.	Brickwork in arches of Piers Nos. 2 and 3	"	460	2 10 0	710 0 0
16.	Masonry in abutments and piers	"	296	2 10 0	67 10 0
17.	Masonry in copes of do.	"	27	1 18 0	2,717 0 0
18.	Granite in bedstones on abutments and piers	"	1,430	4 14 0	155 18 6
19.	Bronze castings in flooring, as per Clause No. 25a	"	33	6 15 0	364 10 0
20.	Gas-pipe hand-rail, 1¼ inches diameter	Lineal feet	54	3 7 0	405 0 0
21.	" " 1 inch	"	120	5 0 1	6 5 0
		"	50	0 1 6	8 0 6
			107		
	Total amount delivered and fixed complete				£16,545 19 0
	Maintenance for twelve months				£200 0 0
	Total —				£16,745 19 0

Corrib viaduct just after completion.

Appendix Two

The Corrib viaduct and other bridges

The major engineering feature on the line was the Corrib viaduct on the outskirts of Galway city.

In 1901, J.H. Ryan, one of the civil engineers appointed to oversee construction work on the Clifden line, gave a presentation to the Institution of Civil Engineers in which he described in detail the construction and make up of the Corrib viaduct. The viaduct consisted of three spans of 150 ft each, with a lifting section which had a lifting span of 21 ft, based on the bascule principle.

The construction was of lattice girders on the large spans. Flooring on the viaduct was of Hobson's patent arched steel floor plates, similar decking being used on other smaller bridges. These were riveted down to the main framework, covered with a thick layer of tar and the track laid on top. The 150 ft spans weighed over 112 tons each.

On account of the opening section, signals had to be provided at each end of the viaduct. Home and distant signals were provided, electrically controlled from Galway Station signal cabin. For local use, the bridge itself had a cabin with five levers at its western end. Opening mechanisms for the bridge were interlocked with the signals so that it was impossible for a 'line clear' signal to show even if the bridge was only slightly ajar, let alone fully open. This was achieved by a break in an electrical connection if the bridge was being opened, or had not been lowered properly after a river vessel had passed below.

The eastern abutment was clear of the water, and had foundations of Portland concrete, while the one next to it had to have a timber cofferdam placed in the river first, inside which the pier was built of masonry footings on top of concrete foundations. The support piers for the lifting section were large wrought-iron pillars, riveted together on staging above the river and then dropped into place. This was not without its difficulties - due to the fact that they were lowered onto a base of large boulders, they proved to be very difficult to arrange into an exactly vertical position. One had to have the brick lining removed and replaced, and eventually divers had to descend under the water level to use explosives to blast some of the boulders in order to level the pillar. A steam 'Goliath' crane was used to lower them, and when it tried to lift one back up again, the pillar had stuck in the heavy clay on the river bed. The experience this gained was put to use with the third and fourth piers, although one of these took 24 days to put exactly in the right place. Eventually, all was rectified, and attention could turn to the completion of the bridge.

The steel and ironwork for the entire structure was all sourced in England, particularly from the firm of T. Butler, Stanningley and another firm named Cochrane & Son.

Special and complex operating instructions for train operations over the bridge, the signalling arrangements, and the organisation of the lifting section were issued to all staff involved. This may be summarized as follows, the extract being taken from documentation supplied in 1894 by the manufacturer of the signals (Railway Signal Company Ltd, Fazakerley, Liverpool).

The bridge is locked in its normal position by Lever No. 3 in Corrib Swing Bridge Cabin. (This was the small signal cabin at the west end of the viaduct.) The bolt cannot be withdrawn without permission of the signalmen in Galway and Moycullen cabins.

When necessary to unlock the bridge, the Bridge Cabin signalman must inform Galway and Moycullen cabins by prearranged code on the Special Bell Circuit. Replies must arrive by the same means. Permission cannot be given if staffs have been taken out of instruments at Galway or Moycullen. Once permission has been granted to open the bridge, signals are exchanged between the three signalmen and once this results in an indicator changing to 'Unlock', the bridge signalman

The Corrib viaduct in Galway shortly after opening of the line. Following closure, the bridge was dismantled and sold for scrap, but the stone piers remain today.

(Both) Hardiman Library, NUIG

Midland Great Western Railway.

SPECIAL BELL CIRCUIT, GALWAY (CORRIB BRIDGE) & MOYCULLEN.

ELECTRIC SWITCH AT CORRIB BRIDGE, GALWAY.

INSTRUCTIONS AND CODE OF ELECTRIC BELL SIGNALS

For Electrically Locking and Unlocking the Corrib Bridge at Galway, in connection with Messrs. Webb & Thompson's Electrical Train Staff Apparatus.

The following Bell Signals are to be used on Special (Bell) Circuit, Corrib Bridge with Galway and Moycullen, when it is necessary to proceed with the operation of Opening or Closing the Bridge, thus:—

1. When a Vessel, Barge, or Boat requires to pass, the Signalman at Corrib Bridge is to send to Galway and Moycullen the Signal (three—pause—two—pause—three) 3—2—3, i.e., "I require to open Bridge."

2. Signalmen at Galway and Moycullen to repeat to Corrib Bridge in reply, the Signal 3—2—3, and if the Section is clear of Trains, they are to send to Corrib Bridge the "All Clear" Signal (two—pause—two) 2—2, which Signal must be repeated by the Signalman at Corrib Bridge, in reply. He must then give the Obstruction Signal—five beats—to Galway and Moycullen to block the Railway, which is to be repeated back; and these two Stations will give permission to unlock the Bridge, by depressing the Tapper Keys on their Staff Instruments, and continue to hold down until they receive permission from the man at the Bridge that they may release by his giving Signal (two—pause—one—pause—two), 2—1—2

3. When the man at the Bridge receives permission as above to unlock the Bridge, he must at once depress the Tapper Key on his Special Switch and watch the indicator, and when this shows "Unlocked" he must turn his Switch handle (at the same time continuing to hold down his Tapper Key) from "Locked" to "Unlocked." When the handle is turned, he must release his Tapper Key, and inform the men at Galway and Moycullen that he has done so, by sending the Signal 2—1—2, on receipt of which the men at Galway and Moycullen may then release the Tapper Keys on their Staff Instruments, and give one beat on the Special Bell Circuit in reply.

4. When the Vessel, Barge, or Boat has passed, the Signalman at Corrib Bridge will close the Bridge, and the obstruction being now removed on the Railway, give the "All Clear" Signal on both sides, which must be acknowledged by a repetition.

5. The Bridge having been restored to its normal position, and the man in the Bridge Cabin having locked the Bridge by putting back Lever No. 3 in his frame apparatus, he must at once inform the men at Galway and Moycullen, by giving the Signal (one—pause—four—pause—one) 1—4—1, "I have closed the Bridge," on receipt of which Signal, the men at Galway and Moycullen must at once depress the Tapper Keys on their Staff Instruments, and continue to hold them down until they receive the Signal 2—1—2 from the man in the Bridge Cabin, and they may then release their Tapper Keys

6. After the man in the Bridge Cabin has locked the Bridge by putting back Lever No. 3, and has informed the men at Galway and Moycullen as above of the fact, he must depress the Tapper Key on his Special Switch, and continue to hold it down until the Indicator shows "Unlocked," when he must turn his Switch Handle from "Unlocked" to "Locked," and then release his Tapper Key.

7. Communication is now restored between Galway and Moycullen, and a Staff may be released from either place, as may be required. It must be proved that Galway and Moycullen are in direct communication, by their giving to each other the "All Clear" Signal on their Train Staff Instrument.

8. Should the Electric Switch Apparatus fail to work, the nearest available Lineman may be called by the Signalmen at Corrib Bridge, giving the Auxiliary Signal (eight—pause—eight) 8—8 to Galway and Moycullen. The former will at once have the message delivered to Lineman, or telegraphed to where he may be found, the latter by telegraph or wire to Galway or elsewhere (by arrangement) and the form of the message will run thus :—

From _____ To _____

"Code 8—pause—8, received from *Corrib Bridge*. Send Lineman."

RECAPITULATION:

TO OPEN CORRIB BRIDGE.

Corrib Bridge to give to Galway & Moycullen	3—2—3	I require to open Bridge
Galway and Moycullen, to repeat this Signal	3—2—3	In reply
Galway and Moycullen to send	2—2	All Clear Signal
Corrib Bridge to repeat this Signal	2—2	In reply
Corrib Bridge to give Galway & Moycullen	5 beats	Obstruction Signal
Galway and Moycullen to repeat this Signal	5 beats	In reply

Galway and Moycullen to depress Tapper Key of Electric Staff Instruments	Hold down	This gives permission to unlock the Corrib Bridge
Corrib Bridge to depress Tapper Key on Special Switch; to watch Indicator, and when it shows *Unlocked*, to turn Switch Handle (continuing to hold down Tapper Key) from *Locked* to *Unlocked*, then release Tapper Key, and give to Galway and Moycullen the Signal ...	2—1—2	To release Tapper Key at Galway and Moycullen
Galway and Moycullen to release Tapper Keys and give on Special Bell Circuit	1 beat	In reply

TO CLOSE CORRIB BRIDGE.

Corrib Bridge to close the Bridge when boat has passed through, and give	2—2	All Clear Signal
Galway and Moycullen to repeat this Signal	2—2	" " In reply
Corrib Bridge to put back Lever No 3, and give to Galway and Moycullen	1—4—1	Corrib Bridge Locked
To depress Tapper Key on Special Switch (and continue to hold it down until Indicator shows *Unlocked*, then turn Switch Handle from *Unlocked* to *Locked*, and release his Tapper Key		
Galway and Moycullen to depress Tapper Keys on Staff Instruments until Signal 2—1—2 is received	Hold down ... 2—1—2	

Corrib Bridge to give to Galway and Moycullen	2—1—2	To release Tapper Keys
Moycullen and Galway to give ...	1 beat	In reply

When this operation is completed, it must be proved that Galway and Moycullen are in direct communication, by their giving to each other the "All Clear" Signal on their Train Staff Instrument.

BROADSTONE TERMINUS,
11th December, 1894.

JOSEPH TATLOW, Manager.

BROWNE & NOLAN, PRINTERS NASSAU-STREET, DUBLIN.

Mem: These instructions are identical with those for Shannon Bridge - Compared with it by me -
GH
14/12/94

must turn a switch handle to 'Unlocked'. When the handle is turned, he must release his tapper key and inform the other two signalmen by a prearranged signal on the Special Bell Circuit.

The effect of the man in the Swing Bridge Cabin turning his handle from 'Locked' to 'Unlocked' has been to cut the line wire between Galway and Moycullen and so prevent a staff being withdrawn from either place until communication has been restored.

On closure of the bridge, the bridge signalman would close and lock it by his lever No. 3, then inform the other two using the same signals as before. Signals confirming all moves were relayed between all three cabins and all acknowledged. At this point, communication was resumed and a staff could be removed from the instruments at Moycullen or Galway station if necessary to allow a train to pass. A lever in the bridge cabin locked the opening span, but there was further control of it from both Moycullen and Galway, both of whose signal cabins had the means to lock it electrically.

Similar procedures were observed at the substantial bridge in Athlone, where the MGWR main line crosses the River Shannon to this day.

The instructions went on,

In the normal state the Bridge is set and locked for the Railway and the electric current passes uninterruptedly through the special Switch at Corrib Swing Bridge cabin between the instruments at Galway and Moycullen.

No incidents concerning potential danger were, in consequence, ever recorded in relation to the operation of the opening span of the bridge.

Details of other bridges on the line, all of which were of conventional design, were as follows. Distances are given in miles (from Galway), as this is the standard used by all railways in Ireland. One mile equates to 1.609 kilometres.

Bridge No.	Name	Location (miles)	Description (Spans given in feet, as originally measured)
1	Forster Street, Galway	$^1/_4$	Over street, 4 spans, three of 30 ft, one of 36 ft. Wrought-iron girders.
2	Prospect Hill	$^1/_3$	'Cut and cover' tunnel, one side of which doubles as town reservoir retaining wall. Lined with brick. Situated on a slight curve. 240 ft in total (73.1 m)
3	Headford Road	$^2/_3$	Single span of just under 29 ft. Girder decking, similar to Forster Street bridge.
4	Corrib viaduct	$^3/_4$	See separate description above - 471 ft span (143.5 m).
5	Woodstock River	$4^3/_4$	Single 30 ft span over river.
6	Ballyquirk Lake Canal (Moycullen drainage canal)	$6^3/_4$	Single 40 ft span.
7	Lough Down (Moycullen)	$8^1/_8$	Single 49 ft span over a drainage canal.
8	Drimcong River	$8^1/_2$	Single 30 ft span over river.
9	Knockbane River	10	Single 23 ft span.
10	Ross Bridge (Rosscahill)	$11^3/_4$	Single 30 ft span.
11	Loughtgannon	$14^1/_8$	Single 30 ft span.
12	Owenriff River	$17^1/_8$	Single 40 ft span.
13	Lead Mines	$18^1/_8$	Single 20 ft span.
14	Glengowla River	$19^1/_8$	Single 40 ft span.
15	Garribaldi River	$19^3/_8$	Single 30 ft span (origin of name uncertain! 'Garri' could come from the Irish word for garden).
15A	Leam River	$20^3/_8$	Single 20 ft span (sometimes quoted as 30 ft).
16	Letterfore River	$22^3/_4$	Single 20 ft span.
17	Bunscanniff River	$28^1/_2$	Single 23 ft span.
18	Bunscanniff Road	$28^3/_4$	Carries main Galway to Clifden road over railway. Masonry construction with arch edged with Bridgwater Brick. Span not recorded.
19	Boheshal River	c. 30	Single 20 ft span.
20	Derryneen River	$32^1/_8$	Single 30 ft span.

Bridge No.	Name	Location (miles)	Description (Spans given in feet, as originally measured)
21	Lissoughter River	33¹/₈	Single 30 ft span.
22	Weir	35³/₄	Single 30 ft span, immediately west of Recess station, near Derryclare Lake.
23	Athry River	37³/₄	Small river bridge, single 20 ft span.
24	Cloonbeg River (Ballynahinch)	40³/₄	Two spans each 50 ft; design similar to spans on on Corrib viaduct.
25	Monga (Munga) Ravine	?	Described in tender as 'Monga Ravine Viaduct'. Same construction as No. 24, except it was planned with three 50 ft spans rather than two. No mileage given.
26	Gowlan (Road Bridge)	46¹/₄	Similar to No. 18; carries main road over railway. Road had to be slightly diverted in order to build it. Span not recorded.
27	Clifden Glen (Road Bridge)	46³/₄	Carries road over railway. Road diverted to avoid having to provide a level crossing. Single span of 17 ft 8 in. on square.
28	Owenglen River (Clifden)	48³/₈	Single 49 ft span, similar to No. 24.
29	Mill Race (Galway)		Located in the townland of Newcastle, west of Corrib viaduct in Galway. Bridges are numbered in order, starting at the Galway end. However, this bridge, despite being numbered 29, was at the start of the line, just west of the Corrib viaduct; this suggests it was a late addition to the tender. It is not known whether it was re-numbered in correct sequence once built, or indeed if it was numbered at all. In the tender document, its planned design is described as being under 'Culverts and Drains'.

Eight of the above were of skewed construction: Nos. 3, 7, 14, 20, 21, 25, 27 and 28. In addition, 13 small accommodation bridges were provided over and under the railway line at various points for the convenience of local landowners. Most were of a standard 12 ft single-span design, with iron tops, and masonry abutments like the larger bridges. Several underbridges remain, the most visible of which is Bridge No. 22 (known as the Weir bridge) just on the Clifden side of Recess station.

Corrib viaduct at low tide, *circa* 1900.   *Hardiman Library, NUIG*

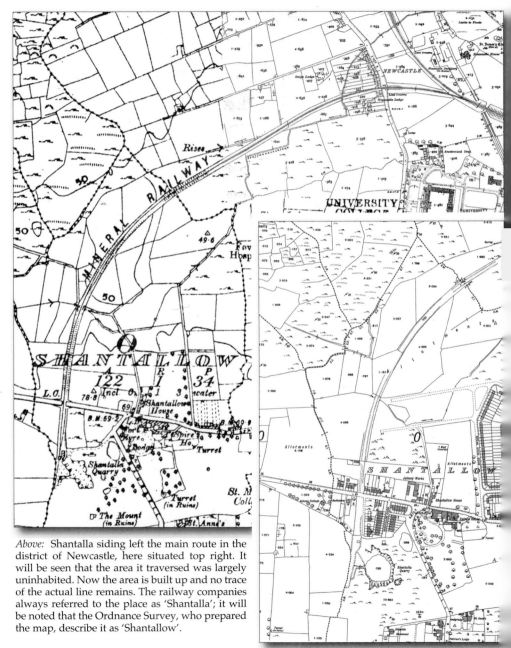

Above: Shantalla siding left the main route in the district of Newcastle, here situated top right. It will be seen that the area it traversed was largely uninhabited. Now the area is built up and no trace of the actual line remains. The railway companies always referred to the place as 'Shantalla'; it will be noted that the Ordnance Survey, who prepared the map, describe it as 'Shantallow'.

Inset: The route of the Shantalla Quarry siding. No track is shown, though the line formation is; this would date the map to just after the siding was lifted, as the area was redeveloped within a short space of time.

Appendix Three

The Shantalla siding

West of Galway city, a number of quarries operated before the railway was ever built. Some had been largely worked out by the time it was built, but one large operation was based at Shantalla Quarry, just south of where the modern day Galway University is located. The stone produced there was described as being 'of a very fine mottled red or pink colour, with very pleasing green shades through it, which can weather in any climate'. Initially, much of the output of the quarry was taken into Galway station where the wagons would be attached to the Galway-Clifden train for onward transit to the Marble Works. At its greatest extent, the quarry occupied a site of some 13 acres, situated where Maunsell's Park is today.

However, some information has survived showing that, in 1912, a year after the siding was opened, the Galway Harbour Commissioners were pursuing a plan to create a deepwater port at Barna, just west of Galway City on the coast. The purpose of this was to attract traffic from transatlantic mail and passenger shipping. The Commissioners thus formally proposed this, in conjunction with Directors of the MGWR. The line would have been some four miles in length, leaving the Clifden branch at Newcastle and travelling through the district of Knocknacarra to a newly built harbour facility at Lenarevagh. Despite having been submitted for Parliamentary approval, the scheme was not proceeded with due to the extremely high costs involved with construction of the harbour.

However, along what would have become the route of this line was the quarry of the Galway Granite & Marble Works which had been opened in 1900 on the site of an earlier quarrying operation dating back to the early 1880s. The attractive marbled stone had been discovered in the late 1800s by a man named Miller, who soon had 20 men employed digging these stones up and polishing them for ornamental use. By degrees a significant quarrying operation built up.

In order to tap at least some of this traffic, a 1½ mile-long line was built to serve this quarry in 1911 at a cost of £2,000. This took the form of a short branch line, simply known as the Shantalla siding. It was connected to the main line just west of the Corrib viaduct in the townland of Newcastle from where it immediately crossed the Newcastle Road before heading due south to the quarry. It was protected by an Annett's Lock key on the Galway-Moycullen staff. The Shantalla Quarry itself had three openings, in the 13 acres or so now occupied by Maunsell's Park.

The MGWR placed a contract with the quarry for over half a million tons of granite ballast for various locations on their system. Unfortunately it was to be a very short-lived operation; the quarry would close within 10 years or so. After the quarry (and a local jail) closed, the quarry was filled in using rubble from the jail. This was to prevent local people drowning in the former quarry, which had now filled up with water.

Operating regulations for the siding were as follows, as this extract from a 1920 *Working Time Table* shows. By this stage, little or no traffic was actually using it:

ARRANGEMENTS FOR THE WORKING OF SHANTALLA QUARRY SIDING, GALWAY
This siding is connected with the Clifden Branch Line, and the points are locked with an 'Annett's Key' on the Staffs for the Galway and Moycullen section.
When the Wagons require to be sent to or from the Quarry, they must be worked by the Galway Shunting Engine, and must be hauled*, the Engine being in front, and a Brake Van in rear for the use of the Guard.
The Siding crosses two public roads, the gates of which are locked with padlocks, and the keys are kept in the custody of the Station Master in Galway, who will give them to the Guard of the Train

before leaving the Station for the Quarry. The train must come to a dead stop before reaching the crossing gates and before latter are opened, to let the Train pass through, care must be taken to stop the traffic on the public road, and for this purpose a Porter must be sent along with the Guard, and one of them will stand on each side of the gates exhibiting a Red Flag until the Train has passed through and the gates are once again locked across the Siding.

Any wagons left in the Siding must be placed in the one at the Quarry† and the points locked.

The Ballast Train will, when required, use this Siding, and the Guard and Ganger will be responsible for the observance of the above instructions.

The Siding must only be used during daylight.#

---

* As opposed to being propelled; while normal in shunting procedures, this would have been too long a trip to involve the locomotive pushing the wagons, with attendant limited visibility. There seems to be no evidence of a run-round loop in the quarry, so it is probable that wagons were shunted by gravity or by horse haulage within the quarry limits in order to place the locomotive at the other end prior to being hauled out again.

† There were at least two sidings at the end of this short branch line.

This appears to have been due to potential danger to road traffic as the train crossed the Newcastle Road, and to railway staff entering the quarry in poor light.

The quarry appears to have ceased operating about 1921, though regular (if not all) rail traffic appears to only have lasted until 1914. The siding fell gradually in disuse after this as a result. The MGWR's management certainly queried why it was still in place as early as 1921, so it is possible that not very much stone had traversed it for some years before that. Certainly, by the time the siding was removed in July/August 1926, it was described by the GSR's Engineer as 'having been in disuse for many years'. No trace of it remains as the entire area of both the siding and the quarry has been completely redeveloped since. It may be taken, however, that the route of the line corresponded closely with the modern Seamus Quirke Road. Just before the quarry closed, a rumour circulated to the effect that the Government was planning to reopen it, but this was not true.

Appendix Four

Tourism and the Recess Hotel

One of the original ideas behind the construction of the railway was its potential benefit to the tourist industry in the area. And so it proved: in the line's first season tourists began to visit Clifden by train. The MGWR already served a number of places which were popular destinations for the holidaymaker, Galway itself being one, and the company was already publishing annual tourist guide books. These were extremely detailed and gave much information about what was to be seen in each area. The 1896 copy was quick to add Clifden and its charms to this guide, quaintly saying: 'There will not be any difference of opinion as to the benefit to the traveller effected by the opening of this extension to the MGWR system'.

The virtues of the local scenery, fishing and hotel accommodation were extolled at length and details of the connecting road coach service to Westport were included, showing how the tourist could take the train to Clifden, then travel onwards via Killary Harbour and Leenane, some of the most spectacular, rugged and unspoilt countryside anywhere in Ireland. At Westport, conveniently, was the MGWR's other recently opened scenic line, that from there to Newport, Mallaranny and Achill. The MGWR had other hotels in Galway and at Mallaranny, and this could be incorporated into all-in package holidays. The Achill line itself traversed beautiful countryside as it skirted the northern side of Clew Bay. The much refurbished Mallaranny hotel is still in use, despite a period of closure in the 1990s, though it has long since left railway ownership.

With immediate effect the MGWR began to issue 'tourist tickets' which included train and coach fares. This suited everybody except the coach drivers, who depended on tips from their passengers, as the coach fare had already been paid by the MGWR to the coach proprietor. By 1906, the railway was granting a subsidy of £135, plus a commission on tickets sold, to Mr R. McKeown of Leenane.

Local drivers of horse-drawn cars would meet trains at various stations, and it was not long before the MGWR agreed to provide shelters for their horses at Ballynahinch and Recess, the latter involving horses owned by the local hotelier. Not all tourists, however, went solely to these places - in 1900 a cycle shed was erected at Clifden station for the benefit of local people and tourists alike, at a cost of £35.

In January 1896, the MGWR made its first proposals for a new hotel at Recess. They sought an existing property, that of a Col Whittle near the station, while a Mr Pyle of Clifden offered a house and lands there as an alternative. Later that year, Whittle's property had been bought. The tenants who managed it were given notice to leave at the end of the season, and the MGWR engaged the well-known Dublin architect, Thomas Deane, to draw up plans for alterations and extensions of the building. By June 1897 almost £2,500 had been spent, with a further £7,400 to follow in two stages.

Now that the hotel was nearing completion, a Miss Gorton was to be transferred from Mallaranny as the manageress, her place taken by a Miss Kilsby from Strabane in Co. Tyrone. Miss Gorton's annual salary was increased from £75 to £100. Almost as an afterthought, a phone was installed in April to connect the hotel with the railway station. On 11th May, 1898 the hotel opened and proved to be a great success immediately. The Mallaranny Hotel was opened in the same year and both were managed by a small committee, which in 1899 felt influential enough to suggest various train timetable alterations for the benefit of the hotel and its guests.

Once the hotel was open, Richard Berridge offered to sell shooting rights to the MGWR for some of his lands in the area for the benefit of tourists, but the company declined his offer. The company was also considering letting the hotel to somebody else to operate and manage, but decided against it.

FRONT ELEVATION

SCALE

INCH

20 FT

Old Great Western Railway Hotel Recess Co. Galway

SIDING AT RECESS HOTEL PLATFORM.

The above Siding will be used exclusively for traffic to and from the Company's Hotel when sent in such quantities as to necessitate the use of separate wagons.

The following instructions in regard to the working must be strictly observed :—

(1) The Points leading into this Siding are locked by means of an Annett's Lock, the key of which is attached to the Train Staff for the Maam Cross-Recess Section.

(2) The Siding will be worked when required by the Down Trains.

(3) The wagons must be placed next Rear Brake Van so as to ensure that the operation of running them into the Siding will be performed as expeditiously as possible.

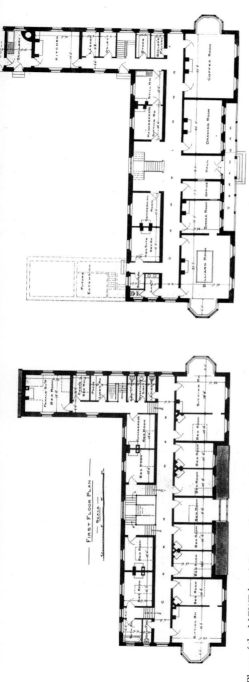

FIRST FLOOR PLAN

Plans of the MGWR hotel, Recess. The layout is interesting, and scarcely believable to a modern hotel guest. There appears to be a single gentlemen's toilet, and a single ladies one, plus another on the ground floor, for the entire guest accommodation. For all staff, one was provided. None contain a wash hand basin. Hand washing was done back in the guest's room, where a jug of water and bowl were provided, and replaced each day. There was no such thing in those days as an *en suite* bedroom, nor were there even wash hand basins in rooms. Servants emptied them and refilled the jugs. There appears to be sufficient bed space for 14 guests, all of whom had to share one bathroom. The servants and staff had none; a room labelled 'Housemaid's Sink' was for washing bed sheets and linen. The 'female servants' shared an average-sized room with three beds, while the 'men servants' room was considerably smaller, and may therefore have contained bunks. The cook had a bedroom, but no other staff had, other than the manageress. She was catered for in comparative luxury, as she would live on the premises all through the season, she had a sitting room and bedroom as well as a room with washing facilities. There was no bar, and no room is labelled as 'dining room', which seems unusual. It might be assumed that the room described as 'coffee room' also served as a dining room or breakfast room. Evenings could be spent in the 'drawing room' (typically by lady guests) and the billiard room (typically by men). The 'smoking room' would doubtless also have been primarily for men. Daytime meetings could be held in a 'commercial room'. The two upstairs sitting rooms appear to be connected to bedrooms as well as having separate doors into the corridor. These two bedroom at opposite ends of the building may be taken as the 'suites', in which hotel guests might receive their own visitors. All but one of the bedrooms had open fires, the middle one being the exception. This room offers some puzzles, as it has no means of heating at all, but also has the large window in the centre of the building occupying almost all of one side of it. It should be remembered that in those days there was no central heating, cavity wall insulation or double glazing. A guest staying here on a cool night would only have extra blankets, and possibly a hot water bottle, to keep him warm. It will be seen that provision was made for future extension of the building as a "west wing"; details of what this might have contained are not to hand.

(All) Author's Collection

RECESS HOTEL&GOLF.W.A.Y. 7355 W.L.

The stretch of line between Recess station and the Hotel Platform Halt about 1900. The hotel may be seen in the distance. The rough stone surface of the
Laurence Collection/National Library of Ireland

Two views of the Railway Hotel shortly after it opened, complete with croquet lawn for its well-heeled guests. No trace of the hotel remains. *NUIG*

The outside of Clifden station about 1911 with the MGWR's tourist bus getting ready to leave. It is likely that this is following the arrival of the 'Tourist Express', with the bus taking its passengers onwards to Westport for transmission by train to the company's hotel at Mallaranny, on the Westport-Achill line. Compare this photogrpaghj to the image top of page 145.
Lawrence Collection/National Library of Ireland

An MGWR tourist bus approaches Recess hotel (in the distance) about 1911. This may be compared with the view on page 170 from approximately the same spot just over a decade earlier.
Lawrence Collection/National Library of Ireland

In 1902, the company arranged with Mr Arnold, of Ballynahinch, for his boats to be brought to Recess - the MGWR would arrange transport. They were to be moored near the hotel on the shore of the lake for the use of hotel guests. In order to assist guests at the hotel and the supply of goods and staff transport, a new request stop was built in 1902 just opposite the hotel entrance where the railway passed. This consisted of a short platform and shelter, though a short siding was added in 1922 for unloading wagons. This siding did not see much use, as the hotel was burned down and the halt abandoned shortly afterwards.

In summer 1903, the MGWR embarked on a new venture, the 'Tourist Train'. This service was designed to carry tourists and first class passengers in hitherto unknown comfort the whole way from Dublin to Clifden and back. The locomotives and coaching stock used on this service were painted in a bold new livery, the locomotives being royal blue with elaborate lining, and the coaches blue and white, with gold lettering. This livery did not wear well, unfortunately, and stock thus painted gradually reverted to the normal lined green for locomotives, and mid-brown for coaches. The Tourist Train was well advertised, and carried a dining car, the only such service on the MGWR system at the time. The MGWR had now started publishing tour guides to the areas it served. These contained train timetables, hotel details, and comprehensive historical and geographical descriptions of the areas through which their lines ran. They were liberally illustrated with scenic photographs from the areas served. The hotels at Recess and Mallaranny featured prominently, and among other things advertised that they had electric light in all rooms; not at all common in these days. In July 1903, King Edward and his entourage landed at Killary Harbour and travelled by motorcade to Recess Hotel, where they stayed overnight, before travelling by train back to Dublin the following day. Now the area became ever more popular with the rich and famous, and the landed gentry, many of whom owned fishing lodges in the area and who would arrive to indulge in recreational river and lake fishing for their summer holidays. One family built themselves a temporary platform at the side of the line just outside Clifden, and occasional unscheduled stops were made there for them.

Significant improvements were made to the hotel in 1904, due to increasing seasonal popularity. More electric lighting was installed throughout, covering areas not previously lit at a cost of £154, and several extra bedrooms were added above the dining room. Following an inspection by the General Manager of the railway, he observed that there weren't enough pictures on the walls, nor postcards available for guests. In these times, production of postcards or photographic illustrations of anything related to the Irish countryside were dominated by the output of the firm of William Lawrence, a commercial photographer in Dublin. The MGWR postcards bear many of his views, and in fact his collection has survived, now in the care of the National Photographic Archive in Dublin. Many of the illustrations in this book of the early days of the railway are Lawrence images.

The 1904 season ended on a high note on 15th October, with newer facilities and a healthy patronage. Many Irish country hotels tended in these times to close at the end of the summer season, though the Mallaranny one remained open all winter in some seasons. In the case of Recess, mid to late October was usually the closure date.

In 1906, a 'motor car house' was provided at the hotel, reflecting the growing phenomenon of wealthy guests arriving by road, few as these would have been. As the tourism trade developed, in 1910 the company decided to replace its long-standing horse-drawn tourist carriages with motorized ones. Three vehicles were ordered and ready for the 1911 season. These were petrol-engined open charabancs, numbered IM 179-181, and each carried 15 first class passengers. The cost, including delivery, for all three was £1,694. Garages were built at Clifden and Westport for stabling them - they would commence operations between the two towns, via Leenane. Their first operation was 1st June, 1911, running to timetable as follows (*page 177*):

MGWR advertisement extolling the virtues of holidays in the West of Ireland. Free fishing was offered Recess; this had resulted from the purchase of local fishing rights by the company. It will be seen from wording that this advertisement was primarily aimed at wealthy English tourists. *(All) Author's Colle*

Midland Great Western Railway of Ireland.

CONNEMARA, GALWAY, ACHILL & THE WEST.

Circular Tour Tickets from Dublin

Issued from DUBLIN (Broadstone Station) embracing Galway, Recess, Clifden, Letterfrack, Leenane, Westport, Mallaranny, and Achill, including Coupons for the Tourist Car between Clifden and Westport, and between Achill Station and Dugort. Reduced Fares for Parties of Two to Four Passengers. Extra Coupons issued for Extended Tours from Dublin (Broadstone) to the North and South of Ireland.

Tourist Tickets from England and Scotland

Are issued during the Tourist Season at the principal Stations in England and Scotland, and at the Offices of the Steam Packet Companies and Tourist Agencies, for Connemara and Achill.

Week-End Excursion Tickets

Are issued on Saturdays, First, Second, and Third Class, at Reduced Fares, from Broadstone to Galway, Recess, Clifden, Westport, Mallaranny, Achill, &c., available for return up to the last Train on the following Tuesday evenings. These Tickets are not available by the Down and Up Limited Mails.

Cycling in Connemara and Achill.

Tourists can take train to Achill, Mallaranny, or Westport, and cycle thence to Galway, via Louisburgh, Dhulough, Delphi, Leenane, Letterfrack, Clifden, Recess, and Oughterard, returning to Dublin by train; or take train to Galway and cycle up to Westport and Achill, returning to Dublin by train. Cycle Tours can also be made from Railway Hotel, Recess, up the Inagh Valley to Kylemore, Letterfrack, Leenane, thence to Clonbur, or from Recess to Cashel, Roundstone, Clifden, and back to Recess via Ballynahinch. From Mallaranny Hotel Tourists can cycle or take train to Achill, and spend the day on the Island, visiting Dugort, which is 9 miles from the Station. The roads throughout Connemara and the West of Ireland are excellent for cycling. Bicycles carried by Rail as Passengers' Luggage:—Up to 50 miles, 6d.; 100 miles, 9d.; 150 miles, 1s. (owner's risk.) Breakfast and Dining Cars run between Dublin and Galway per Down and Up Limited Mail Trains.

Tourist Cars run from June 1st to September 30th between Clifden and Westport, passing through Letterfrack for Renvyle, Kylemore, and Leenane; and from 1st July till 30th September the Midland Great Western Railway Co.'s Tourist Cars will run between Achill and Dugort, distance 9 miles. Fare, 2/6. Steamers ply on Galway Bay, during the Tourist Season, to Aran Islands, to Ballyvaughan, and also on Lough Corrib.

Application for Time Tables, New Illustrated Tourist Guide to Connemara (price 6d.), Tourist Programmes, and information as to Fares, Routes, and Hotels, &c., may be made to the Co.'s Agents, Mr. J. Hoey, 50, Castle-street, Liverpool and Mr. J. F. Ritson, 180, Buchanan-street, Glasgow; or to the Superintendent of Line, Broadstone, Dublin.

JOSEPH TATLOW, Manager.

Broadstone Station, Dublin.

The Railway Hotel in Clifden was not actually part of the railway establishment. Many towns had a 'Railway Hotel', however. This one was in the centre of the town. The advertisement gives a good idea of what a well-heeled traveller might expect about 1900, from which time this advertisement dates. Some advertisements of the day refer to the town as 'Clifden-on-Sea', implying miles of golden beaches in the town, which was not the case!

		pm			*pm*
Clifden	*dep.*	1.30	Westport	*dep.*	1.55
Letterfrack	*dep.*	2.29	Leenane	*dep.*	4.55 (approx.)
Leenane	*dep.*	3.30	Letterfrack	*dep.*	5.55 (approx.)
Westport	*arr.*	6.30	Clifden	*arr.*	6.55

The Clifden departure was timed to meet the incoming Limited Mail train from Galway and Dublin. In 1911/12, these coach services were extended to serve Recess and Mallaranny Hotels as well, and as a result garages were built for these vehicles at each hotel. After a few years, a car for local use was provided at Recess, in which guests could be given lifts to local places by arrangement. Mallaranny hotel received another.

A further improvement had been the complete redecoration of the hotel in time for the 1908 season. With tourists beginning to bring their own cars now, the sale of petrol ('motor spirit') was commenced from both hotels from September 1909.

In July 1911, the hotel gardener asked the company for a gun with which to control rabbits. The request was granted on the condition that he was to understand that the gun was strictly railway company property!

In August 1914, World War I broke out, and fuel shortages were acute as a result. The railways were placed under Government control and the tourist car services were suspended indefinitely from 1st September. Lights were not to be used unless necessary, and fires were not to be lit with coal, except in railway station waiting rooms in exceptionally cold weather. Coal was also rationed in the hotel which did what it could to bring in supplies of local wood and turf to maintain heat (and cooking!) in the building.

By 1918, wartime inflation had eaten into pay scales, and the hotel manageress had her salary increased to £200 per annum, plus £25 for managing the fishing rights and activities associated with the hotel guests. Richard Berridge and the MGWR entered into legal agreements whereby the former leased fishing rights to the latter, and thereby the hotel customers, for nine years at an annual rent of £50. A separate agreement under these terms existed for both Ballynahinch Fishery and for Lough Inagh.

In July 1919, the railway management discussed the purchase of extensive grounds in the hotel estate from Mr Berridge. They obtained a valuation of £3,500, but only offered him £3,000. Berridge said that he would sell for £5,000, which the MGWR declined. He later offered it for £4,500, but the company was not interested in this price. Berridge subsequently changed his mind anyway, so it became a moot point.

Between 1915 and 1919, the cars and coaches owned by the company were replaced by newer models; all was looking good. A lorry for carrying turf for hotel heating fuel was acquired in 1920. By 1921, the external Great War had ended, but the internal War of Independence was in full swing, and the Connemara area was not to escape unscathed. Apart from the incidents mentioned elsewhere in relation to attacks on the railway line, the life of Recess Railway Hotel was to come to an abrupt end on the morning of 6th October, 1922, when the Irregulars* burned it to the ground, having given staff and guests half an hour to vacate the premises. The building was destroyed and what was left had to be demolished completely. Another nearby hotel was also destroyed. The reason for this destruction was to prevent the military using such places as local headquarters. A windmill at Recess was severely damaged at the same time - this was used for pumping water. It is unclear whether the damage was weather related or a by-product of the burning of the hotel, but the MGWR repaired it for possible use elsewhere.

All that was left for the MGWR to do was to claim compensation, which they finally received in June 1925, when the Government agreed to pay £16,670 5s. 8d. in full and final settlement. As mentioned earlier, the company had claimed £50,000 compensation. Recess railway station would remain open for primarily local use until the line was closed in 1935. With the demise of the hotel, its dedicated Hotel Platform Halt also fell into disuse, though some remains of it may be seen to this day.

---

* The 'Irregulars' were a semi-militarised force sent by the British to quell nationalist activity in 1919/20.

Some figures have survived which show samples of how many tourists visited the MGWR's Recess and Mallaranny hotels. These were compiled by taking one week from each of the following months:

In one week in the month of	Recess	Mallaranny
Sep. 1898	42	93
Jul. 1902	54	58
Aug. 1904	74	129
Apr. 1905	14	31
Oct. 1908	3	11
Oct. 1909	6	12
Oct. 1910	20	29
Oct. 1911	17	10

Mallaranny Hotel was significantly larger than that at Recess. While most of the above figures relate to off-season periods, and were probably gathered to examine the viability of keeping the hotel open very early or late in each season, it will be seen that summer figures in 1902-04 were very respectable.

In terms of tourism, probably the most famous person to use the line was an Indian gentleman, the Maharajah of Nawanagar. His name was Ranjitsinji, and he was also a famous cricketer. In 1924 he purchased Ballynahinch Castle and extensive lands around it, and spent frequent holidays in the area as he was a keen fisherman and many local lakes had salmon in them. His arrival at Ballynahinch was a colourful and memorable event, with his Indian staff - servants and cooks - all arriving with him, and placing fire crackers along the line to welcome him as his train approached the station.

CLIFDEN.

RAILWAY HOTEL,
Clifden-on-Sea.
CONNEMARA.

Every comfort and convenience. Bath Rooms. Billiard Room. Certified Sanitation. Moderate Terms. Magnificent Walks and Drives. Invigorating Atlantic Breezes. Lake and Sea Fishing. Good Rough Shooting. The Marconi Wireless Station is within one mile from from Hotel.

Address, Manageress.

Appendix Five

Traffic Statistics 1929

In 1929/1930, the GSR undertook a detailed analysis of the financial position of lines known to be likely loss makers. Galway-Clifden came under scrutiny, and the following figures give a very interesting picture of how the line was then used. They may be taken as reasonably typical for the GSR era. Six days were picked during each of the three summer months, with a census taken of passengers travelling on the line. The first thing that strikes us is that the passenger traffic was very much heavier leaving Galway, than leaving Clifden. This suggests that many people found other means to get into Galway during the day, but used the train to go home. This could be related in some cases to local people accompanying goods or livestock they planned to sell in Galway by road, and returning by train. However, the first train each day left Galway on five occasions out of 18 without a single passenger, and never with more than seven. The largest number recorded in a day was 161 - a very respectable number - on the 6.50 pm down train on 31st August. This was exceptional, and thus probably due to some special event, but the two preceding Saturday evening trains also had large numbers. It may be taken, therefore, that in summer months, a single train in one direction, once a week, was the only one carrying a reasonable payload. In winter, the situation was much worse, as no tourists would be among them. Unfortunately for the railway, it seemed that as far as passenger traffic was concerned, a bus was normally sufficient to cover all services except one single journey per week!

By this stage, while first and third class were both available on trains (second having been abolished in 1914), few passengers used first class.

Passengers carried on each train on selected dates, summer 1929

	Leaving Galway – Down trains			Leaving Clifden – Up trains		
June 1929	7.40 am	11.05 am	6.50 pm	7.35 am	12.20 pm	5.40 pm
3rd	2	35	26	6	9	9
4th	2	14	22	2	10	5
5th	3	12	34	9	6	7
6th	-	7	22	3	5	8
7th	1	9	27	7	4	-
8th	-	42	117	6	26	34
July 1929						
15th	4	29	47	5	13	4
16th	6	34	56	3	7	40
17th	5	25	41	8	9	3
18th	6	20	20	6	7	8
19th	-	18	88	11	8	12
20th	-	31	147	9	20	40
August 1929						
26th	7	20	27	3	10	17
27th	4	22	35	8	9	5
28th	6	17	60	3	12	13
29th	4	16	15	3	9	8
30th	4	9	30	4	12	14
31st	-	56	161	7	42	31

Appendix Six

Some staffing details

Some details have survived relating to staffing levels on the line. A modern railway is organized with as much automation as possible, but in the past railway operation was labour intensive. At various times the staff shown below were employed on the line although this is by no means a complete list of all staff. It is simply reproduced in case it may be of interest to some. A complete record of staff employed on the Clifden line has not survived. In addition, in the case of locomotive drivers, firemen and train crews it should be borne in mind that some are likely to have worked in from Galway and Athlone, and on days of special trains probably other places too. For those researching the careers of ancestors, it must be borne in mind that a driver based in Galway may never have driven to Clifden - many Galway drivers spent their entire careers on trains to Dublin, Tuam, or other points east. Equally, a driver or other member of staff who is known to have traversed the line on at least one occasion may have been based elsewhere, possibly some distance away, and only visited the line once when providing relief cover for a regular on the line.

A typical rural railway station would have had a full staffing of a station master, with the following staff under him: booking office clerk, goods office clerk, one-two signalmen (one on duty at any one time); foreman, one-three porters, often 'junior staff' boys aged between 14 and 18. Milesman, gangers and permanent way staff - possibly a permanent way gang based at the station, responsible for daily inspections of track over a defined stretch of line. A permanent way inspector might also have his office in a station where a track gang was based.

If a terminus, e.g. Clifden, a steam raiser, locomotive cleaner, one-two drivers and fireman, and train guards. If a large or important station, e.g. Galway, an inspector and other clerical staff might be based there.

The following is a list of known employees on the line. Galway station has been excluded as (a) no meaningful record survives, and (b) the majority of the staff based in Galway would not have worked on the Clifden line.

Name	Position	Dates known	Notes
All stations			
Michael Foley	Manager's Office	Early 1900s	Visited stations regarding personnel matters. Native of Farranfore, Co. Kerry.
Moycullen			
? Wisdom	Station master	1895-1900	Probably transferred from elsewhere when line opened.
? McDonnell	Station master	1900-1905	
? Stewart	Station master	1905-????	
? Murray	Station master	At closure	
? Burke (Rineen)	Gatekeeper/milesman	1896	Gatekeepers/milesmen were based at the nearest station.
P. Cranny	Gatekeeper	1903	
H. Bristley	Station master	1892	Salary £200 pa.
O. Perry	Station master	?	Salary £170 pa.
G. Peters	Station master	1898	Transferred from Ross, 1924. Subsequently transferred to Carrick-on-Shannon, Co. Leitrim. Salary £200 pa.

Name	Position	Dates known	Notes
Ross			
Michael McHugh	Station master	1901	Native of Dublin.
William Nolan	Station master	c.1905-1911	Native of Roscommon.
? McKeown	Station master	At closure	
John Harris (& wife Mary)	Railway policeman	1901	Natives of Wicklow. Mary was probably the gatekeeper as they lived in the gatehouse at Killaguile, a mile from Ross in the Oughterard direction.
Michael Joyce (& wife Mary)	Linesman	1911	Listed as living in same Killaguile gatehouse in 1911; Mary was probably the successor to Mary Harris (above). Natives of Oughterard.
G. Peters	Station master	1898	Salary £180 pa; increased to £200 in 1923. Transferred to Moycullen 1924.
W. Kavanagh	Station master	1924	Salary £180 pa.
Oughterard			
? Hackett	Porter	c.1908	
? Murray	Station master	At closure	
Francis McGuinness	Porter	1900	
Patrick McLoughlin	Porter	1896	Probably from opening of line.
James Malone	Porter	1896	Probably from opening of line.
W. O'Gara	Station master	1895	On opening of line; probably transferred from elsewhere.
Joseph Monaghan	Foreman	1895	On opening of line; probably transferred from elsewhere.
P. Smallholme	Station master	1899	Salary £200 pa 1920-3.
James Potts	Station master	1893	Salary £200 pa.
Maam Cross			
? Kelly	Boy porter	1900	'Boy' = junior, c.14/15 years old.
? Gerrard	Station master	At closure	
? Conneely	Gate keeper	1896	To Moycullen by 1904.
? Keavy	Station master	Early 1900s	
? Coghlan	Station master	Early 1900s	
J. Kelly	Station master	1899	Salary £200 pa.
Recess			
Michael Kelly	Porter	1896	
? Kelly	Station master	At closure	
Thomas Tobin	Porter	1896	
? Plunkett	Signlaman/porter	1905	Junior signalling position. A station of this size would not warrant a full time signalman, so the signalman/porter was expected to assist with general station duties in between trains.
? Goslin	Gatekeeper	1896	
M. Sullivan	Station master	1911	Salary £170 pa, increased to £200 in 1921.
J. Griffin	Station master	1921	Salary £200 pa in 1923.
Ballynahinch			
? Mahoney	Station master	At closure	Previously Clifden.

Name	Position	Dates known	Notes
Clifden			
P.J. Lambe	Driver	1895	Transferred from elsewhere on opening of line. A driver would have previously worked up the ranks from cleaner and fireman.
Robert Copperwhite	Driver	1895	Ditto.
James Connolly	Driver	1896	Ditto.
Edward Stankard	Foreman	1935	May have opened Stankard's newsagents in the town
Michael Grogan	Station master	At closure	Replaced Mahoney, see Ballynahinch
John Dwyer	Porter	1896	
G. McKeown	Porter	1896	
G. Fury	Porter	1896	
? Ward	Porter	1896	
B. Grogan	Porter	1896	
P. Smallhorne	Goods clerk	1905	
? Toole	Milesman	1905	Lyons' Crossing
(Mrs) ? Hussey	Gatekeeper	1896	Bunnakyle Crossing
Unknown location (some based at Galway)			
William Blackmore	Driver	1895-1903	Employed as driver within this period. Some or all were probably drivers outside this period too and are likely to have been transferred into the area from elsewhere when the line opened.
John McClean	Driver	1895-1903	Ditto.
J. Maguire	Driver	1895-1903	Ditto.
P. Morrisey	Driver	1895-1903	Ditto.
Owen McIntyre	Driver	1895-1903	Ditto.
(?) Banks	Driver	1895-1903	Ditto.
(?) Forbes	Driver	1895-1903	Ditto.
(?) Corley	Driver	1895-1903	Ditto.
Patrick Clavin	Guard	1896	
(?) Reap	Guard	c.1904	
James Mooney	Guard	c.1904	
J. Horan	Guard	c.1904	
(?) McGlynn	Guard	c.1904	
(?) Jennings	Inspector	1896	Probably based in Galway.
(?) Conway	Inspector	1905	Probably based in Galway.
(?) Kelly	Ganger	1909	Track maintenance.
(?) Mullarney	Porter	1909	
John Kerrigan	Foreman	c.1898	
J. Shine	Shunter	1900	
(?) Browne	Painter	1900	
P.J. Rourke	Station master	1908	Possibly Galway; salary £230 pa in 1920.
J. Finnegan	Station master	?	Salary £210 pa in 1924.
P. Halfpenny	Clerk	1914	Salary £120 pa in 1920.
J.J. Kelly	Clerk	1915	Salary £140 p.a. in 1920.
S.G. Cunningham	Clerk	1920	Salary £120 p.a. in 1924.
P.K. Brady	Clerk	1919	Salary £170 p.a. in 1924.

For those interested in tracing family history, the archives of the Irish Railway Record Society in Dublin contain much of the surviving information on the careers of former railwaymen. They are listed according to surname and may be consulted by arrangement with the society.

Appendix Seven

The Ulster & Connaught Light Railway

In 1905, one of the more unusual railway proposals ever made in Ireland involved a main 3 ft gauge line running from Clifden to Shrule, where one branch would run north to Ballinrobe, and another south to Galway, before continuing up towards Co Leitrim. There, an end-on connection would be made with the Cavan and Leitrim Railway, from whose far end this meandering 'main line' would proceed towards Co. Tyrone, connecting into the Clogher Valley Railway (CVR) in a similar fashion. At the far end of the CVR, the railway would head for the south Armagh town of Keady, where it would pass under the Great Northern Railway's (GNR) Armagh-Castleblayney line through a short tunnel, before heading eastwards through Newry and on to Greenore in Co. Louth.

This scheme was bizarre even by the standards of the day but is worth repeating both for that, and the fact that it managed to have an Act of Parliament passed to authorise most of its construction. The impetus came from the other end of the line, as in 1899 a company called the Newry, Keady & Tynan Light Railway applied for powers to build the stretch between these three places and Greenore, from where ferries operated to England. Even this short section was circuitous, and the only local benefit was the connection of the Clogher Valley with the Bessbrook & Newry Tramway, itself likely to have become part of this route. Even a connection such as this would have connected no place of significance with port facilities at Newry. The Newry-Greenore section was proposed as a dual gauge section of the 5 ft 3 in. gauge Dundalk, Newry & Greenore Railway. Ambitious as even this local project was, the Act authorising its construction was

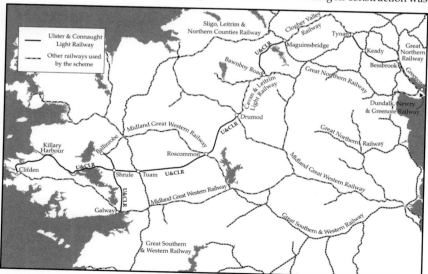

Map of the proposed route of the Ulster & Connaught Light Railway, probably the most far-fetched of many ideas to bring the railway to Clifden. From coast to coast, this line would have avoided virtually every centre of population within reasonable reach of its route!

finally passed in 1900, with an extension granted in 1902 to cover all the various extensions all the way back to Clifden. The name of the proposed railway was changed to the Ulster & Connaught Light Railway (U&CR).

By 1905, no construction had taken place and the powers had only been obtained for the section to Tynan from Greenore. However, an extension to the Act was obtained. By 1909 the company had reverted to its original name and the extensions west of the Clogher Valley line appear to have been abandoned. However, even this truncated version was to be stillborn; while a working agreement with the Clogher Valley Railway had been made, and the tunnel under the GNR station in Keady actually built, the whole scheme was abandoned around 1910. Thus Clifden, and Ireland, was deprived of one of its most imaginative railway schemes. Had it been built, Clifden would presumably have seen the departure of long narrow gauge trains setting out on a 234 mile (351 km) journey to Greenore, via a very indirect route serving nowhere with a population exceeding 4,000 (and most with a fraction of that) other than Newry. Galway would be served too, but only at the end of a branch line! A main line of this length would have been by far the longest in Ireland, both in distance and time, and corridor trains with dining cars would have been necessary. It can be estimated that a through journey would have taken at least 10 hours even by express train, assuming, that is, that through services would have been provided. No other single railway journey in Ireland ever came anywhere near that timescale.

It is safe to suggest that such an undertaking would have been spectacularly unwieldy and uneconomic to operate, and would have probably failed within a few years. Construction would have taken perhaps five to seven years, by which time the creation of the Irish border, which it would cross in two places, was imminent. The effect of the border killed off the GNR's Keady to Castleblayney line in 1923 after just 10 years operation. The U & C R would have done well to even last this long; it is mentioned here simply to complete the record of potential railways serving Clifden.

Appendix Eight

The Marconi Railway, Clifden

In 1905, Guglielmo Marconi planned to launch the first wireless transmitter to link Ireland and the USA from a site on Derrygimlagh Bog, a short way outside Clifden. Having conducted much experimentation over several years, Marconi (whose mother was Irish) decided that the location off the Ballyconneely Road was the best place, as the shortest distance possible from Ireland to the United States of America was preferable. But the site was remote, and only reached across bogland, so he laid a light railway of 2ft gauge for 1½ miles (2.41 km) across the bog to transport personnel and equipment to the chosen site from the nearest road, that from Clifden to Ballyconneely. Construction of the transmitter and railway commenced in 1905 and was complete by 1906.

The boilers for the boiler house came by train to Clifden, from where they were slowly moved by road trolleys out to starting point of the light railway. The railway had an 0-4-0T steam locomotive of 3 tons weight, built by Dick, Kerr & Co., Kilmarnock, Scotland. In 1906 the Viceroy of Ireland, Lord Aberdeen visited. He and his wife were carried out to the telegraph station by a train hastily put together, consisting of the locomotive hauling a wagon with two seats bolted onto it. Normally this railway was used for moving staff and supplies about; several short sidings went off into the bog to enable turf to be transported to the station for fuel in the boilers.

Guests travel on the railway around the time of the opening of the wireless station *circa* 1907.   *Author's Collection*

In 1907 the wireless link successfully began the world's first wireless service between Ireland and America. The wireless operator was Jack Phillips, later to serve (and die) on the ill-fated *Titanic* on its maiden voyage in 1912.

The area around the station was to become famous for another reason. In 1919, a competition was staged for a race by air across the Atlantic. Pioneer aviators John Alcock and Arthur Whitten Brown took off from St Johns, Newfoundland, at 1.45 pm on 14th June, arriving at the Co. Galway coast at 8.40 am on 15th June, 1919, not far from their intended landing place, after less than 16 hours flying time. The aircraft was damaged on arrival because of an attempt to land in what appeared from the air to be a suitable green field but which turned out to be the bog. Neither of the airmen were hurt, and were taken to the roadside by the narrow gauge railway. Having made it across the Atlantic they were feted as heroes. They had won the race, and the prize of over £13,000. As the first British subjects to fly the Atlantic Ocean, they were knighted a few days later by King George V. The plane landed adjacent to Marconi's wireless station.

In 1922, during the Irish Civil War, the station was destroyed by fire. Like the MGWR's hotel at Recess, it was not rebuilt.

Today, the route of the railway is still traceable, and suitable signage indicates where these events took place.

After their crash-landing in Derrygimla Bog outside Clifden in June 1919, the pioneering pilots John Alcock and Arthur Whitten Brown, drove this improvised railcar on the 2km Marconi Railway on 14th/15th June, 1919 from the capacitor building to the receiving house. Here they are pictured in the driving seat; a very different machine from their transatlantic aeroplane! *Author's Collection*

Appendix Nine

The Galway & Salthill Tramway Company

To complete our look at the railways around Galway and Connemara, the tram line to Salthill (Bóthar na Trá = the street of the strand (beach), in Irish) is worthy of inclusion. As city tramways go, this line was small by any standards, covering a distance of only 3.6 km (2.25 miles) between Galway's city centre and the then outlying village of Salthill.

The city had expanded greatly in the period after the Great Famine in the mid-19th century. By 1872, a steamboat service was operating to the Aran Islands, and commercial boat routes had also opened up on Lough Corrib to the north west of the city. It was only a matter of time before proposals would be made to expand local transport facilities, as the outlying village of Salthill began to expand.

In 1877 the Galway & Salthill Tramway Co. was formed to connect the village with the city centre, adjacent to Eyre Square and the MGWR railway station. It was proposed to build the line to the 3 ft (914 mm) narrow gauge as had been proposed for several of the abortive schemes for railways to Clifden. The line was very well constructed with track of a section more suited to the heavier traffic associated with a light railway. Given the difficulty of gaining financial support for many railway schemes at the time, it may be concluded that the track might have been completed more cheaply, but it may be assumed that the company had its eye on other proposals at the time, which could have resulted in a narrow gauge line to Clifden, or further along the coast. Thus, had considerably heavier traffic appeared, the lines would not have had to be relaid.

Construction proceeded without incident with track being laid in well-constructed limestone setts which were quarried in Menlo Quarry, west of the city. One hundred men were employed in this work alone. The line was complete and ready for opening to the public on 1st October, 1879. The Salthill terminus therefore became Europe's most westerly tram terminus.

The line commenced at the tram depot in Forster Street, a minute's walk from both the railway station of the MGWR, and the city centre at Eyre Square. The terminus was a property previously owned by a Capt. Blake-Forster and which had been adapted for the purpose, with stables added for the horses. The line proceeded along the east and south sides of the square, before heading towards the west of the city via Shop Street and Dominick Street. Beyond there it crossed a bridge before heading along the Salthill Road, then a rural thoroughfare with open fields and thatched cottages. In fact, the final third of the route was entirely rural in character. It remained as a roadside line the whole way with a terminus opposite the Eglinton Hotel. No facilities at all were initially provided at the terminus – the line simply stopped and the horse was switched to the other end for the return trip. Since it was an exposed and then bleak spot, by 1880 the company had at least erected a waiting shelter for prospective passengers.

The line was single throughout, but to cope with heavy traffic had eight passing loops spaced 250 yards (228m) apart. The overall cost of the entire tramway as built was £15,990. Apart from one very short but steep gradient at Kingshill, where an extra horse was usually needed to assist uphill trams, the line was level.

Trams were always horse drawn. Electricity had not come to Galway when the line was built, and when it did, about 1890/91, the company's finances were not sufficiently healthy to invest in electric propulsion for its trams, as was done in other cities in such circumstances. Initially, five were ordered from the firm of Starbuck Car & Wagon Company, Birkenhead, a company which would be absorbed into the famous tram manufacturing firm of George F. Milnes, Fallowfield, Manchester in 1886. The first trams arrived by ship into Galway port just in time for the opening of the line. It may be assumed that later orders of trams came from this firm which was better known for building some of the iconic electric tramcars in the Isle of Man, many of which are still in use.

Each tram had a seating capacity of 36 and required two horses to pull it. The lower deck was enclosed but the upper deck was open with bench seating. While the company did not accept goods for carriage, passengers were allowed a significant 'baggage allowance' of 28 lb. (13kg) per person. By the standards of the day, the trams must have been quite comfortable, as seats were cushioned and lit by oil lamps. Given the rural nature of the Salthill area, trams could see piglets, ducks, chickens and other small livestock being carried in to markets in the city. Fares were set in consultation with Galway Town Commissioners and were initially between one and two pennies per full journey.

Galway and Salthill Tramways Company.

BALANCE SHEET, 31st JULY, 1895.

Paid up Capital of Company	..	£15,990 0 0	Tramways	...	...	£12,889 10 8	
Accumulated Profits per			Premises	...	...	1,182 17 6	
last account	.. £13 4 1		Rolling Stock	...	...	1,110 12 4	
Reserve Fund per last			Rail Material	..	..	219 5 5	
account	... 58 15 7		Machinery	...	...	84 5 5	
	£71 19 8		Office Furniture	...	...	15 11 5	
			Harness	..	...	78 1 9	
Loss for Half-year end-			Horses	...	...	371 19 4	
ing 31 July, 1895,	98 11 9		Cash in Bank	...	...	100 10 6	
			" Hand	...	...	11 7 7	
Balance to Contra	£26 12 1		" Bank to meet unclaim-				
Dividends unclaimed ..	..	3 7 6	ed Dividends ...	...		3 7 6	
Sundry Creditors	... ...	416 6 3	Forage in Stock	...	...	27 6 8	
			Post Cars and Harness	...		115 6 0	
			Materials for Repairs	...		10 0 0	
			Manure	..	...	10 6 0	
			Punches and Tickets	...		5 0 0	
			Sundry Debtors	...	...	53 2 4	
			Posting	...	...	50 14 4	
			Rent	... ..	...	0 2 8	
			Repairs a.c, carried forward to				
			next half-year	..		65 0 0	
			Rates and Taxes. do.		...	30 0 0	
			Balance deficiency for Contra			26 12 1	
		£16,409 13 9				£16,409 13 9	

Nothing has been written off the amount due for posting, £50 14s. 4d. to meet bad debts. We bring forward to next half-year proportion of Repairs, &c, £65, and proportion of Rates and Taxes, £30. We have examined the above Accounts and Balances for 31st July, 1895, have compared same with the Books and Vouchers of the Company and certify them to be correct.

73 Dame street, Dublin, 27 Sept, 1895.

M. CROWLEY & CO.
Chartered Accountants and Auditors.

Balance Sheet for the Galway & Salthill Tramways Co., 31st July, 1895. It will be seen that in the preceding six months the company made a loss of £98 11s. 9d.   *M. Semple*

By 1888 traffic had reached saturation point for the five original tramcars, and several more were ordered. These differed in design being covered single-deck vehicles only. As such, they were popular in winter when lower numbers of people travelled and covered accommodation was more necessary. By 1909 a further five cars were ordered, of a more similar design to the originals. It is likely that at some stage most or all of the original cars were withdrawn, as it was recorded that in 1901 only seven tramcars were in use.

The earliest double-deck trams and the later ones were painted dark olive green and white, while the single-deck 'winter' trams were plain grey.

However, receipts were falling due to gradual improvement of the roads for early bus services and the line became financially unviable. In addition, during World War I, the company's best horses had been commandeered by the military authorities to accompany the British Army to the battle fields of Flanders. Let us hope that they survived such horrors.

By the end of 1918 the writing was on the wall, and services ceased entirely on 1st October, 1919 after 39 years and 2 months. The tracks were removed and sold for scrap soon afterwards. However, by this stage Salthill had developed considerably, and had the city authorities taken it over and invested in electrifying it, a further lease of life might have been possible. Certainly, a rapid transit system today would certainly benefit the area as Salthill has nowadays become a bustling suburb of the city.

After the tramway closed, the Galway General Omnibus Company was registered (August 1919) and this successor commenced bus services over the same route. Their initial stock was of nine buses, ranging from 20 to 49 seaters. Some years later, these services would be absorbed into the Great Southern Railway's road service section. Today, Galway's city bus services are in the hands of the GSR's successor, Bus Éireann.

The old trams were all scrapped, except for two of the bodies which were sold as fishing lodges on the shore of Lough Corrib. It is uncertain where they were placed, though it is likely that today they are long gone.

The Salthill tram makes its way along Shop Street in 1904.   *NUIG*

Acknowledgements and Bibliography

A publication of this nature depends heavily on archival material, as very few people alive today have any detailed memory of the railway - at the time of writing it is well over 80 years since Clifden last heard a steam locomotive whistle. The railway only operated for 40 years.

I would like to thank Ian and Jane Kennedy (formerly of Oakwood Press) for encouraging me to carry out this work, albeit many years before I managed to get around to it. By the time I did, I am glad to also thank Richard Stenlake for further encouragement, after his publishing firm took over from Oakwood. This volume may therefore be taken as a natural follow-up to my earlier book on the railway from Westport to Achill (*Rails to Achill*, Oakwood Press, 2002).

First and foremost, I would like to thank the late Padraig O'Cuimín of Craughwell, Co. Galway, for his early encouragement and assistance with various areas of research. Padraig was kind enough to let me have his collection of copious notes he had made over the years on this line and others. He also led me towards several illustrations. Ernie Shepherd (Co. Wexford) was also of great help in directing me towards certain archival material which I might otherwise have overlooked. His comprehensive history of the whole Midland Great Western Railway system also makes reference to the line. Retired Galway locomotive drivers John Foy and Robert Healy were also of assistance, as was their friend and colleague, the late Billy Lohan of Tuam, Co. Galway. Billy lived to be in excess of 100 years old, and his vivid and graphic stories of life on the railway brought to life a period now so long forgotten, as he recalled starting work in 1914. I am grateful to Frank Dawson of Tuam for putting me in touch with these gentlemen.

I would also acknowledge assistance given by Owen Quinn and Donagh O'Donoghue of Galway, and Ivor Hamrock, of Castlebar Library.

When I started research on this project some years ago, the only way to view old newspaper reports and articles was in person, at places like Galway University and the National Archives in Dublin. Now, much of this nature can be accomplished online, but I am grateful for time saved by reference to notes and indexing of old newspaper articles prepared previously by several of those named above.

Some archival material relating to the line is in the hands of the Irish Railway Record Society (IRRS) in Dublin. Among their members who provided assistance and granted permission for the publication of various material were Brendan Pender, Herbert Richards the late Norman McAdams. IRRS members Barry and David Carse, Paddy O'Brien, Gerry Conmy and Peter Rigney were also of help. I am grateful to Col Eugene Field of the IRRS and the National Railway Museum, York, for copies of tickets issued for the line, and background details about them.

Some other useful information was provided by Bill Scott, of Belfast.

Photographic material regarding the line is sparse. Given the infrequent train service, the remote countryside covered, and the difficulties in carrying out a return day trip from Dublin, camera equipment in hand, few railway enthusiasts visited the line. We are therefore lucky that even two photographers covered the line in any detail. The first was William Lawrence of Dublin, whose vast photographic collection is housed in the National Photographic Archive, Temple Bar, Dublin. Lawrence (and his assistants) visited the line in its early days. At the other end of the life of the railway, the prolific English railway photographer, Henry Casserley, visited the line in its last year of operation. Illustrations from both the Lawrence and Casserley collections are included with thanks to the current copyright holders of both.

Given the scarcity of other photographs of the line, it has been felt necessary to reproduce as many as possible of the illustrations from the above two collections, despite the fact that most have been published before. I am grateful to Hassard Stacpoole (London) for his assistance in sourcing several important illustrations.

Any illustrations in this book which are not credited in the captions are from the author's own archive.

Some research material was accessed through the offices of CIÉ (Ireland's state transport company, of which Irish Rail/Iarnród Eireann is a subsidiary). I am grateful to Marcella Doyle, Heuston station, for her direction some years ago in this regard.

I am especially grateful to Jim Deegan (Co. Laois) for other material relating to the line, and for checking some details in the text. Jim has family connections with the area through which the line ran. In that connection, I would also acknowledge very valuable assistance given to me by Shane Joyce, of Clifden, and Tom Kenny, of the well known Kenny's Bookshop, Galway. Kenny's has for generations been a major resource for rare and specialist books in the city. All three above have been of immense help.

Previous published material on the Clifden line includes a booklet produced by renowned local historian Kathleen Villiers-Tuthill for the Station House Hotel, Clifden, which is built itself around the former railway station.

I would like to thank Lord O'Neill, Shanes Castle, Co. Antrim for permission to reproduce the painting of the 'Tourist Train' train at Ballynahinch, which is on the front cover.

To all who assisted in any way, please accept my thanks, and my apologies if I have left anybody out.

Finally, I must mention an extremely rare co-incidence. It is not normal to include an anecdote amongst acknowledgements, but to this day I can hardly believe what follows ...

While researching in CIE archives, I spent several days making notes of the convoluted negotiations between the Midland Great Western Railway and various landowners along the proposed route of the railway. This was heavy going, as some aspects of research can be, and it took much patience to make sense of the minutae of what had unfolded back in the 1890s. Central to the theme of my research that day was negotiations between the railway company and two landowners named Lynch and Berridge. The former is a well-known name not only in the area, but elsewhere in Ireland too. The latter is a name which would be extremely unusual in Ireland; it is of English extraction.

As I made my way home that evening, I stopped off for a fast food carry-out en route. As I queued, a group of young men were in front of me, speaking to each other in what I thought were accents from the west of Ireland. I struck up a conversation, asking them were they from Co. Mayo, by any chance, as I knew the area quite well?

Yes, several of them replied. 'Where in Mayo?', I asked them out of curiosity. They mentioned one particular town. I simply replied that while their accent had sounded recognisable, I did not know anybody from their home town, intending to leave it at that.

'I'm not from Mayo!', piped up one of the others, 'I'm a Galway man'.

'Where in Galway – the city?', I asked, making conversation. 'No', he replied, explaining that he was from 'out in Connemara' originally. He mentioned Ballynahinch, expecting me not to have heard of it, something to be expected given its remoteness. I commented that I had spent the day researching the origins of the railway and was aware where Ballynahinch was.

We agreed that this was a massive coincidence. But then the punch line came; 'My great-grandfather sold land to the railway to build the line'.

I told him that this was precisely what lay in the copious pile of papers and notes I had in my bag beside me. 'What was your ancestor's name?', I asked, expecting it to be either Lynch or a name I had not heard of.

'Berridge'.

Now, as mentioned, this is not a common name in Ireland. In fact, not only in my own experience, but that of the young man I spoke with, it is the only instance we had ever heard of the name occurring in Ireland!

I told him, all those years ago, that I would include the background to our almost supernaturally-ordained meeting in the book, so there it is.

Index

Single line staff for the Maam Cross-Recess section. Staffs were exchanged at stations where trains left the section of track concerned, and entered a new one. This meant that only one train could be in each section at a time, as there was only one; thus avoiding accidental instances of trains meeting head on! This example is believed to be the sole remaining staff from this line, and was discovered during renovations of the former level crossing gatekeeper's house near Recess station. *Jim Deegan*